Wittgenstein as Philosophica

STUDIEN ZUR ÖSTERREICHISCHEN PHILOSOPHIE
Gegründet von Rudolf Haller
Herausgegeben von Mauro Antonelli

BAND XLV

WITTGENSTEIN AS PHILOSOPHICAL TONE-POET
PHILOSOPHY AND MUSIC IN DIALOGUE

BÉLA SZABADOS

Amsterdam - New York, NY 2014

Die Reihe wird gemeinsam von Editions Rodopi, Amsterdam - New York
und dem Verlag Königshausen und Neumann, Würzburg herausgegeben.

The paper on which this book is printed meets the requirements of "ISO
9706:1994, Information and documentation - Paper for documents -
Requirements for permanence".

ISBN: 978-90-420-3857-8
E-BOOK ISBN: 978-94-012-1099-7
©Editions Rodopi B.V., Amsterdam - New York, NY 2014
Printed in the Netherlands

MIX
Paper from
responsible sources
FSC® C109576

Printed by Printforce, the Netherlands

For Heather

Musicians

I pass a bunch of musicians in the street.

It's about 12.30, rehearsal just over, they're

standing around outside the side door of the church.

A good rehearsal; and it's April. They're laughing,

horsing around, talking about shoes, or taxes, where

to go for lunch, anything

except what their heads are full of.

It's a kind of helplessness, you can see

they are still breathing almost in unison, like people

the search light has passed over

and spared, their attention

lifts, swerves, settles; even

the gravel dust stuttering at their feet is coherent.

Jan Zwicky

Table of Contents

Acknowledgements

Special thanks to Andrew Lugg, Alex Rueger, Heather Hodgson and John Lehman who read through the entire manuscript and offered valued suggestions for improvement. I am also grateful to Steven Burns, Daniel Steuer, Roger Shiner, Bill Perks, Tricia Bond, Eleanor Akins and Gord Gault for helpful comments on particular chapters, as well as to Monika Horn for discussing with me English translations of several passages from the German text of *Culture and Value*. Latest but not least among my helpers was Donna Grant, whom I thank for the preparation of the manuscript. Ancestral versions of the sections on irony and on Mahler were presented at meetings of the Western Canadian Philosophical Association, with Justin Horn and Victor Rodych as respondents. A previous version of "Wittgenstein on Musical Irony" was published in the journal *Wittgenstein-Studien* and "Wittgenstein's Reception of Wagner" is a revised contribution to the collection *Wittgenstein Reading,* edited by Sascha Bru, Wolfgang Huemer and Daniel Steuer (De Gruyter, 2013). I am grateful to the editors for permission to reprint. The poem *Musicians* by Jan Zwicky is from her collection *Songs for Relinquishing the Earth* and is reprinted here with her kind permission.

Béla Szabados
Regina, Saskatchewan

Introduction

"I often think that the highest I wish to achieve would be to compose a melody".[1] This is a striking and surprising remark coming from Ludwig Wittgenstein, the iconic philosopher of the twentieth century. Surprising, for it is not the sort of thing we expect from someone who spent his life doing philosophy and in the process re-oriented Western philosophy's self-conception and direction. Striking, for it suggests a closer connection between music and philosophy than philosophers in the analytic tradition would be comfortable with or allow. Perhaps this enigmatic remark is a suitable start to a book about Wittgenstein and music.

In this book I paint a portrait of Wittgenstein as a musical philosopher. Although he regarded music an important part of his life and relevant to his philosophical activity, his many remarks on music are scattered throughout the *Nachlass* and thus little known, largely unexplored, and, in general, not given the significance they deserve in Wittgenstein-studies. Certainly, what Wittgenstein says about music and composers in his diaries and notebooks are in themselves interesting, but admitting this still allows for their dismissal as a curiosity. However, the remarks suggest a many-sided Wittgenstein who is very different from conventional portraits that narrowly depict him as exclusively interested in technical questions about language and logic, meaning and method. Not only do they express his love of music and sketch its role in his life, they show a keen engagement with musical and aesthetic issues that bear the characteristic stamp of his later philosophy and motivate his philosophical practice. Thus they deserve to be taken seriously and to be related to his philosophical perspective.

There is a tension between the conventional reception of

---

1 Ludwig Wittgenstein, *Public and Private Occasions*, eds and trs James Klagge and Alfred Nordmann, Lanham, Maryland: Rowman & Littlefied, 2003, 17.

Wittgenstein's remarks on arts and aesthetics on the one hand, and the way he viewed his own work in relation to arts and aesthetics on the other. The conventional view is that arts and aesthetics are on the periphery of his concerns, while he says that he is not interested [as a "modern" philosopher is expected to be] in scientific questions but only aesthetic and conceptual questions are at the center of his interest. I elaborate and provide textual support for the view that for him the arts, especially music, but also aesthetics, were a focal concern both biographically and philosophically.

Wittgenstein is conventionally read as providing a powerful critique of the whole project of traditional philosophy, recommending instead a family resemblance approach to philosophical reflection on aesthetic concepts. On this reading, Wittgenstein's lectures and remarks on aesthetics fall into place as mere applications of the big themes of the *Tractatus Logico-Philosophicus* and the *Philosophical Investigations* with their lessons about meaning, mind and method. Thus we have the themes of anti-essentialism, anti-reductionism, and anti-scientism applied to fundamental questions about the nature of art and beauty, of aesthetic experience and aesthetic appreciation. It is almost as if Wittgenstein, having arrived at his purely philosophical methods independently of the arts and aesthetics, was curious about how they might work when applied to the arts and questions of aesthetics. Viewed this way, it is natural to say that Wittgenstein's concerns with the arts and aesthetics did not lie at the centre of his interest, but rather at its margins, since for him the core of philosophy had to do with questions of language and understanding. While a wealth of good work was done under the umbrella of this perspective, there are remarks throughout the *Nachlass* that suggest a deeper and more fruitful way of approaching Wittgenstein's relation to the arts and aesthetics.

In my reckoning Wittgenstein was a philosopher whom we can think through profitably when reflecting on musical/philosophical issues. In reading Wittgenstein's remarks on music I highlight and remain faithful to biographical and historical materials, to cultural context and official philosophical texts. Since Wittgenstein's writing style has a beauty and crisp elegance all its own, it does not easily lend itself to paraphrase. Scholars who indulge in "executive summaries" cut themselves off from the rich rewards of a close reading that opens up Wittgenstein's texts to questions and the discernment of various voices.

I quote the relevant texts on music from Wittgenstein; partly because they have not been gathered, arranged or properly attended to, partly to see their upshot for the questions of musical aesthetics and philosophy, and partly because of their austere beauty and suggestiveness. This way, as I twist and turn with the texts, readers do not lose their grip on Wittgenstein. Although he doubted if, "in the darkness of this time", he would be understood, he had enough confidence in the reader to say—"Anything the reader can do for himself, leave it to [him]".[2] As well, Wittgenstein made demands of the reader: "I should not like my writing to spare other people the trouble of thinking. But, if possible, to stimulate someone to thoughts of his own".[3] Indeed, the deeply dialogical character of the *Philosophical Investigations* is intended to promote these goals and to engage the reader in the practice of philosophy as he considers the various voices in the conversations about the ideas and questions it brings up.

Many of Wittgenstein's remarks are about the relation of music to language, about the nature of musical understanding, about the concepts of representation and expression, about melody, irony and aspect-perception. Other interesting and incisive remarks are comments on, or assessments of, composers belonging to the Austrian-German tradition from Bach and Beethoven, through Mendelssohn, Schubert, Schumann and Brahms, to Wagner, Bruckner and Mahler, including the neglected Josef Labor. The comments on Wagner, Mahler, and Mendelssohn are especially fertile, provocative and vulnerable to misunderstanding. Hence they receive longer discussion. Yet other remarks are concerned with questions about music and the character of Wittgenstein's own philosophical activity. I shall take up these questions as well as the question of the role music played in his life and highlight his keen interest in music as philosophy's other. I discern in Wittgenstein's remarks about composers a distinctive practice of music criticism that resonates with Richard Wagner's essays on music, but with the ugliness removed. In discussing Wagner's influence on Wittgenstein, I discuss its implications for Wittgenstein's music criticism, especially in his

---

2   Ludwig Wittgenstein, *Culture and Value*, ed. G.H. von Wright, tr. Peter Winch
    (1980), revised 2nd edition ed. Alois Pichler, Oxford: Basil Blackwell, 1998, 88.
3   Ludwig Wittgenstein, *Philosophical Investigations,* revised 2nd edition, ed. and
    tr. G.E.M. Anscombe, Oxford: Basil Blackwell, 2001, 10.

remarks on the musical achievements of Mendelssohn and Mahler with whom, I claim, he identifies.

I begin by making a few observations about the lack of interest in music in the history of philosophy, and point to Wittgenstein's strikingly different attitude. I continue by gathering—from his diaries and notebooks as well as from biographical fragments reported by friends and students—the body of music Wittgenstein listened to that show the important role music played in his life. Then, I revisit Wittgenstein's Vienna to situate his musical tastes and sketch his relation to Eduard Hanslick's musical formalism, arguing that the early Wittgenstein was a musical formalist, but not the later Wittgenstein. Next, I look at his criticism of the foundations of musical aesthetics—beauty, work of music, and the aesthetic attitude—contending that he navigated between two extremes: those who regard these notions as foundational and those who want to dispose of them altogether. The landscape of musical aesthetics, I argue, is refreshed through Wittgenstein's rather different way of looking at things. What appear to be mere side-glances acquire critical significance when seen against the backdrop of the musical/aesthetic tradition. This backdrop has at its core the reductionist idea of essence—the musically beautiful, the essence of a musical work, and a unique attitude for listening to music. Wittgenstein raises questions about the importance of the musically beautiful in our critical vocabulary, about musical essence, and about received views of what it is to listen to music with understanding. The remarks about these issues are not to be understood as proposing some theory or even a sketch of it, and hence reinforce the anti-theoretical thrust of his later work.

In conjunction with his critique of the tradition, there follows a change in Wittgenstein's perception of music in the early 1930s, which I connect with the transition from the Tractarian view of language to that of the later philosophy of the *Philosophical Investigations*. Through a close reading of his remarks on musical irony, I argue that the later Wittgenstein is no formalist who eschews music's expressive character: for him, music is not alone but connects and resonates with our cultural forms of life. I continue by considering his relation to composers, especially to Richard Wagner and Gustav Mahler.

This discussion naturally leads to a question that concerned him deeply: How to do philosophy and compose music in the breakdown of tradition? I turn to consider how his remarks on music relate to his philosophical activity and its aim of therapy. I look at the brothers Wittgenstein, Ludwig and Paul, and notice family differences and similarities concerning their attitudes to modern music. I ask whether Paul got on while Ludwig was left behind the musical journey of the West. I go on to argue that Ludwig's later philosophical perspective, unlike his conservative musical sensibility and taste, is congenial to compositional/musical experiments. Philosophy cannot be reduced to the life of the philosopher, even though the life is relevant to the philosophy. I conclude with remarks on some affinities between Wittgenstein and John Cage, including the theme of therapy as a goal in music and philosophy.

The reader will notice that throughout my discussion I issue reminders of Wittgenstein's major philosophical themes and make use of recurring quotations. Such repetitions are in mostly different contexts and are meant to bring attention to, and shed new light on, different aspects of the themes and quotations. Also, I speak, without embarrassment, of the early, middle/in transit, and later Wittgenstein. For me these are useful and convenient, rough and ready, ways of referring to Wittgenstein's changing style and line of thinking in his works. By speaking this way, I aim to bypass the scholarly party lines between Orthodox Wittgensteinians: those who accentuate the discontinuities, and New Wittgensteinians: those who emphasize the continuities between the early and later works. Surely we can do both and thus decline to join either party. There is, of course, only *one* Wittgenstein: one who keeps on thinking and who is always there as a conversation partner

Chapter I
A Life in Music

1. An Appetite for Music

"When I imagine a piece of music", Wittgenstein wrote in a 1937 diary entry,

> something I do every day & often, I rhythmically grind my upper & lower front teeth together. I have noticed it before but usually it takes place quite unconsciously. Moreover it's as though the notes in my imagination were produced by this movement. I think this way of hearing music in the imagination may be very common. I can of course also imagine music without moving my teeth, but then the notes are much more blurred, much less clear, less pronounced.[1]

This entry confirms Wittgenstein's passionate, although as we shall see later, highly discriminating, appetite for music which is in sharp contrast to an absence of desire for music in the history of philosophy in general. Philosophers, as Michael Tanner observed, have on the whole shown little interest in music as raw material for philosophy, partly because most of them had little appetite for it. There are exceptions, however, such as Plato and Schopenhauer, and two of Schopenhauer's ambivalent descendants, Nietzsche and Wittgenstein. Nietzsche's philosophy, as Tanner recognized,

> tends to have music as background, and Wittgenstein certainly thought of music as a deep phenomenon, though it is commonly thought that he wrote little about it and what he did write is of questionable value.[2]

---

1 Wittgenstein, *Culture,* 32.
2 Michael Tanner, *Schopenhauer,* London: Phoenix, 1999, 43.

Observations such as these are on the mark as far as rough generalizations go. However, what is said about one of the exceptions, namely, Ludwig Wittgenstein, raises questions: where is Wittgenstein's writing about music supposed to be found and why is most of it deemed without value? What is the "little that is valuable" and why? Why did Wittgenstein think of music as a deep phenomenon? These questions cry out for discussion that may be of interest to students of musical aesthetics and those interested in the idea of a dialogue between music and philosophy, Wittgenstein scholars, and lovers of music in general.

To make evaluations about Wittgenstein on music we must track down and gather his remarks about it. He wrote many substantive remarks about music but we cannot survey or take stock of their significance, as long as his remarks are scattered over his entire oeuvre. While the masterworks that bear his imprimatur, namely, the *Tractatus Logico-Philosophicus* and the *Philosophical Investigations*, contain allusions to music, *Culture and Value* and the Wittgenstein *Nachlass* unexpectedly presents us with a wealth of material on, or related to, music. These materials have not been assembled or arranged, nor have they received due scholarly attention. Unless we gather and carefully reflect on them, any assessment of their value seems premature. So the project of assessment requires a gathering of the fugitives; a serious consideration and connecting of those remarks that either eluded philosophers or which philosophers generally tend to dismiss or take lightly. Either way, they have been reluctant to pay them the sort of sustained attention given to Wittgenstein's other remarks on issues of meaning, reference, intention, and so on. This tendency is manifest not only in the lack of an appetite for music, but also in the unwillingness to take seriously the possibility of music's relevance for philosophy or, better still, for Wittgenstein's philosophy. Wittgenstein's attitude to music was completely different.

2.   Music's Place: Biography or Philosophy?

When he was working on what now appears as the second part of the *Philosophical Investigations*, Wittgenstein said to his friend Drury: "It is impossible to say in my book one word about all that music has meant in my life", adding, "How then can I hope to be understood?"[3] This remark relates the significance of music for Wittgenstein to its significance for understanding his philosophy, since the conversational context makes it clear that "How then can I hope to be understood?" is an allusion to his philosophical work.

Wittgenstein's comment does not sit well with the analytical tradition's sharp divide between biography and philosophy, according to which whether a philosopher loves music and regards it as an important stimulus for his work is merely of biographical interest, a matter external to philosophical activity. If a philosopher is passionate about music, that's *simply* a biographical fact about them having little or no relevance to their practice of philosophy. Another philosopher's predilection may be for backgammon, chess or sport, and obviously these have no bearing on philosophy. In opposition to this commonly received view, Wittgenstein's remark holds forth the prospect of music having philosophical import (at least for understanding his own philosophy), thereby straddling the conventional divide between biography and philosophy.

The theme of what can and cannot be said with sense—a major theme of the *Tractatus*—is also struck in the conversation with Drury, since the sentence "It is impossible to say in my book one word about all that music has meant in my life" resonates with proposition 7 of the *Tractatus*: "Whereof one cannot speak, thereof one must be silent". The early work asserts that ethics and aesthetics are one, and part of what this means is that through music (or the other arts) the sense and value of human life is *shown*, but nothing can be sensibly *said* about this in a book of philosophy. This apparently simple knock-down objection to taking up the question of music's relation to philosophy an objection based on an internal feature of Wittgenstein's early philosophy— suggests that Wittgenstein himself discouraged this sort of direction for investigation. What music has to teach us would thus have to be stated propositionally, and this is not possible, for the value music has to offer cannot be sensibly said but only shown. Anyone who contravenes the

3 *Ludwig Wittgenstein Personal Recollections*, ed. Rush Rhees, Oxford: Oxford University Press, 1981, 94.

above call to silence not only talks pernicious nonsense but succumbs to the "great temptation to want to make the spirit explicit".[4]

This interpretation seems plausible if we have the *Tractatus* in front and centre of our attention, focusing on its assertion to talk about nothing but the propositions of natural science. But since the Tractarian admonishment about what can and cannot be said depends on the show/ say distinction, and since the later Wittgenstein recast this distinction, the remark to Drury needs to be understood somewhat differently. In any event, Tractarian strictures do not hamper the later philosophy and the "knockdown objection" rings hollow if we look at the remarks on music in the *Nachlass*. There we see that Wittgenstein wrote many remarks about music and composers in notebook entries that range from the late 1920s to the late 1940s. Even if these remarks do not add up to a sustained meditation on the Austrian-German classical tradition in music, they do constitute an attempt toward it. Although scattered, once gathered and arranged, Wittgenstein's remarks display much of the character and approach of the remarks in the *Philosophical Investigations*.

One way to understand the remark to Drury is to connect it to the later philosophy's negative view of explanation and reduction: "We must do away with all explanation and allow only description to take its place".[5] Of course, the target of such a negative attitude to explanation is "out of place" explanations, such as theoretical explanations in philosophy. Wittgenstein had no aversion to 'explanation' where it clarified meaning. In the case of the meaning of music, neither a scientific-theoretical, nor a verbal explanation suffices, and obviously no description is a substitute for listening. If someone were to ask: What is valuable in a Beethoven sonata? The sequence of notes? The feelings Beethoven had when he was composing it? The state of mind produced by listening to it?

> I [Wittgenstein] would reply, that whatever I was told, I would reject, and that not because the explanation was false but because it was an explanation: If I were told anything that was a theory,

---

4   Wittgenstein, *Culture*, 11.
5   Wittgenstein, *Investigations*, §109.

> I would say, No, no! That does not interest me—it would not be
> the exact thing I was looking for. [6]

This sort of remark, of course, allows room for observations that throw
light on how we can hear the music as expressive of the human: of the
tragic, of the heroic, of the ironic and so on. And he could not say in
his philosophical book how much music meant to him, for that suggests
that an explanation could accomplish this, when what is required is
attentive listening. What we have here is a "Listen and hear" analogue
to the "Look and see" attitude in philosophical inquiry. What then can
we expect in the writings of a philosopher with a passionate appetite for
music? We can at least expect evidence not only of philosophizing about
music but *through* music, thinking of philosophical issues through the
ears of music. Wittgenstein does this by drawing analogies between
a meaningful sentence and a musical theme, by putting philosophical
and musical issues side by side, by letting each shed light on the other.
The treatment of such particular analogies in Wittgenstein's works is a
demanding task worthy of being investigated.

Nor need our expectations be confined to content only but
may be extended to style as well. This line of thinking is reinforced
by Wittgenstein's reflections on his own style of doing philosophy
complaining that his style is *"like* bad musical composition".[7] Notice
his complaint is not that his style is *like* musical composition, but that it
is like *"bad* musical composition". One feature of the musical character
of Wittgenstein's later philosophical writings is their contrapuntal
character: instead of the monotone of the traditional univocal essay or
text book, we have a polyphony of voices: of the tradition, of its critic
and of the commentator who exposes distortions and attempts to do
justice to the measure of truth in each voice, as it were, thus aiming for
a kind of balance.

Another feature is the absence of footnotes or references in
general—unless one counts the occasional allusion in the text to
Augustine, Plato, Frege or Russell. It is tempting to attribute this absence
to a disregard for, or indifference to, scholarly convention, but it's better

---

6   Ludwig Wittgenstein, *Ludwig Wittgenstein and the Vienna Circle: Conversations
    Recorded by Friedrich Waismann*, ed. Brian McGuinness, trs Joachim Schulte
    and Brian McGuinness, Oxford: Basil Blackwell, 1979, 116.
7   Wittgenstein, *Culture*, 45.

seen as a deliberate strategy reminiscent of music. A particular theme—derivative or original—is struck, elaborated, improvised on, and undercut in the distinctive way of the individual philosopher/composer; its source or relevance is not announced, but is to be identified by or made his own by the discerning listener. The theme haunts us, recurring in different variations in different musical/philosophical contexts:

> Each sentence that I write is trying to say the whole thing, that is, the same things over and over again & it is as though they were views of one object seen from different angles.[8]

Again, Wittgenstein's books and writings, early and later, may profitably read as an arrangement of notes he wrote to himself (and others):

> If I am thinking just for myself without wanting to write a book, I jump about all round the topic; that is the only way of thinking that is natural to me. Forcing my thoughts into an ordered sequence is a torture for me. Should I even attempt it now? I squander untold effort making an *arrangement* of my thoughts.... [9]

The allusions to music and composers have implications for Wittgenstein's philosophical perspective—how to do and write philosophy:

> I believe I summed up where I stand in relation to philosophy when I said: really one should write philosophy only as one writes a poem. That, it seems to me, must reveal how far my thinking belongs to the present, the future, or the past. For I was acknowledging myself, with these words, to be someone who cannot do what he would really like to be able to do.[10]

By putting music and philosophy side by side, we can see affinities between them. Both identify and unearth tensions and problems with the aim to resolve or dissolve them. Like a composer who scores tensions and then resolves them, so Wittgenstein identifies and dissolves

---

8   *Ibid.*, 9.
9   *Ibid.*, 33.
10 *Ibid.*, 28.

the tensions in philosophy. As philosophical tone poet, he attends to troublesome concepts, sketches tones of everyday life and language games, aims at clarity of expression:

> In this world (mine) there is no tragedy & with that all the endlessness that gives rise to tragedy (as its result) is lacking. It is as though everything were soluble in ether. There is no hardness. This means that hardness & conflict do not become something splendid but a *defect*. Conflict is dissipated in much the same way as is the tension of a spring in a mechanism that would melt (or dissolve in nitric acid). In this solution tensions no longer exist.[11]

If music means a lot to a person then we expect him to listen to and appreciate music. Wittgenstein did so whenever he had a chance. And he could not say in his philosophical book how much music meant to him, for that suggests that some reductive explanation could accomplish this, when what is required is attentive listening. The claim that music was an important part of Wittgenstein's life has strong support from diverse sources: reports of his friends and family, his diaries, and the frequent allusions to music in his philosophical lectures and works. Here is a recollection of Maurice Drury's:

> To watch Wittgenstein listening to music was to realize that this was something very central and deep in his life. He told me that this he could not express in his writings, and yet it was so important to him that he felt without it he was sure to be misunderstood. I will never forget the emphasis with which he quoted Schopenhauer's dictum, 'Music is a world in itself.'[12]

I now turn to Wittgenstein listening to music, dividing things into early and later listening, the two being rather different in that the early listening is rarely accompanied by comments or reflections of a philosophical nature while the later ones often are. This is remarkable for it attests to yet another discontinuity between the Tractarian and the later philosophy in that from the early 1930s the hold of a rigid

---

11 *Ibid.*, 12.
12 K.T. Fann, *Ludwig Wittgenstein: The Man and His Philosophy*, New York: Dell Publishing, 1967, 67-68.

transcendent take on the say/show distinction is abandoned. Apparently, more can be said about music than he had previously thought.

3. Young Wittgenstein Listens to Music

What then is the kind of music that Wittgenstein imagined, hummed or whistled every day and often? What sort of music put a spring in his step? We get a good idea of this by looking into respective biographies of Wittgenstein by Brian McGuinness and Ray Monk which allude to his enthusiasm and passion for music, even though the presented material is fragmentary in nature and, in general, unrelated to his philosophical activity. To provide some cultural context: he came from a musical home in which there were several grand pianos. Recall the boy Wittgenstein in Derek Jarman's film echoing what Wittgenstein said, in a rather testy conversation, to the literary critic F.R. Leavis: "In my father's house there were seven grand pianos".[13] This is probably the right number, McGuinness comments, if the pianos in Karl Wittgenstein's other houses are included.[14] In any event, the Wittgenstein family played music together and arranged for performances in their home where Johannes Brahms, Josef Labor, Gustav Mahler and other Viennese musical notables were frequent guests. The mother played the piano, the father the violin. Wittgenstein's eldest brother committed suicide when his ambitions as a concert pianist were, apparently, thwarted by the father. Paul, another brother, had been a concert pianist. After losing his right arm in World War I he commissioned piano works for the left hand from famous contemporary composers, notably Ravel who composed a piano concerto for left hand especially for him. It is noteworthy that while studying engineering in Berlin young Ludwig is reported to have attended Wagner's *Mastersingers* at least a dozen times. What could he have heard in it that so engaged him? Perhaps the source of attraction, as McGuinness proposed, was that Wagner's opera treats problems in music and life together and it solves these problems by invoking the

---

13   *Ludwig Wittgenstein Personal Recollections*, ed. Rush Rhees, 54.
14   Brian McGuinness, *Wittgenstein: A Life, Young Ludwig*, Berkeley: University of California Press, 1988, 19.

need for rules—even in spontaneity. These themes parallel some of Wittgenstein's philosophical preoccupations.

Although Ludwig took piano lessons as a child he got nothing out of them and abandoned them. He did not learn to play an instrument until much later, when in the early 1920s he entered Teachers' College, where one of the requirements for the diploma was the ability to play an instrument. He chose the clarinet, which he could teach himself. His sister, Hermine writes:

> Music, too, came to have an ever stronger attraction for Ludwig. In his youth he had never played an instrument, but as a teacher he had to acquire this skill and chose the clarinet. I think that only from then on did his strong musical sense become really developed; at any rate, he played with great musical sensibility and enjoyed his instrument very much. He used to carry it around in an old stocking instead of in a case, and... he often cut a curious figure.[15]

Paul Engelmann, whom Wittgenstein met during the Great War and who became a good friend, provides a few more details. He tells us that when they first met during the great war, Wittgenstein:

> played no instrument; later he learned to play the clarinet, and played it very well; I once heard him in Schubert's *Shepherd on the Rock*. Instruments apart, he whistled beautifully. On one occasion, when the conversation turned to the viola part in the third movement of a Beethoven string quartet, he whistled the part from beginning to end, with a tone as pure and as strong as that of an instrument. I have repeatedly heard him perform such feats.[16]

How appropriate the practice of whistling the air is for a philosopher who has regard for, and builds on, the everyday! Engelmann also notes that Wittgenstein had a detailed knowledge of the whole Western European musical repertoire, and this was so before he learned an instrument. Running in the family then, music was, and Ludwig was

---

15   *Ludwig Wittgenstein Personal Recollections*, ed. Rush Rhees, 9.
16   Paul Engelmann, *Letters from Ludwig Wittgenstein with a Memoir,* Oxford: Blackwell, 1967, 89-90.

actively engaged in music making, thus having had a participant's understanding of it through the natural practice of whistling.

There is earlier testimony for Wittgenstein as whistler in David Pinsent's Diaries from 1912 to 1913, published as *A Portrait of Wittgenstein as a Young Man.* Having met Wittgenstein at a Cambridge social, Pinsent later observed that:

> Wittgenstein is very musical with the same tastes as I, which explains why we get on so well together despite having known each other only for three weeks.[17]

They are both "mad about Schubert" and start performing Schubert songs together, Pinsent taking the piano part and Ludwig whistling the part for the voice. Pinsent's diary is full of delightful concrete details about two trips he and Wittgenstein took: one to Iceland and one to Norway. They set out for Iceland on Saturday, September 8th, 1912. The boat called the 'Sterling' resembles an ordinary Channel steamer. "Lunch was at 11.0—consisting of sausagy sorts of things, cold, laid on the table to be chosen from. Afterwards we strummed the piano—for there is one on the ship—mostly Schubert songs, of which we have an edition with us". Then there is the trip to Norway. On August 30th, 1913, they sailed on the Wilson Line S.S. 'Eskimo' from Hull bound for Christiania. "The sea seems to be absolutely calm—but it is foggy and the hooter is making an awful row every quarter of a minute".[18] Soon after landing, Wittgenstein went off to Bergen and acquired two volumes of Schubert songs some of which they performed "in our customary manner".[19] By September 21st, 1913 Pinsent reports: "We have now a repertoire of some 40 Schubert songs—which we perform—Ludwig whistling the air and I playing the accompaniment".[20]

There is regular and frequent attendance at the Cambridge University Musical Club with Pinsent and others, including Bertrand Russell. Wittgenstein's reactions to the program are indicative of his musical tastes. Bach, Mozart, Handel, Beethoven, Schumann, Schubert

---

17   David Pinsent, *A Portrait of Wittgenstein as a Young Man,* Oxford: Basil Black-
      well, 1990, 5.
18   *Ibid.,* 61.
19   *Ibid.,* 73.
20   *Ibid.,* 78.

and Brahms compositions are usually received with enthusiasm, while those of Richard Strauss usually avoided. On October the 4th, 1912, for example, Wittgenstein and Pinsent attend a concert "with Brahms' *Requiem* "splendidly performed—those climaxes in it are simply indescribable—W said he had never enjoyed it more—and he has heard it pretty often.... The second half of the concert began with two selections from Strauss' 'Salome': W refused to go in for them, and stayed outside till the Beethoven.... The Beethoven following was the 7th symphony—gorgeous".[21] Again at the Cambridge University Musical Club, on October the 4th 1913, they attend Beethoven's *Septet* and Schubert's *Octet*—the performance was a bit wooden but enjoyed enormously, especially the *Octet*—"wonderfully mystic and romantic".[22]

That Wittgenstein gave a miss to the Strauss may indicate aversion or indifference, or, alternatively an awareness that at any one time he can take in only so much music. There are, he later remarked, an extraordinary number of different kinds of appreciation—the broad, the narrow and deep, and his was concentrated and circumscribed. The fact is however that Wittgenstein considered Strauss a modern composer and, as we shall see later on, he had serious misgivings about "modern music". The attitude to Strauss is in sharp contrast to Mozart and Beethoven whose biographies he recommended to Bertrand Russell. In a letter to Russell the young Wittgenstein wrote: "I am glad you read the lives of Mozart and Beethoven. These are the actual sons of God".[23] When, on another occasion, Wittgenstein went to hear Beethoven's *Choral* symphony with Russell, he described it as "a turning point in my life". That this event was Beethoven's *Ninth Symphony*, celebrating human fraternity, suggests the deep ethical significance of the event for young Ludwig. The cryptic remark is full of promise, but the tendency to explain or justify is resisted.

In London, about a week later, Pinsent and Wittgenstein hear Beethoven's *Violin Concerto* and Brahms' *First Symphony* with Steinbach conducting. On November the 7th at the Guildhall they hear Mozart's *Sonata for 2 pianos*, and "W was very enthusiastic about the

---

21   *Ibid.*, 34.
22   *Ibid.*, 36.
23   Brian McGuinness, *Wittgenstein in Cambridge: Letters and Documents, 1911-1951,* Oxford: Basil Blackwell, 1995, 4.

Mozart".[24] Two days later, at the Cambridge University Musical Club, they attend Dohnányi conducting Beethoven's Piano and Violin Sonata, no. 4. If we look at the intervals, we realize that it was not unusual for Wittgenstein to attend concerts as often as twice a week. There were also "informal" concerts, as on Saturday, April 12, 1913, where they heard a Chopin fugue, a Bach Fugue, a movement of a Brahms' *Sonata for Piano and Violin* and a Mozart trio.[25] And on April the 9th, they went to the Guildhall:

> The programme was splendid and included Bach's *Chaconne*, a Mozart *Sonata for 2 pianos*, the *Kreutzer Sonata* of Beethoven and Brahms' *Variations on a Theme by Haydn*. The latter was amazing—the most wonderful thing I had heard for a long while. The theme itself is indescribable—the variations typical of Brahms at his very greatest, and finally when at the end the theme emerges once more, unadorned, *fortissimo* and in tremendous harmonies, the effect is to make one gasp and grip one's chair![26]

During this period of 1912 and 1913 Wittgenstein was also associated with the Cambridge experimental psychology laboratory, where, with David Pinsent as subject, he conducted experiments on the various factors in music appreciation, such as pitch, rhythm and the property of being musically meaningful. Another noteworthy feature of their friendship is that they argued against "modern music" with other musically minded students—taking up all and sundry.[27] Singled out as a student who supported modern music, was W.M. Lindley: [T]hen [Lindley] and Wittgenstein got arguing about modern music, which was rather amusing. Lindley used not to like modern stuff, but has been corrupted!"[28] Again, "Wittgenstein and Lindley came to tea: there was a lot of animated discussion about modern music—Lindley defending it against us two—which was great fun".[29]

Dirge: Wittgenstein enlisted as a volunteer in the Austrian army

---

24   Pinsent, *A Portrait*, 39.
25   *Ibid.*, 43.
26   *Ibid.*, 53.
27   *Ibid.*, 42, 46, 55.
28   *Ibid.*, 42.
29   *Ibid.*, 46.

in August 1914 and served to the end of the war when he was taken prisoner. David Pinsent, serving as a military test pilot, died in an airplane accident on the 8th of May 1918. Wittgenstein dedicated the *Tractatus* to his memory.

4. Later Listening

Returning to Cambridge some eleven years later Wittgenstein began a new life in philosophy and, for our purposes, we might add, in music—a period that biographer Ray Monk refers to as the "Second Coming". Music continued to play an important part in his life, for its own sake and as a way of interacting with friends and students. What is different about the later listening is the discussion or commentary, no matter how brief, after hearing the music, suggesting that the austere Tractarian attitude, bidding silent reverence, was fading or at any rate less pronounced. Drury recollects a 1930 meeting of the Moral Sciences Club in C.D. Broad's rooms at Cambridge: "Before the meeting began, Wittgenstein and I stood talking looking out of the window; it was a dull grey evening just getting dark. I told Wittgenstein that I had been listening to Beethoven's *Seventh Symphony*, and how impressed I had been by the second movement. Wittgenstein: 'The chord with which that slow movement opens is the colour of that sky' (pointing out of the window). 'At the end of the war, when we were retreating before the Italians, I was riding on a gun carriage and I was whistling to myself that movement. Just at the very end of the movement Beethoven does something which makes one see the theme in an entirely different light".[30] This comment not only gives us a striking image, but also embodies the method of juxtaposition: a sky-scape is put side by side with a piece of music to bring out their respective expressive powers.

The idea of a dialogue between philosophy and music offers a sharp contrast with the way analytical philosophy draws disciplinary boundaries: philosophy in one category and music in another. Such a cultural difference is illustrated by the recollections of John King— another student of Wittgenstein in Cambridge in the early 1930s. In King's memoirs we find more evidence for the easing of the "Whereof

---

30 *Ludwig Wittgenstein Personal Recollections*, ed. Rush Rhees, 130.

one cannot speak, thereof one must be silent" attitude, in the sense that music is discussed and put side by side with philosophy or ideas, even though the memoirist mistakes the import of his own memory when he says that "Music, indeed, was the chief topic of conversation—never philosophy". Music, King recalls:

> was one of the great passions of the Norfolk Rectory where I was born and brought up; and I kept up my choral singing in various choirs in Cambridge. I also had a portable gramophone in my digs at Portugal Place; and Wittgenstein came several times to hear some of the few records which I had. Two records in particular called forth remarkable comments. I once put on the 2nd, 3rd, and 4th movements of Beethoven's *Quartet in C sharp minor, opus 131*, played, I believe, by the Lener String Quartet. He was rapt in his attention and most excited at the end of the playing. He jumped up as if something had suddenly struck him and said: 'How easy it is to think that you understand what Beethoven is saying' (and here he seized a pencil and a piece of paper), 'how you think you have understood the projection' (and he drew two kinds of a circle, thus) and then suddenly (and here he added a bulge) 'you realize that you haven't understood anything at all.'[31]

Another fragment from King's memoirs is equally striking:

> The second comment came from a playing of my then most recent acquisition, Brahms's *String Quartet in B flat Major, opus 67*. I told him that I particularly liked the 3rd movement where a superb and hauntingly lovely theme is given over to the viola. After this movement, he said with his characteristic rapt look—drawing breath, shutting his eyes and gathering his brows, and drawing down his chin with mouth closed, just as if he were savouring something exquisite, 'How strange it is that musicians at that time were so much concerned with the 'cloven hoof'. These comments took my breath away: I remained tongue-tied, and have cursed myself ever since for not questioning him about what he meant.[32]

---

31   *Ibid.*, 84-85.
32   *Ibid.*, 85.

At least two things are of interest here. What is ironic about King's apparent recollection—that music, never philosophy, was the chief topic of conversation—is that it constitutes an unwitting self-refutation of the announced view, namely, the exclusive disjunction of music and philosophy. The very comments that he finds fascinating and describes as rendering him tongue-tied are about *both* music *and* philosophy. The comments about the Beethoven Quartet acquire philosophical significance if they are put side by side with Wittgenstein's work at the time on problems concerning meaning and truth, about how we relate propositions to the world through "the method of projection". The comments about the Brahms *String Quartet* and the 'cloven hoof' have cultural import, for Wittgenstein evidently puts music and cultural/ religious ideas side by side. It seems then that while the exclusive disjunction between music and philosophy may have come naturally to King, it was alien to Wittgenstein. Also of note is the advent of the gramophone record, a change in the technology of music that made mechanical reproduction possible and thus the listening to records in students' 'digs'. The downside was the palpable loss of musical communing, being together in the concert hall or the Guild Hall.

The substance and tenor of King's musical recollections are confirmed and expanded on in the memoirs of another student. Theodore Redpath recalls that "[f]rom time to time in conversation Wittgenstein made illuminating (or at least thought-provoking) comments on the general drift of a musical work or passage. I recall two which seemed to me particularly striking. One day I had been listening to the *Ninth Symphony* of Beethoven and he asked me what I considered the drift to be. I said it seemed to me to represent a revolution. He agreed with that, but with a modification: 'Yes, but an *ideal* revolution.'"[33] No doubt, the "modification" was meant to remind Redpath of the joyful reconciliation at the end of the symphony—where the uplifting choral part in unison affirms human solidarity and thus resolves conflict.

Concerning Beethoven, there is more. Redpath recalls Wittgenstein saying:

---

33 Theodore Redpath, *Ludwig Wittgenstein: A Student's Memoir*, London: Duck-worth, 1990, 57.

> 'I have no doubt that anything the old man wrote was good,
> but it doesn't *mean* much to *me*—except for the symphonies'.
> I could not even get him to agree to listen to the wonderful
> slow movement of Beethoven's last *String Quartet, Op. 135*,
> which I had from schooldays on an HMV 78 rpm gramophone
> record for which it had been played by the Flonzaley Quartet.
> I could not conceive of his having difficulty in responding to
> that movement, but he obstinately refused to listen to it. In all
> fairness, however, it must be added that he may well have tried
> the whole work before and got nothing out of any of it.[34]

This recollection is not quite in sync with comments Wittgenstein made
in conversation with other students, since it suggests that Wittgenstein's
appreciation of Beethoven was confined to the symphonies and excluded
the late quartets. This is at odds with King's vignette of Wittgenstein
deeply engaged with one of Beethoven's late quartets, namely, *Quartet
in C sharp minor, opus 131*. The more likely explanation is that at the
time of Redpath's offer, Wittgenstein had reasons of his own for his
refusal to listen to Beethoven's last *String Quartet, Op. 135*—reasons
other than *not* being able to get anything out of the late works. To say
that he appreciated the late quartets is, of course, not to deny that all
things considered he may have preferred the symphonies.

On another visit to Redpath's "digs" Wittgenstein heard him
practicing the top part of Mozart's *Fugue in G Minor for Four Hands* and
asked what Redpath "imagined it to mean. I said I have no idea. 'Well',
he replied, 'it's the eternity of the damned!'" This is a partial echo of
a remark Wittgenstein made on a previous occasion in a conversation
with Drury to the effect that "Mozart believed in both Heaven and Hell,
whereas Beethoven only believed in Heaven and nothingness".[35] Also,
there is the passion for Brahms: "I vividly remember", Redpath writes,

> walking with him one afternoon in the town. We were about to
> pass in front of the Great Gate of St John's College when we
> heard through an open window of the Music Room a passage
> from the *Third Symphony in F Major*. The passage was from the
> third movement, the *Poco allegretto*, in C minor. He stopped,
> and motioned to me to stop too. He seemed spellbound. As

---

34   *Ibid.*, 54-55.
35   *Ludwig Wittgenstein Personal Recollections*, ed. Rush Rhees, 126.

the wonderful lyrical crescendos unfolded, he drew his breath, and his facial expression responded to the music with striking sensitivity. We stood there for about a minute, I should say, till the movement ended. He was radiant with enthusiasm and satisfaction.[36]

Nor did Wittgenstein's love of Schubert and lieder diminish in later life. His careful attention to details of performance and interpretation are born out by another Redpath recollection which gives us a lively sense of how those Schubert songs may have been performed in Wittgenstein's early days in Cambridge—with Pinsent playing the piano and Wittgenstein whistling, as mentioned before. Redpath had been exploring *Der Leiermann*—the last song of Schubert's cycle *Die Winterreise*. The song, we might recall, is about an old organ grinder who stands at the end of a village monotonously turning the handle of his barrel-organ with fingers stiff with cold and tottering barefooted on the ice. Wittgenstein happened to drop by and:

> asked me to play the piano accompaniment. When I started off with a few bars he criticized my *tempo* for not being quite regular and monotonous enough. He was also insistent that the semiquaver rests should always be brought out clearly, and he was keen that the accentuated beats should suggest the mechanical hiccups of the hurdy-gurdy. We went through the whole accompaniment, and once it seemed to him in order he whistled the song part right through, admirably. As far as the text was concerned he wanted me to be aware of the monotony of the repetitions, and he also noted the balance of the realism of the happenings and the clam tolerance of the old man. The wistfulness of the ending did not seem to him sentimental but buoyant, and he threw in the comment that, though Schumann's music was sometimes sentimental, Schubert's *never* was.[37]

To be sure, these recollections by Wittgenstein's friends in the 1930s support my claim that by this time he thought that questions about "the drift" or "meaning" of a musical work or passage were legitimate and interesting questions. As well, the recollections capture

---

36 Redpath, *A Student's Memoir*, 56.
37 *Ibid.*, 58-59.

his seriousness about music and the way it should be played. For instance, Wittgenstein was invited to tea and to hear Redpath and his friend Basil Willey play Mozart's piano duets including the *Theme and Variations in G Major* (K. 501):

> We had barely started that piece when, in the eighth bar, Basil, who was playing the bass part, executed the closing arpeggio in a light-hearted, even jaunty way. Wittgenstein was livid: 'Is that a joke or something?' he rapped out.[38]

Such comments give a rather grim and one-sided impression of his personality.

Redpath's memoir, however, also brings a much needed balance. A lighter and somewhat unexpected aspect of Wittgenstein comes through vignettes which show that Wittgenstein's range was not confined to the Austrian-German classical repertoire but included some French composers and performers as well:

> An amusing musical episode, trivial but significant, occurred one day when he was talking with me about Bizet. He evidently liked Bizet, and he told me that Bizet had appealed to Nietzsche as 'Southern music', in contrast with the 'Northern music' of Wagner. I had recently been playing to myself through a piano score of *L'Arlésienne* and had enjoyed the work keenly. I told him how much I had liked it, and he said he liked it too. I asked him if he remembered the opening theme of the Overture, and I started to hum it. He said I had not got it quite right, and he tried to whistle it correctly, as he thought. He was very proficient at whistling and sometimes whistled splendidly to piano accompaniment. This time, though, he didn't get the melody right, and I had the face to say so and tried to whistle it correctly myself. My whistling was not as technically skillful as his, but this time I am pretty sure that it was at least accurate. He was annoyed and burst out: 'We are a couple of asses!'[39]

---

38 *Ibid.*, 89.
39 *Ibid.*

And now to a recollection of an evening of unequivocal delight for "a couple of asses": In May 1938 Redpath was invited, perhaps as a reward for a favour he did for Wittgenstein, to the Cambridge Festival Theatre to hear the *diseuse* Yvette Guilbert, who was about 71 at the time and whom Wittgenstein described as "a very great artiste".[40] The songs she performed covered a wide period—medieval religious and secular songs through feudal times to the seventeenth century and onwards. Wittgenstein, Redpath reports, was strongly impressed and buoyant with delight. He preferred the narrative of Christ's Nativity to the Passion; relished the secular songs, enjoying the piquancy of the protest by the unhappily married woman who complained that her husband beat her and appreciated the racy outburst in the other song in which the woman was planning to get rid of her husband. In the second half of the programme Wittgenstein was particularly delighted by *Les Deux Notaires*, a duet between two lawyers in high spirits reminiscing about their youth and, especially, by an eighteenth century monologue '*Mais oui, Mesdames*', which Yvette Guilbert had herself set to music. The latter is about a lively woman who had been jilted by her lover after a six and a half month courtship, '*Mais oui, mais, oui.*'

> The story she tells intermingles confessions of her passion for the man with assertions of proud independence and of mockery for the faithless rascal. The '*Mais oui, mais oui* ' and '*Mais oui Madames*' are strewn through the song and function sometimes as appeals for the sympathy of the ladies to whom she is telling the story and sometimes simply to underline the facts and intentions. The sounds in their varying intonations still ring in my [Redpath's] ears over fifty years later…. Yvette Guilbert's was a brilliant *virtuoso* performance. Understandably, Wittgenstein was strongly impressed and buoyant with delight. At the end of the whole performance he applauded with great enthusiasm and was anxious to visit Yvette Guilbert to present her with a magnificent bouquet of scarlet carnations…. The whole occasion brought out for me another side of Wittgenstein's personality, and I found it both astonishing and refreshing.[41]

---

40   *Ibid.*, 59.
41   *Ibid.*, 59-64.

Now that we have achieved a more or less balanced view of Wittgenstein's musical profile from the available materials, I proceed with the task of gaining a better understanding of the roots of Wittgenstein's musical sensibility by situating it in the distinctive context and cultural sensibility of 19th-century and *fin de siècle* Vienna.

Chapter II
Early Views: Wittgenstein's Vienna Revisited

1. Eduard Hanslick and a Tradition in Music

The importance of cultural context and tradition—whether understanding a person, a language or a work of art—is a basic premise in Wittgenstein's mature philosophical perspective. We are reminded of this in his lectures on aesthetics: "[t]o describe appreciation you have to describe a whole culture", a remark that encourages the retrieval of tradition and context in understanding his reflections on music and its appreciation. I now situate Wittgenstein's attitude to and remarks on music in the larger context of Austrian-German musical aesthetics and criticism, with particular reference to Eduard Hanslick. Sketching this background also helps us with the task of providing a perspective on Wittgenstein's discriminate musical preferences and his practice of listening to music.

The first thing to do is to put right up front the intimate relationship between music and philosophy in Austrian-German culture. "Unlike much Anglo-American philosophy", Steven Burns aptly observed:

> nineteenth century German philosophy is in constant dialogue with literature, theology, and politics, and that a full understanding of this period cannot be realized by attending to the officially philosophical works alone.[1]

This is especially true, Burns continues, of the dialogue between philosophy and music, in which Wagner engages Schopenhauer, and in turn Nietzsche engages Wagner. Burns' observation makes sense of Wittgenstein's otherwise strange acknowledgement of Robert

---

1 Steven Burns, "A Flock of Nightingales: Wagner's Music and German Philos-ophy", *AE Canadian Aesthetics Journal,* 2002 (online).

Schumann, a composer of the nineteenth century, as a possible source of his cultural ideal:

> I often wonder whether my cultural ideal is a new one, i.e. contemporary, or whether it comes from the time of Schumann. At least it strikes me as a continuation of that ideal, though not the continuation that actually followed it then. That is to say, the second half of the 19th Century has been left out. This, I ought to say, has happened quite instinctively & was not the result of reflection.[2]

In light of this I suggest that Wittgenstein saw himself as, among other things, a participant in the dialogue between music and philosophy, a dialogue in which justice, meaning, truth, and community, beauty, the good and the right were themes for music as well as philosophy. Wittgenstein forcefully reminded us that the arts not only entertain, they instruct and cultivate our humanity. Thus we forget at our peril the tradition of a conversation between philosophy and music that is required to make sense and appreciate the importance of Wittgenstein's remarks about music. A central and influential participant in that conversation was Wittgenstein's Viennese elder, Eduard Hanslick, a renowned critic and an original philosopher of music.

Allan Janik's and Steven Toulmin's masterly retrieval of the cultural context of Wittgenstein's philosophy in *Wittgenstein's Vienna*, as well as Janik's more recent *Wittgenstein's Vienna Revisited*, both identify Hanslick as a dominant figure in 19th and early 20th century music criticism and aesthetics. Surprisingly, these books do not take up the topic of Wittgenstein on music nor do they relate Wittgenstein to Hanslick, so I propose to extend their retrieval. Hanslick's book *On the Musically Beautiful: A Contribution towards the Aesthetics of Music* underwent fifteen editions between 1854 and 1922, and through his role as music critic for the influential Viennese newspaper *Neue Freie Presse*, he was a dominant figure in Viennese and German musical culture for more than half a century. He took sides in the Brahms versus Wagner/Liszt controversy and was a warm supporter of Brahms and a hostile critic of Wagner and Liszt. When Wagner drew the figure of Beckmesser in the *Mastersingers of Nuremberg* he clearly had Hanslick

---

2   Wittgenstein, *Culture*, 4.

in mind, since in two early sketches of the libretto the name 'Hans Lich' appears instead of 'Beckmessser'. No Viennese seriously interested in music, even if they wanted to, could avoid reading or discussing Hanslick. All this would have been known to the Wittgenstein household and presumably to Ludwig.

In one sense there is no direct evidence linking Hanslick to Wittgenstein: His name does not appear on the list of influences Wittgenstein drew up, even though the names of the architect Adolf Loos, of the culture-critic Karl Kraus, of the philosopher and psychologist Otto Weininger, as well as of the philosopher of history Oswald Spengler are on the list. This of course does not settle the matter of influence, since Freud's name is not on the list, even though Wittgenstein for a period described himself as a "disciple or follower" of Freud. With such a highly critical student, one might say, who needs any disciples? The case with Hanslick is different, however, in that his name does not appear in any of Wittgenstein's writings nor does he explicitly draw upon actual quotations from Hanslick, while Freud is referred to by name and his ideas are critically discussed in Wittgenstein's lectures and notebooks. So it might be said that Hanslick's influence, unlike Freud's, is likely to be indirect, perhaps part of Wittgenstein's "early nursery training" consisting of general affinities such as a distinctive taste, of a cultural sensibility, an attitude, an approach. To establish a stronger connection with Hanslick we need to draw on common themes, textual parallels or affinities, shared points of view, and on instructive differences as Wittgenstein reacts to his reading or hearing about Hanslick. I begin with the early nursery training and continue by sketching family resemblances and differences.

There is, in another sense, a direct connection between Hanslick and the Wittgensteins, for what could be more direct than knowledge by acquaintance? Hanslick was a regular guest at the Wittgenstein musical soirées (with the Wittgenstein children included) which were, as Wittgenstein's sister Gretl described them, "always festive occasions, almost solemn, and the beautiful music was the essential thing". Attesting to such a direct connection is Hanslick's reply to a letter from Mrs. Wittgenstein concerned about his health:

> Dear and esteemed and gracious lady,
> Your letter, so beautiful, touched my heart with such warmth, a

sentiment that it happily and gratefully retained for the whole day. Those splendid evenings for which I have you to thank passed in lively reminiscence before my eyes. The magnificent music, the toasts, anticipated with pleasurable excitement, given by your sage and eloquent husband, the deep pleasure you took in rapt attention to the music and the rest! My health, which seems to maintain a certain equilibrium, allows me to hope that I shall be able to thank you in person in May for so kindly inquiring about me.

With the greatest respect, yours, Ed. Hanslick. [3]

With Hanslick's presence at the musical soirées established, we established a direct connection to the Wittgensteins that legitimately motivates further exploration of the question of Hanslick's work as an influence on Wittgenstein's musical sensibility and aesthetics.

Wittgenstein and Hanslick share a conception of music and a musical tradition in which their lives in music was grounded, thereby providing the backdrop for their reactions and assessments. For Hanslick, the history of music began with Bach and Handel, continued with Mozart and reached its summit with Beethoven, Schumann, and Brahms. For Wittgenstein too, music seems to include that spanning from Bach through Mendelssohn to Schumann and Brahms. "Music", he said to his friend Drury, "came to a full stop with Brahms; and even in Brahms I can begin to hear the sound of machinery". But then there was Josef Labor, the blind composer of late Romantic music, who was later but composed as though earlier, whom Ludwig singled out for high praise as one of the six great composers along with Mozart, Haydn, Beethoven, Schubert and Brahms. In any event, this tradition shapes Wittgenstein's musical responses and sets limits to his musical appreciation and understanding. Appreciation and understanding may be difficult, if not impossible, outside one's musical tradition, unless one acquires an insider's understanding of another tradition. His 1914 diary entry about linguistic and moral meaning foreshadows this perspective about Chinese speech as inarticulate gurgling except to those who understand Chinese. Similarly, he often did not recognize

---

3   Alexander Waugh, *The House of Wittgenstein: A Family at War,* New York: Doubleday, 2008, 30-31.

the human being in someone. No doubt he would have said the same thing about music.

Not only is the previous remark applicable to music in general but it also throws light on the young Wittgenstein's attitude to "modern music". Not only can music from another culture be perceived as mere noise, certain developments in one's own musical culture—such as atonality—can foreclose discernment of musical meaning. This gives us reason to think the early Wittgenstein was influenced by Hanslick's pro-Brahms/anti-Wagner criticism that also opposed those composers who adopted Wagner's style and methods, for instance, Richard Strauss and Gustav Mahler who radically departed from the musical tradition of Mozart and Brahms. As we have seen earlier, the young Wittgenstein's attitude to "modern music" is evident in several entries in David Pinsent's diaries. Modern music was something Wittgenstein and Pinsent enthusiastically argued against when at Cambridge. Regrettably, we do no have any indication of the actual content of their debates. So: what could they have meant by "modern music"? To us the obvious candidates are the composers Schoenberg, Berg and Bartók on the Austro-Hungarian side, and perhaps Berlioz, Debussy, Ravel from France, and Stravinsky from Russia. To be sure these composers would have been within Wittgenstein's compass, if not within Pinsent's judgement, but at the time the ground breaking compositions of the Austro-Hungarians were still nascent or at least looking for an audience. As for French composers, Wittgenstein rarely mentions or discusses them. So, who were the composers Wittgenstein and Pinsent had in mind when they were arguing against modern music?

The proposed Wittgenstein-Hanslick connection suggests Richard Strauss and Gustav Mahler represented "modern music" for them, and were at least then the bête noire to be blamed for the threat to and impending collapse of the tradition. Consider the aversion to Strauss palpable in an entry in Pinsent's diary we have seen already: "The second half of the concert began with two selections from Strauss's *Salome*: Wittgenstein refused to go in for them, and stayed outside till the Beethoven, which followed. He went out after that and went back to Lordswood by himself". Recall that after hearing the Strauss, Pinsent comments: The *Salome* was rot, but very clever and amusing in consequence. We can speculate that Wittgenstein gave the Strauss a miss because of his aversion to his compositions, but he missed the

Bach which ended the concert, because he reached the limits of his ability to listen further. As to Mahler, the other "modern" composer, Wittgenstein's assessment of his music seems brutal: "worthless", he said. One way to explain such overall musical preference and sensibility is to say that Wittgenstein was a musical formalist á la Hanslick, a suggestion that needs support of substantial and compelling thematic and textual connections—a task to which I now turn.

2. Was the Early Wittgenstein a Musical Formalist? Affinities to Hanslick

What then were some specific themes in the dialogue between music and philosophy that Wittgenstein took up and put his stamp on? A central theme in the conversation between music and philosophy had to do with the question of the meaning of music and included theorizing about the relation between music and language. In the course of doing so, Hanslick criticized Romanticist views that music is a language of emotion/feeling and put forth and defended a formalist view of music as sound in motion. He argued for the autonomy of music and against reductionist theories that sought to locate musical meaning in matters external to music. In particular, Hanslick effectively combated theories that equated musical meaning with representation of nature, as well as widely received Romanticist views that would reduce meaning in music to the expression of emotions/feelings internal to us. Neither the expression of emotion nor any sort of representation, Hanslick argued, are essential to music; on the contrary, they are often a distraction both to musical experience and understanding. His conclusion is striking and strangely satisfying: "We cannot *say* what music means; in music", he claimed, "there is both meaning and logical sequence, but in a musical sense; it is a language we speak and understand, but which we are unable to translate".[4] Music has meaning in a purely musical sense: unique, self-contained, having an autonomous meaning of its own.

This austere stance resonates with Wittgenstein's treatment of the question of musical meaning in the 1914–1916 *Notebooks* and the

---

4   Eduard Hanslick, *On the Musically Beautiful*, tr. Geoffrey Payzant, Indianapolis: Hackett, 1986, 30.

Tractatus and renders intelligible his frequent juxtaposition of remarks about the meaning of a theme in music and the meaning of a proposition or a sentence. In the *Tractatus*, language—whether in everyday speech, dictionary entries or musical notation—veils the logical form required for understanding, and once the form is uncovered, the way is open to understanding. Consider *Tractatus* 4.002 and 4.0031:

> Language disguises thought. So much so, that from the outward form of the clothing it is impossible to infer the form of the thought beneath it, because the outward form of the clothing is not designed to reveal the form of the body, but for entirely different purposes…. It was Russell who performed the service of showing that the apparent logical form of a proposition need not be its real one.

The general form of a proposition is identified as 'This is how things stand': "A proposition is a picture of reality" (4.01). "If a proposition has meaning, then it pictures or represents the existence or non-existence of states of affairs" (4.1).

The early Wittgenstein approaches questions of meaning within the framework of the picture theory and presents an essentialist theory of language. Since tones and themes in absolute music do not picture or represent things in the world, they have no meaning in the way factual propositions do. However, "a tune is not a mere jumble of notes", we are told in the early *Notebooks* as unmusical people think" just like "a proposition is not a mere jumble of words",[5] since both propositions and tunes can be articulated and followed. (This is echoed in *Tractatus* 3 141· "A proposition is not a medley of words.—Just as a theme in music is not a medley of notes".) Therefore, musical meaning needs to be understood differently.

"Musical themes", Wittgenstein says, "are in a certain sense propositions. Knowledge of the nature of logic will for this reason lead to knowledge of the nature of music".[6] In what sense are musical themes propositions then? Since they are unlike factual propositions, the analogy has to be with propositions of logic which in turn are said to be "tautologies", empty of content and not about anything: "All

---

5 Ludwig Wittgenstein, *Notebooks 1914-1916,* Oxford: Basil Blackwell, 1961, 41.
6 *Ibid.,* 40.

tautologies say the same thing—namely, nothing" (4.461). "A tune is a kind of tautology, it is complete in itself; it satisfies itself".[7] Neither logic nor music *say* anything; rather, logic *shows* the structure of the world, while tunes and themes *show* the structure of music. The early Wittgenstein was indeed a musical formalist: he saw music, or better still, heard music, as a formal system only with no possibility of interpretation or translation. Hanslick may be read as having performed a similar service for music that Russell performed for logic: he made us realize that underneath the deceptive surface of music is its real structure to be unearthed.

Wittgenstein and Hanslick are also at one in their rejection of causal theories of musical meaning. Hanslick acknowledges that the experience of music may cause emotions, and making music may be caused by emotions, but the immediate experience of music is not an emotion. Nor are the thoughts involved in making or composing music emotions. Then he specifies a necessary condition for listening to music aesthetically: "that we hear the piece for its own sake.... The instant music is put to use merely as a means to produce a certain mood in us or as an accessory or an ornament, it ceases to be effective as pure art". When Shakespeare's dying Henry IV called for music:

> it was not with the intention of really listening to the performance, but for the purpose of letting it lull himself into a dreaming state by means of its mere sound. In all these instances, it is entirely a matter of indifference what piece of music it is, provided it has... the required basic attributes.... Only the person who retains not just the general aftereffects of feeling, but also the... specific image of just this particular piece of music, has heard it and enjoyed it.[8]

"If all that matters is the effect the music causes," then, Hanslick argues, "we could without much alteration substitute 'poetry,' 'art,' or indeed 'beauty,' for 'music' in such situations".[9]

Wittgenstein, in his characteristic manner, engages Hanslick's

---

7   *Ibid.*
8   Hanslick, *On the Musically Beautiful*, 66.
9   *Ibid.*, 67.

insight into the issue of "substitutivity" by imagining another culture where music plays a different role:

> Here there is something you might call music, since it has notes. They treat music like this: certain music makes them walk like this. They play a record to do this. One says: "I need this record now. Oh, no, take the other, it is just as good. If I admire a minuet I can't say: 'Take another. It does the same thing.' What do you mean? It is not the same. One can't say: 'Now play Mozart, it does just as well.[10]

These ways of arguing against causal theories of music in general, and against "substitution" in particular, parallel many of Wittgenstein's remarks in substance and vocabulary. *Tractatus* 5.1361 asserts that "Belief in the causal nexus is superstition" and later on, in 1930, he remarks: 16 years ago when I had the thought that the law of causality is insignificant in itself & that there is a way of regarding the world that does not bear it in mind, I felt the beginning of a New Era".[11] Giving up the principle of causality seems to have liberated him to look at things differently and thus do philosophy differently.

Rejection of causal theories in general is a hallmark of the *Tractatus* and of the later philosophy, and resistance to causal theories of music in particular also appears in Wittgenstein's lectures on aesthetics. The point that aesthetic explanations are not causal explanations is echoed several times, perhaps most explicitly in the following passage:

> The sort of explanation one is looking for when one is puzzled by an aesthetic impression is not a causal explanation, not one corroborated by experience or by statistics as to how people react You cannot arrive at the explanation by means of psychological experiment. One of the characteristic things about psychological experiments is that they have to be made on a number of subjects. It is the agreements of Smith, Jones and Robinson which allows you to give an explanation—in this sense of explanation, e.g., you can try out a piece of music in a psychological laboratory

---

10   Ludwig Wittgenstein, *Lectures and Conversations on Aesthetics, Psychology and Religious Belief*, ed. Cyril Barrett, Berkeley: University of California Press, 1967, 34.
11   Wittgenstein, *Public and Private*, 29.

> and get the result that the music acts in such and such a way
> under such and such a drug. This is not what one means or what
> one is driving at by an investigation into aesthetics.[12]

What motivates Wittgenstein's critique is not only his intention to
remove a basic misconception about aesthetics, but also his concern
that the *scientistic attitude* of the age mistakes a contingent matter of
convention for inexorable necessity. "[T]he insidious thing about the
causal point of view", Wittgenstein complains, is that it leads us to say:
'Of course, it had to happen like that.' Whereas we ought to think: it
may have happened like that—and also in many other ways".[13]

    Another affinity emerges when we consider what Hanslick has to
say regarding the question of musical understanding:

> The most significant factor in the mental process which
> accompanies the comprehending of a musical work and makes
> it enjoyable will most frequently be overlooked. It is the mental
> satisfaction which the listener finds in continuously following
> and anticipating the composer's designs, here to be confirmed in
> his expectations, there to be agreeably led astray.... Only such
> music as brings about and rewards this mental pursuing, which
> could quite properly be called a musing of the imagination, will
> provide fully artistic satisfaction.... [M]usic is characteristically
> this type of activity, for the reason that its achievements are not
> static; they do not come into being all at once but spin themselves
> out sequentially before the hearer, hence they demand from him
> not an arbitrarily granted, lingering, and intermittent inspection,
> but an unflagging attendance in keenest vigilance. This
> attendance can, in the case of intricate compositions, become
> intensified to the level of spiritual achievement.[14]

Even though Wittgenstein may raise his eyebrows at Hanslick's idea of
"comprehending music as a mental process", there are several features
of this key passage that would resonate with him. First, there is the
connecting of the question of musical meaning with the question of
musical understanding. Secondly, there is the retrieval of agency in

---

12 Wittgenstein, *Lectures*, 21.
13 Wittgenstein, *Culture*, 45.
14 Hanslick, *On the Musically Beautiful*, 64.

musical understanding: the listener imaginatively and attentively follows as the composer takes him on a journey of the familiar and the strange so that he or she is reassured and in turn surprised. Third, aesthetic enjoyment involves listening and attending to the music, rather than in some passive experience of disengaged rapture. All this suggests that the author of the *Tractatus* was a formalist both in the philosophy of language and the philosophy of music. He held that the logical form has to be dug out from the surface grammar of language and that the structure of the composition has to be unearthed from the morass of feelings and irrelevant associations the music brings in its wake.

3. Whistling the Inexpressible: Wittgenstein, Hanslick and Schopenhauer

If we cannot *say* what music means, how does a formalist perform or listen to music so as to get a grip on its form? One might respond: Theories of music make no difference here. A performer should just perform-play the notes; a listener should just listen-hear the notes. However, for Wittgenstein, things are not so simple: "We must not forget", he says that:

> even our more refined, more philosophical scruples have a foundation in instinct. E.g. 'We can never know....' Remaining receptive to further arguments. People who couldn't be taught this would strike us as mentally inferior. *Still* incapable of forming a certain concept.[15]

What then is the instinct that drives the "scruple" of formalism in music? The instinct is the fear of losing the music to words (literature/poetry) or to feeling/emotions. Unless we think in a clean and precise manner, we miss what is unique and distinctive to music, namely, tonal forms. This fear is palpable in what Hanslick had to say and the way he argued: "The starting point of all the creative activity of the composer is not the intention to portray a specific feeling [or concept or image] but the devising of a particular melody.... There resounds in the mind

---

15   Wittgenstein, *Culture*, 83.

of the composer a theme, a motif.... *We have to accept it simply as given"*.[16] Music can be grasped only as music and can be understood and enjoyed only from itself, from its own resources.[17] The performer can deliver only what is already in the composition, and this demands not much more than playing the notes.[18]

One way for a formalist to perform songs then is to erase words as extraneous and get at the music itself through an instrumental rendition, and if we do not play or are without an instrument, whistling or humming as "bodily instruments" suffice. Perhaps they are even to be preferred, since the expressive bodily rendition is closer to the music while an instrument somewhat distances it. Whistling or humming is close to what Hanslick calls "an inner singing, not a mere inner feeling, [that] induces the musically gifted person to construct a musical artwork".[19] Wittgenstein, as mentioned before, was a master whistler who often whistled pieces from the classical repertoire, including Schubert songs. How striking and appropriate it is for a philosopher, who throughout his life had respect for the ordinary, to adopt the ordinary practice of whistling as a mode of performance.

If you think this goes without saying, imagine Wittgenstein entering the London underground whistling the finale of Brahms' *First Symphony* and coming across Theodor Adorno's icy stare and critique: "The man who in the subway triumphantly whistles loudly the theme of the finale of Brahms' *First Symphony* is already involved with its debris".[20] The climaxes and repetitions, Adorno continues, render the disconnected fragment memorable, and thus we can make it our own, treating it as if it were our own *property*. What Adorno really objects to is not the triumphant or loud whistling, but the "bourgeois" tendency to transform music into a commodity. Since "the symphony as a whole, spontaneously experienced, can never be appropriated",[21] we dismember it for *prêt-a-porter* possession.

---

16   Hanslick, *On the Musically Beautiful*, 32.
17   *Ibid.*, 30.
18   *Ibid.*, 49.
19   *Ibid.*, 47.
20   Theodor Adorno, "On the Fetish Character of Music and the Regression of Listening" in *The Philosophy of Art Readings Ancient and Modern,* eds Alex Neill and Aaron Ridley, London and New York: Continuum, 1995, 530.
21   *Ibid.*

Is this, one may wonder, a principled objection or an ideological bias? Adorno's reduction of multiple possible motives for whistling the Brahms finale to one, namely, the desire for possession, smacks of a theoretical prejudice: as if Wittgenstein's motive is necessarily a "triumphant possessiveness", rather than, say, a way of resisting despair in a time of desolation; or his sheer enthusiasm for Brahms' music; or a way of sharing, through his whistling, the beauty of the music with his companion. In any event, whistling as a way of performing *least* distracts the listener or performer from the purely musical journey the composer intended to take us on and dovetails with the distinction drawn in the *Tractatus* between what can be said and what can only be *shown*. Wittgenstein could not say anything about what music meant to him because what music has to teach us—the value of music—cannot be stated but can only be shown. Anyone who contravenes the bid to silence not only talks pernicious nonsense but succumbs to the "great temptation to want to make the spirit explicit".[22]

This interpretation seems plausible if we have the *Tractatus* in front and center of our attention, focusing on its assertion that "It is clear that ethics cannot be put into words. Ethics is transcendental. Ethics and aesthetics are one and the same" (6.421) and on its prescription to talk about nothing but the propositions of natural science (6.53). Thus in a Tractarian mood we might whistle, with the young Wittgenstein, what we cannot put into words. On Wittgenstein's return to Cambridge in 1929, Frank Ramsey became a valued friend and conversation partner who prompted Wittgenstein's critical reassessment of the *Tractatus*. If the core proposition of philosophy is that philosophy is nonsense, then, Ramsey bluntly said, "we must take it seriously that it is nonsense".[23] Later he added: "But what we can't say we can't say, and we can't whistle either".[24] The response is made in a different context but is directly applicable to the last proposition of the *Tractatus*: "Whereof one cannot speak thereof one must remain silent".

The pianist who gives a repeat performance after being asked for the meaning of a short piece he had just played is bringing attention to limits. Repetition, in music and language, plays an important role of

---

22 Wittgenstein, *Culture*, 11.
23 F.P. Ramsey, "Philosophy" in *The Foundations of Mathematics*, ed. R.B. Braithwaite, London: Routledge and Kegan Paul, 1931, 263.
24 *Ibid.*, 238.

gesturing to the limits of what can be described. Listening to music we sometimes say that:

> '[t]he impression made by this melody is completely indescribable.'—that means: a description is no use (for my purpose); you have to hear the melody. If art serves 'to arouse feelings', is, perhaps, perceiving it with the senses included amongst these feelings?[25]

Similarly, "[t]he limit of language manifests itself in the impossibility of describing the fact that corresponds to a sentence without simply repeating the sentence".[26]

But why, it might be asked, bring Hanslick into this discussion about the issue of being linguistically silent so as to hear "the meaning of music" pure, if not simple? After all, Arthur Schopenhauer is the original source for the perspective that both Hanslick and Wittgenstein are espousing, namely, that "music speaks its own language" and "if it tries to stick too closely to the words and to mould itself according to the events, it endeavors to speak a language not its own".[27] Wittgenstein acknowledged Schopenhauer's influence on the *Tractatus*, referring to him in the text as well as including him among the writers who influenced him.[28] Also, Schopenhauer regarded music as the most powerful and penetrating of the arts, since "it bypasses ideas, is quite independent of the phenomenal world, positively ignores it, and [....] could still exist even if there were no world at all, which cannot be said of the other arts...".[29] Unlike the other arts that "copy the ideas" and thus are limited to the phenomenal world, music "speaks" of the essence of the world, an essence we have access to only through music; hence it has special philosophical significance.

In this vein, Schopenhauer attempts to grasp music's relation to emotion/feeling as well as its universality. Music for him is expressive and bound up with emotion but:

---

25   Wittgenstein, *Culture*, 42.
26   *Ibid.*, 13.
27   Arthur Schopenhauer, *The World as Will and Representation*, tr. E.F.J. Payne, Indiana Hills, Colorado: The Falcon Press, 1958, Vol. I, 262.
28   Wittgenstein, *Culture*, 16.
29   Schopenhauer, *World as Will*, Vol. I, 257.

does not express this or that particular and definite pleasure, this or that affliction, pain, sorrow, horror, gaiety, merriment or peace of mind, but joy, pain, sorrow, horror, gaiety, merriment, peace of mind themselves, to a certain extent in the abstract, their essential nature, without any accessories, and so also without the motives for them. Nevertheless, we understand them perfectly in this extracted quintessence.[30]

In this passage Schopenhauer conjures up a strange yet philosophically familiar view of emotions as feelings without any need for what they are about in order to identify and understand them. As if emotions were distinct mental states or processes we can identify through introspection—by looking into ourselves. As if we could tell anger apart from indignation, fear from awe or anxiety, shame from embarrassment, without knowing their intentional objects or their context. Implicit in Schopenhauer is a crude Cartesian theory of emotions, and Hanslick, who only alludes to Schopenhauer, is on to the theory's shortcomings early on. Claiming that music cannot express particular emotions, Hanslick argues, almost as if he were one of our contemporaries, that expressions of "specific" emotions require thoughts about their specific objects, and music cannot represent such thoughts. Therefore, to say that a musical composition expresses a specific emotion, say, awe, is absurd, for *nothing* could be said in response to the question: in awe of what?

As to music's universality and its relation to the other arts: Schopenhauer took notice of our inclination to relate music to particular things by way of analogy:

[O]ur imagination is easily stirred by music, and tries to shape that invisible, yet vividly aroused spirit-world that speaks to us directly, to clothe it with flesh and bone, and thus embody it in an analogous example. This is the origin of the song with words, and finally of the opera…. It is just this universality which belongs uniquely to music, together with the more precise distinctness, that gives it that high value as the panacea of all our sorrows. Therefore if music tries to stick too closely to the words, and to mould itself according to the events, it is endeavouring to speak a language not its own. No one has kept

---

30   *Ibid.*, 261.

> so free from this mistake as Rossini; hence his music speaks its own language so distinctly and purely that it requires no words at all, and therefore produces its full effect even when rendered by instruments alone.[31]

Since many people don't like Rossini, or even classical music as such, 'universality' here cannot mean that it appeals to everyone. Perhaps it comes to the twin claims that music transcends linguistic boundaries and it inspires us to relate it to our world by way of analogy, despite the impossibility of capturing it thus.

In his allusion to Schopenhauer Hanslick does not name or quote him, but makes similar points in a crisp but metaphysically sparse manner:

> Since music has no prototype in nature and expresses no conceptual content, it can be talked about only in dry technical definitions or with poetical fictions. Its realm is truly not of this world. All the fanciful portrayals, characterizations, circumscriptions of a musical work are either figurative or perverse. What in every other art is still description is in music already metaphor. Music demands once and for all to be grasped as music and can be only from itself understood and in itself enjoyed.[32]

Wittgenstein is reported to have echoed this view with awe when he said to his friend Drury that music is a world in itself. But there is an important difference: In the later Wittgenstein's hands, the mist of the underlying metaphysics of other-worldliness—Schopenhauer's "spirit world", even Hanslick's "a realm not of this world"—is stripped away.

Unlike Hanslick, Wittgenstein takes seriously the aesthetic theory that "the aim of music is to communicate feelings", and extracts a measure of the truth it contains. Consider what he says about a classic theory of art as expression:

> There is *much* to be learned from Tolstoy's false theorizing that the work of art conveys 'a feeling'. And you might really call it, if not the expression of a feeling, an expression of feeling,

---

31   *Ibid.*, 261-262.
32   Hanslick , *On the Musically Beautiful*, 30.

or a felt expression. And you might say too that people who understand it to that extent 'resonate' with it, respond to it. You might say: the work of art does not seek to convey *something else*, just itself. As, if I pay someone a visit, I don't wish simply to produce such & such feelings in him, but above all to pay him a visit, & naturally I also want to be well received. And it does start to be really absurd, to say the artist wishes that, what he feels when writing, the other should feel when reading. Presumably I can think I understand a poem (e.g.), understand it in the way its author would wish, but what he may have felt in writing it, that doesn't concern me at all.[33]

The shift between Wittgenstein's early and later philosophy runs parallel to the shift between an admiring and a critical attitude to Schopenhauer. Consider:

One could call Schopenhauer a quite crude mind. I.e., he does have refinement, but at a certain level this suddenly comes to an end & he is as crude as the crudest. Where real depth starts, his finishes. One might say of Schopenhauer: he never takes stock of himself.[34]

Well, what is so crude about Schopenhauer? What does he fail to notice about himself—i.e. what is he saying? The error Schopenhauer falls into is an a priori dogmatism that Wittgenstein delineates by a homely example:

'Yes, that's how it is,' you say, 'because that's how it *must* be!' (Schopenhauer: the real life span of the human being is 100 years.) 'Of course, it *must* be like that!' It is as though you have understood a creator's *purpose*. You have understood the *system*. You do not ask yourself 'How long do human beings actually live then?', that seems now a superficial matter; whereas you have understood something more profound.[35]

This sort of philosophical self-deception is also at the heart of the *Tractatus* and could be leveled at the young Wittgenstein: The real form

---

33   Wittgenstein, *Culture*, 67.
34   *Ibid.*, 41.
35   *Ibid.*, 30

of the proposition (the real use of language) is 'This is how things are.' Or music as such consists in the formal structure of the composition. You do not ask yourself about 'How do human beings actually understand or use language or music?' How to avoid this sort of "prejudice"? We need to

> posit the ideal as what it is, namely as an object of comparison—a measuring rod as it were—within our way of looking at things, & not as a preconception to which everything must conform. This namely is the dogmatism into which philosophy can so easily degenerate.[36]

Schopenhauer's name is also mentioned as Wittgenstein compares language and architecture:

> Phenomena akin to language in music and architecture. Significant irregularity—in Gothic e.g. (I have in mind the towers of St. Basil's Cathedral.) Bach's music is more like language than Mozart's & Haydn's. The double bass recitative in the 4th movement of Beethoven's 9th Symphony. (Compare too Schopenhauer's remark about *universal* music composed to a *particular* text.)[37]

The young Wittgenstein admires Schopenhauer's otherworldly musical metaphysics with the proviso that it can't be talked about, but needs to be shown. Music stands alone and speaks a language of its own. To ask for an explanation for what the music means is misguided and the only legitimate response is "Play it again, Sam", as the protagonist says to the pianist in the film *Casablanca*. The later Wittgenstein rejects the otherworldly metaphysics, but retains the insight about the importance of music for philosophy but not because it shows the intentional objects of emotion or feeling—"the reality of the will". While Schopenhauer separates the arts and makes music stand alone, Wittgenstein brings the individual arts together in a family—the sister arts—with their affinities and differences acknowledged, retaining the view that music is expressive of feeling and emotion, in the sense that "felt expression" is a feature of the music. So, the music does not

---

36   *Ibid.*, 30.
37   *Ibid.*, 40.

express a particular emotion or feeling that can be identified in terms of
its intentional object, but shows a particular expressive face, or makes
a particular gesture that may be the same despite the fact that the face
is younger or older, fatter or leaner. "A theme no less than a face wears
an expression".[38] If we look at the later Wittgenstein's remarks on these
themes, we find that in some respects he is much closer to Hanslick than
to Schopenhauer. Like Hanslick, he repudiates Schopenhauer's picture
of emotion, he rejects the metaphysics, declines the role of paradigm
Schopenhauer proposed, but adopts the use of analogy and metaphor to
aid musical understanding and appreciation. Amidst the harsh criticism,
it's easy to forget what was kept.

How did the shift between Wittgenstein's early and later
perspective come about? This is a question that has received much
scholarly attention and I engage only its neglected aesthetic aspect since
it has relevance to understanding Wittgenstein's remarks on music. Now
I go on to look at the transition period in which Wittgenstein struggles
with the tradition as he tries to find a new way of looking and listening.

---

38 Wittgenstein, *Culture*, 59.

Chapter III
Wittgenstein in Transit: A Critique of the Tradition

1. Is Beauty All It's Cracked Up to Be?

"Today as I was thinking about my work in philosophy & said to myself: I destroy, I destroy, I destroy",[1] reads a 1931 diary entry as Wittgenstein is engaged in dismantling the philosophical tradition which, of course, includes the aesthetic tradition. At the core of the aesthetic tradition are the foundational ideas of the beautiful, of the work of music, and of an attitude of listening that Hanslick endorsed, applied and clarified in his work and criticism. "It is objectively certain", he asserts, "that what rightly pleases in a composition, be it the strictest fugue of Bach or the dreamiest nocturne of Chopin, is the *musically* beautiful".[2]

The early Wittgenstein subscribed to this view of art in general: "The essence of the artistic way of looking at things", he wrote in a 1916 entry in his notebook:

> is that it looks at the world with a happy eye. Life is serious, art is gay…. For there is certainly something in the conception that the end of art is the beautiful. And the beautiful *is* what makes one happy.[3]

When Wittgenstein wrote this he, like Hanslick, still had Plato's idea of finding the general idea lying behind all particular meanings of a word, whereas, in sharp contrast to Hanslick's and his own early views, the later Wittgenstein thinks of the meanings as like the fibres of a rope. One may run the whole way through, but none may.[4] He also rejects

---

1   *Ibid.*, 19.
2   Hanslick, *On the Musically Beautiful*, 40.
3   Wittgenstein, *Notebooks*, 86.
4   Wittgenstein, *Public and Private*, 387.

the idea of the beautiful as foundational for aesthetics and remarks: "The way whole periods are incapable of freeing themselves from the grip of certain concepts–e.g. the concept 'beautiful' & 'beauty'".[5] While Hanslick lumps all good music together under the rubric of the "musically beautiful", Wittgenstein, in opposition to this, contends that the idea of the beautiful does not play a uniquely significant role in musical appreciation or discernment. Moreover, when invoked, "the musically beautiful" may cause a lot of mischief, since it stresses the primacy of classicistic norms, and neglects, for instance, the importance of improvisation and dissonance. As a consequence, the role and significance of irony in music may be missed or underappreciated.

As mentioned before, a salient difference between Hanslick and the later Wittgenstein has to do with the role of "the beautiful" in aesthetics. Hanslick's "intention is to elucidate fully the 'musically beautiful' as the vital issue of our art and the supreme principle of its aesthetics". Wittgenstein rejects the idea of the beautiful as foundational for aesthetics and claims that the preoccupation with the idea of the beautiful has done harm in aesthetics. In this vein he speaks of the "inane role the word 'beautiful' plays in aesthetics" and cites as an instance of such inanity the comment that the repeat of a musical theme is necessary because the piece just sounds more beautiful with the repeat".[6] The concept of the beautiful has done a lot of mischief. The word 'beautiful' idles, it hardly plays a role in genuine discourse about art: "It is remarkable", Wittgenstein observes in the early 1930s, "that in real life, when aesthetic judgments are made, aesthetic adjectives such as 'beautiful', 'fine', etc., play no role at all". Are [such] aesthetic adjectives used in actual music criticism? "You say: Look at this transition", or "The passage here is incoherent".[7]

Nor was this view confined to the early 1930s but was reiterated as late as 1947 in Wittgenstein's Saturday Discussions. Here are the notes of Gilbert Harris Edwards who attended the discussions:

> The word beautiful is bad. The reason is that it is hardly ever
> used outside classes in aesthetics. Wittgenstein said he hardly
> ever applied it to anything he appreciated. It misleads us and

---

5 Wittgenstein, *Culture*, 91.

6 *Ibid.*, 59.

7 Wittgenstein, *Lectures*, 3.

levels out the great difference between appreciating different matters; it is like calling all pictures green or all dishes by the name of the sauce spread over them. To say 'I see the beauty', 'I appreciate it because it is beautiful' is just to use so many words.[8]

These remarks may be seen as direct criticisms of musical aesthetics as presented by Hanslick, who takes the "musically beautiful" as the central term, construes it as an adjective, and then looks for a single property in the music that corresponds to its correct application. According to Wittgenstein such a move is a ground-floor mistake. "The use of such a word as 'beautiful' is even more apt to be misunderstood than the use of most other words if you look at the linguistic form of sentences in which it occurs. "Beautiful' (and 'good') is an adjective, so you are inclined to say: 'This has a certain quality, that of being beautiful'". Wittgenstein challenged such an essentialist account of 'beautiful'. Consider a notebook entry as early as 1933 that point out the importance of asking the question "A beautiful *what*?" when trying to get clear about the intended meaning of beautiful:

> If someone says 'A's eyes have a more beautiful expression than B's', then I want to say that he certainly does not mean by the word 'beautiful' what is common to everything we call 'beautiful'. Rather he is playing a game with this word that has quite narrow bounds. Perhaps I shall not even want to compare the beauty of expression in a pair of eyes with the beauty of the shape of a nose.[9]

He goes on to say that If we had two words for 'beautiful' in the case of 'A's eyes have a beautiful expression' and in the case of 'A's nose has a beautiful shape', so that there is no indication of anything common to these cases, nothing would be lost of the sense of what we wanted to say if we used the two specialized words instead of 'beautiful'.

The absurdity of the essentialist idea that the meaning of 'beautiful' when attributed to diverse things refers to a common property is driven home when we ask what do these beautiful eyes have in common with a Gothic church that we also find beautiful? Certainly not the almond

---

8   Wittgenstein, *Public and Private*, 403.
9   Wittgenstein, *Culture*, 27.

shape, the long lashes, the delicate lids! Well then what? The best
procedure here is to seek the reasons we have for calling something
beautiful and then the peculiar grammar of the word 'beautiful' will be
evident in this in this instance.[10] A neglected aspect of seeing or hearing
something beautiful is its setting. Not even a crystal is beautiful in just
any setting or at least not equally so. Analogously, if we think of a
movement in music as developing from a melody and both Hanslick
and Wittgenstein seem to do—then the musical setting or surroundings
acquire unexpected importance. Drawing a connection between this and
the beauty of mathematical demonstrations as experienced by Pascal,
Wittgenstein remarks that within that [Pascal's] way of looking at the
world those demonstrations had *beauty*, but not what the superficial call
beauty. These remarks are also instructive concerning the meaning of
words: If the context of a conversation has to do with money matters,
then when the word 'bank' is used, its sense is best understood as
'financial institution' rather than 'river bank'.

At this point it might be said, quite rightly, that Hanslick in a sense
rejected Platonism: "the delusion that the aesthetics of any particular art
may be derived through mere conformity to the general, metaphysical
concept of beauty" and avowed that "each particular art demands to be
understood only of itself, through knowledge of its unique technical
characteristics. System-building", he continued, "is giving way to
research firmly based on the axiom that the laws of beauty proper to
each particular art are inseparable from the distinctive characteristics of
its material and technique":[11]

> Where is the Platonism in this? Granted that the general
> metaphysical concept of beauty is rejected for the purposes of
> musical aesthetics, but in another sense Platonism is upheld,
> nay, insisted on, concerning the "musically beautiful.[12]

So, Hanslick's critique of Platonism in aesthetics does not go far
enough. The later Wittgenstein then finds Hanslick's attempt to make
the idea of the *musically beautiful* "the supreme principle of musical
aesthetics" radically misguided on three counts: it is an instance of

---

10   *Ibid.*, 28.
11   Hanslick, *On the Musically Beautiful*, 1-2.
12   *Ibid.*, 2.

Platonist essentialism that causes mischief and distortion in aesthetics; as if the whole edifice of music were to collapse if 'beauty' as foundation crumbles; and last, it forgets or neglects that beauty is not a stand alone concept, but needs an appropriate setting if it is to shine forth.

Before going on to discuss the "work of art", let's consider another idea in Hanslick that sets off alarm bells for Wittgenstein, namely, the idea of *scientism* in musical aesthetics to the effect that at bottom aesthetics is really a kind of science. Consider:

> The striving for as objective as possible a scientific knowledge of things, of which the effects are being felt in all areas of knowledge in our time, must necessarily also have an impact on our investigation of beauty.... If it is not to be wholly illusory, this investigation will have to approach the method of the natural sciences, at least to the point of attempting to get alongside the [beautiful] thing itself.[13]

Hanslick's emphasis on objectivity and science—in particular on physiology—creates a tension with his own assertion that music and its appreciation is a "spiritual achievement". This idea of the role of science was a characteristic feature of the second half of the 19th century and, with the immense success of the sciences, has become a prominent feature of our 20th and 21st century civilization, as well as the *bête noire* of Wittgenstein's later cultural criticism. Wittgenstein's stand against *scientism* puts many of his remarks on science and culture in proper perspective. In this connection an important thing to recognize is that Wittgenstein's remarks about science, here and elsewhere, are not to be taken as anti-science but rather as *anti-scientism*—part of his critique of the idols of the age. Modernism has been successful in destroying many idols and superstition, but in the process seems to have succumbed to the idolatry of science. "All that philosophy can do", Wittgenstein remarked, "is to destroy idols. And that means not creating a new one".[14] If Wittgenstein is a modernist, he is a critical modernist.

---

13   *Ibid.*, 1.

14   Ludwig Wittgenstein, *Philosophical Occasions 1912-1951*, eds James C. Klagge and Alfred Nordmann, Indianapolis and Cambridge: Hackett, 1993, 171. For an overview and assessment of Wittgenstein's critique of scientism, see Peter Campbell and Béla Szabados, "Wittgenstein on Self-Deception in Science, Psychology and Philosophy", *Wittgenstein-Studien* IV/1 (2012).

Hanslick speaks of an "objective, scientific musical aesthetics" in the sense that advancing science will in the future form the foundation of a musical aesthetics. Once this idea gets a hold on the culture, people will speak of "a scientific investigation" in connection with aesthetics— as if aesthetics, in particular musical aesthetics, is a science telling us what's beautiful—a notion that Wittgenstein regards as "almost too ridiculous for words".[15] Wittgenstein, alarmed at the cultural malaise of scientism raising its ugly head even in musical aesthetics, criticizes *psychologism*—a particular form of scientism—that would reduce aesthetics to experimental psychology:

> People often say that aesthetics is a branch of psychology. The idea is that once we are more advanced, everything—all the mysteries of art—will be understood by psychological experiments. Exceedingly stupid as the idea is, this is roughly it. I wish to make it clear that the important problems in aesthetics are not settled by psychological research, but in an entirely different way.[16]

If we think of psychology, say, as a mechanics of the soul, then the idea is that we could predict the reactions of human beings to works of music. Suppose we could do so. Such an achievement would not solve what we feel to be aesthetic puzzlements, for, unlike psychological explanation, aesthetic explanation is not a causal explanation.

> The sort of explanation one is looking for when one is puzzled by an aesthetic impression is not a causal explanation, not one corroborated by experience or by statistics as to how people react. One of the characteristic things about psychological experiments is that they have to be made on a number of subjects. It is the agreements of Smith, Jones and Robinson which allows you to give an explanation in this sense; e.g. you can try out a piece of music in a psychological laboratory and get the result that the music acts in such and such a way under such and such a drug. This is not what one means or what one is driving at by an investigation into aesthetics.[17]

15　Wittgenstein, *Lectures and Conversations*, 11.
16　*Ibid.*, 11.
17　*Ibid.*, 21.

He would say much the same thing about recent attempts at neurological or biochemical reduction as suggested by the following passage: Suppose we knew the nature and mechanism of the molecules in the brain, and the sequence of notes in the music, then we could show that this sequence of notes causes a person to smile and say: 'Oh, how wonderful'. This would enable us, by calculation, to predict people's musical likes or dislikes and give an account of their reactions. We are not so much interested in the effect of a work of music but, rather, why do these bars give me such a peculiar impression? What we really want to solve this sort of aesthetic puzzlement is certain comparisons, certain ways of grouping things. We want an arrangement of certain musical figures, comparing their effect on us.

> If we put in this chord it does not have that effect; if we put in this chord, then it does…. If you played syncopated music of Brahms and asked: 'What is the queer rhythm which makes me wobble?' 'It's the 3 against the 4.' One could play certain phrases and he would say: 'Yes. It's this peculiar rhythm I meant.'[18]

The work of music and the impression it leaves are to remain at the centre of our attention.

2.   Do Works of Art Have an Essence?

A second foundational idea of the aesthetic tradition is the concept of art—the concept of art-music in the context of this discussion. In the later Wittgenstein the great tradition of music from Bach to Brahms became one among others—with the proviso that he himself had his roots in this cultural tradition and identified with it. This tradition shapes Wittgenstein's musical responses and sets limits to his musical appreciation and understanding. Appreciation and understanding may be difficult, if not impossible, outside one's musical tradition, unless one acquires a participant's understanding of that other tradition. There is a 1914 diary entry about linguistic and moral meaning that foreshadows this perspective:

---

18   *Ibid.*, 20-21.

> If we hear a Chinese we tend to take his speech as inarticulate
> gurgling. Someone who understands Chinese will recognize
> language in what he hears. Similarly I often cannot recognize
> the human being in someone etc.[19]

This remark is equally applicable to music and sheds light on the young
Wittgenstein's (and his friend's David Pinsent's) attitude to what they
called "modern music". Not only can music from another culture
sound like mere noise, certain developments in the music of one's own
culture—such as atonality for instance—can foreclose discernment of
musical meaning.

As the essence fragments in Wittgenstein, so does language
and music. The plurality of musical traditions is suggested in a 1932
notebook entry which is not merely about possible changes of musical
forms but signals the anti-essentialist approach of the *Philosophical
Investigations*. In this entry Wittgenstein is speculating about the
"music of the future":

> I shouldn't be surprised if the music of the future were in
> unison. Or is that only because I cannot clearly imagine several
> voices? Anyway I can't imagine that the old large forms (string
> quartet, symphony, oratorio etc.) will be able to play any role
> at all. If something comes it will have to be—I think—simple,
> transparent. In a certain sense, naked. Or will that hold only for
> a certain race, only for *one* kind of music (?)[20]

Another important difference between Wittgenstein and Hanslick
emerges when we consider the implications of Hanslick's purely
formalist perspective. In his anxiousness to protect music's integrity
and autonomy against what he sees as attempts to reduce it to "nothing
but a means for the generation of musical configurations"—Wagner,
Liszt, and Berlioz seem to be Hanslick's targets here—he disconnects
music from any "extraneous or extra-musical context". This view leaves
music alone in that it isolates it from the other arts, such as literature
and painting, and gives the impression that music has nothing to do
with expression, ideas, thought and argument. A similar if not identical

---

19   Wittgenstein, *Culture*, 3.
20   Wittgenstein, *Public and Private*, 49.

view of music was held by Igor Stravinsky in the twentieth century who claimed that music does not teach or express anything at all.[21] Their theories involve an evaluation masquerading as a description: they conflate what they see as worthwhile music with how things are in music. To make sense of their views we need to remind ourselves of the context of such theories of music. Both Hanslick and Stravinsky, in their different ways, wrote polemics with program music as a target or backdrop. There is something curiously self-defeating about such theories: you keep on writing against one sort of music and at the same time you deny its existence. If we adopt such a formalist picture of music we lose the connectedness of the application of expressive predicates to music and their central use in our talk about human beings.

In sharp contrast with Hanslick and formalism Wittgenstein held musical meaning and understanding to have connections with the language games in the culture in which the music originates:

> Does the theme point to nothing beyond itself? Oh yes! But that means:—the impression it makes on me is connected with things in its surroundings—e.g. with the existence of the German language & of its intonation, but that means with the whole field of our language games. If I say e.g.: it's as if here a conclusion were being drawn, or, as if here something were being confirmed, or, as if *this* were a reply though someone were expressing agreement, or as though this were a reply to what came earlier,—then the way I understand it clearly presupposes familiarity with conclusions, expressions of agreement, [question], replies, etc.[22]

Another thing to notice here is the later Wittgenstein's anti-essentialism about the twin claims that music is a language and that no music is like language. There is a respect for differences in music, a "listen and appreciate" approach rather than an approach that lumps all music together. That some music bears a similarity to language is remarkable and shows that this feature cannot be simply a definitional matter. "We should like to call music a 'language'; no doubt this applies to some music—& to some no doubt not…. Bach's music is more like language

---

21   Igor Stravinsky, *Autobiography,* London: Calder and Boyars, 1975, 53-54.
22   Wittgenstein, *Culture*, 59.

than Mozart's & Haydn's".[23] Moreover, the actual playing, the execution or interpretation is also important. Consider what Wittgenstein said about the Austrian composer and organist Josef Labor:

> Think about how it was said of Labor's playing 'He is *speaking*'. How curious! What was it about his playing that was so reminiscent of speaking? And how remarkable that this similarity with speaking is not something we find incidental, but an important & big matter!—We should like to call music, & certainly some music, a language; and no doubt this does apply to some music—& to some no doubt not. (Not that this need involve a judgment of value!)[24]

Wittgenstein repeats his observation that we are inclined to call music a language, and that some music is more like language than other music, and gives Labor as an additional example of composers whose music and playing is like speech. The repetition signals the weight Wittgenstein attaches to the theme and the examples he gives of particular composers and features of their music that strike us as language-like show a cautious, discerning attitude concerning our inclination to generalize.

Repetition, whether in music or philosophy, sometimes has a useful role to play. It needn't be tedious or redundant, rather it may serve as a device to bring out the expressive power or importance of a theme:

> 'The repeat is *necessary*.' In what respect is it necessary? Well, sing it, then you will see that it is only the repeat that gives it its tremendous power.—Don't we feel then as though the theme only approached it, corresponded to it, in reality, & as though the theme only approached it, corresponded to it, once this part is repeated? Or am I to utter the inanity: 'It just sounds more beautiful with the repeat?'[25]

These and similar remarks straddle a middle way between two sorts of essentialists about music—those who reduce it to language or poetry or literature on the one hand, and those who say it has nothing to do with

---

23   *Ibid.*, 40.
24   *Ibid.*, 71.
25   *Ibid.*, 59.

language, on the other. To relate them somewhat crudely to methods, or rather, caricatures of composing: one extreme is thinking we compose from "word to note"; the other extreme is thinking we compose from note to word. To be sure, the dichotomy is over-simple and does not do justice to the complex practice of composition, but nevertheless they indicate something. Examples of composers who frequently worked under a literary stimulus are Schumann—who indicated this by his titles—and Schubert who if a poem appealed to him, it would at once suggest its own musical setting.[26] The idea that we compose from note to word seems to be suggested by some passages in Hanslick where he speaks of "an inner singing [that] induces the musically gifted person to construct a musical artwork" and that "each and every [composition] will have been created for its own sake as purely musical autonomous beauty". To protect the purity of the "composer's kind of constructing", he adds for good measure, "Even further removed from the character of a musical work as such are the social and political conditions which dominate its time".[27]

Wittgenstein rejects in equal measure both theories as extreme and unwarranted generalizations about compositional practices since they fail to do justice to the diversity and complexity of compositional practice as it manifests the diversity and complexity of being human. He attends to individual composers. Attesting to his awareness of this diversity is a 1931 note:

> Pieces of music at the keyboard, those by thinking with the pen
> & those composed just with imagined sounds must be of quite
> a different kind and make quite different kinds of impression.
> I am sure that Bruckner composed just in his head, imagining
> the orchestra playing, Brahms with his pen. Of course this is an
> oversimplification. But it does highlight one feature.[28]

Later on in the same year, identifying with Brahms' method, Wittgenstein draws a parallel between the way he thinks philosophically and the way

---

26 Percy A. Scholes, *The Oxford Companion to Music,* 10th edition, ed. John Owen Ward, London: Oxford University Press, 1970, 220.
27 Hanslick, *On the Musically Beautiful,* 47.
28 Wittgenstein, *Culture,* 14.

Brahms composed: "I really do think with my pen, for my head often knows nothing of what my hand is writing".[29]

From all this we may get the impression that an unmusical philosopher (and this includes most philosophers in the tradition) becomes an object of suspicion for philosophical reasons, since he seems to be out of touch with reality in the sense that they lack *one* significant way of being in tune with "the given" or suppress in themselves the resonance of the forms of life and culture manifest in the music. This may be glossed as a variation on Schopenhauer's idea that music is the deepest of the arts because it is iconic of the will: it does not represent, but it reverberates with, life. The bold idea is that an unmusical philosopher then does not embody "the acceptance of the given—of forms of life"[30]—and hence is at a disadvantage when engaging philosophical problems.

This may be true of philosophers working on issues in the philosophy of music, but is it not an over strong claim about philosophers in general? After all, the "acceptance of the given" may be shown through non-musical ways—for instance, through our acting in the world and language use. So having a musical ear cannot be a necessary condition for the "acceptance of the given". Wittgenstein does not believe that the tone-deaf can't "get it"; nor does he believe that the musically astute and appreciative necessarily "get it". His ambivalent remarks about the brilliant young logician and philosopher Frank Ramsey indicate that Ramsey was musically sensitive and appreciative:

> He truly relished music & with understanding. And one could see by looking at him what effect it had on him. Of the last movement of one of Beethoven's late quartets, a movement he loved perhaps more than anything else, he told me that it made him feel as if the heavens were open. And that meant something when he said it.[31]

Ramsey was also a penetrating critic of ideas, yet, in Wittgenstein's view, there was something philosophically deficient about him. What, we may ask. Is Wittgenstein not demanding too much here?

---

29 *Ibid.*, 24.
30 Wittgenstein, *Investigations*, 192.
31 Wittgenstein, *Public and Private*, 17.

Surely, in a sense Ramsey "got it": Six weeks after his death in 1930, Wittgenstein wrote: "I had a certain awe of R[amsey]. He was a very swift & deft critic when one presented him with ideas". Fifteen years later, in the preface—written in 1945—to the *Philosophical Investigations* the assessment is repeated with the particulars of indebtedness: Ramsey was acknowledged for his "always certain and forcible" criticism that helped Wittgenstein "to recognize grave mistakes" in the *Tractatus*. However, in Wittgenstein's 1930 remarks, another aspect of Ramsey's personality, as Wittgenstein saw it, came into view, suggesting that Ramsey did not fully get it after all:

> Ramsey's mind (*Geist*) repulsed me. ...[his] incapacity for genuine enthusiasm or genuine reverence, which is the same, finally repulsed me more & more.... his criticism didn't help along but held back & sobered. That short period of time, as Schopenhauer calls it, between the two long ones when some truth appears first paradoxical & then trivial to people, had shrunk to a point for R[amsey]. And so at first one laboured arduously for a long time in vain to explain something to him until he suddenly shrugged his shoulders about it & said this was self-evident, after all. He had an ugly mind. But not an ugly soul (*Seele*).[32]

What was it about this towering Cambridge genius who died so young, that drove Wittgenstein—with such apparent lack of gratitude and reverence—to criticize him? We get an idea of this from another notebook entry made in the same year:

> Ramsey was a bourgeois thinker. I.e. he thought with the aim of clearing up the affairs of some particular community. He did not reflect on the essence of the state—or at least did not like doing so—but on how *this* state might reasonably be organized. The idea that this state might not be the only possible one partly disquieted him and partly bored him. He wanted to get down as quickly as possible to reflecting on the foundations—of *this* state. This was what he was good at & what really interested

---

32   *Ibid.*, 15-17.

him; whereas real philosophical reflection disquieted him until
he put its result (if it had one) on one side as trivial.[33]

Both Ramsey and Wittgenstein accept the given, the forms of life,
but Ramsey, unlike Wittgenstein, is impatient with, or uninterested
in, exploring the possible foundations of other "buildings". Thus, in
contrast with Ramsey, Wittgenstein was concerned with "having the
foundations of possible buildings [states] before [him]".[117]

This concern is of interest to us for, when we extend it to music,
we expect Wittgenstein to be interested in the foundations of possible
music, while a Ramsey would be interested only in the foundations of
this (of classical European) music. Yet, contrary to our expectations,
on the face of it, Wittgenstein's remarks on music *show* Ramsey-like
behaviour, as if he is interested only in *this* (classical) music and not
even interested in exploring the possible foundations of new music
which is a successor to the classical tradition. "Every defilement I
can tolerate", Wittgenstein wrote, "except the one that is bourgeois".
Presumably, by 'bourgeois', he meant an easy conformism, a buckling
under existing conventions. He thought he detected this in Ramsey, but
the intensity of the remark suggests that the eggshells of a bourgeois
attitude were sticking to Wittgenstein himself, and this seems to come
to a head in his attitude to modern music. In my last chapter I shall take
up this issue explicitly and try to come to grips with it. But for now
I turn to Wittgenstein's relation to the "aesthetic attitude"—the third
building block of the aesthetic tradition.

3. "As If from a Great Distance": Uncovering an Aesthetic Attitude?

While Wittgenstein's influence on twentieth century contributions
to the question "What is Art?" is widely recognized his more direct
contributions to other central questions of traditional aesthetics,
namely, the questions of aesthetic experience and the aesthetic attitude,
have received little scholarly discussion. Perhaps philosophers see his
remarks on these topics as side glances scattered throughout his personal

---

33   Wittgenstein, *Culture*, 24.

notebooks. Such remarks are of significance for my purpose, since they are sometimes made in the context of music and have relevance to musical aesthetics.

I now revisit Wittgenstein's philosophical journey arguing that throughout his writings he adopts an aesthetic attitude. As well, I trace the 'secularization' of that attitude in his later works and diary entries. I claim that in the *Tractatus* he adopts a full blown transcendent aesthetic point of view; in the transition period he holds a qualified view of an aesthetic attitude; and in the later period he offers a deep critique of theories of the aesthetic attitude and experience reminiscent of George Dickie's critique two decades later.[34] Let's begin by uncovering an aesthetic attitude in the *Tractatus*.

The traditional answer to the question 'What makes artworks worth attending to?' was: 'Having an aesthetic experience'. The official way to access such experience was through adopting a distinctive attitude that takes one out of the world of our everyday practical concerns and thus enables us to look at an object or phenomenon in an impersonal, "disinterested" way. One might say, in aesthetic experience the self drops out. This is reminiscent of Schopenhauer's proposal that to appreciate things for and in themselves is to contemplate them in a pure and detached manner free of the demands of the will and the constraints of our individual personality. As mentioned before Wittgenstein included Schopenhauer on his list of writers who influenced him, although the placement of Schopenhauer's name on the list indicates that influence to be largely on the early philosophy of the *Tractatus*.

Equally noteworthy is that Edward Bullough, the father of the modern English version of the theory of the aesthetic attitude, was Wittgenstein's contemporary at Cambridge. Both conducted experiments in the psychology of the arts in the laboratory headed by C.S. Myers, a pioneer of British experimental psychology. Bullough's influential 1912 essay, 'Psychical Distance: As a Factor in Art and an Aesthetic Principle', appeared in the *British Journal of Psychology* where he claimed that to have an aesthetic experience we need to "distance" the object or phenomenon. Bullough's instructive example is a fog at sea:

---

34 George Dickie, "The Myth of the Aesthetic Attitude" in *American Philosophical Quarterly*, I/1 (1964), 56-66.

> Imagine a fog at sea…. In the fog, the transformation of Distance
> is produced… by putting the phenomenon, so to speak, out
> of gear with our practical, actual self; by allowing it to stand
> outside the context of our personal needs and ends.[35]

There are, for Bullough, two stages of distance: in the negative stage our practical concerns are dropped concerning the object and in the positive stage we attend to features of the object itself. It would be surprising if Wittgenstein had not read Bullough's essay or heard it discussed since he was in the hub of the action and had a keen interest in aesthetics.

Is there something similar to an aesthetic attitude in Wittgenstein's philosophy? Here we must ask: Which Wittgenstein? Which philosophy? The Wittgenstein of the *Tractatus* alludes to 'the disinterested gaze' when he says: "To contemplate the world *sub specie aeterni* is its contemplation as a limited whole" (6.45). "The sense of the world lies outside the world" (6.41). "It is clear that ethics and aesthetics cannot be put into words, since they are one and the same: they are transcendental" (6.421). There are things that can be said, namely, the propositions of natural science. And there are, indeed, things that cannot be put into words. They make themselves manifest. They are what is mystical (6.522).

Linked to *Tractatus* 6.45 is a proposition where Wittgenstein characterizes the mystical as "*feeling the world as a limited whole*". As we have seen, the cognitive core of this feeling is *viewing* the world as a limited whole. This description of the mystical can be put beside some remarks in the *Lecture on Ethics*, where he speaks of the sense of wonder at the existence of the world, the sense of feeling absolutely safe whatever happens, and ethics/aesthetics as being a matter of intrinsic/absolute value. It would seem then that experiences of the sort Wittgenstein mentions in the *Lecture on Ethics* constitute experiences close to the arts. Moreover, he explicitly says in the *Notebooks* of 1914–1916 that the connection between art and ethics is that "[t]he work of art is the object seen *sub specie aeternitatis* [under the aspect of eternity], and the good life is the world seen *sub specie*

35　　Edward Bullough, "Psychical Distance as a Factor in Art and as an Aesthetic
　　　Principle" in *The Philosophy of Art Readings Ancient and Modern*, eds Alex
　　　Neill and Aaron Ridley, New York: McGraw Hill, 1995, 298-299.

aeternitatis".[36] Developing this idea, he goes on to say that the usual way of looking at things sees objects as it were from the midst of them, the view *sub specie aeternitatis* from outside but with the whole world as background. As a thing, each thing lacks significance, but as a world each one is significant. And "[t]he world is *my* world: this is manifest in the fact that the limits of language (of that language which alone I understand) mean the limits of *my* world" (*Tractatus* 5.62). We need to adopt an aesthetic attitude towards the world, look at it from outside, so as to experience wonder at the existence of the world. Both the mystical and aesthetic/ethical offer a sense of wonder, so it is no surprise that Wittgenstein thought so highly of the arts. "One might say", he later remarks, that "art shows us the miracles of nature. It is based on the *concept* of the miracles of nature. The blossom, just opening out. What is *marvelous* about it? We say: 'Just look how it's opening out!'"[37]

Discernible in both the *Tractatus* and the *Lecture on Ethics* is an attitude that has a strong family resemblance to the aesthetic attitude. Having said this, caveats are in order. The Tractarian attitude that enables us "to see the world aright", is not to be arrived at through any kind of theory or the employment of such psychological devices as Bullough's special mental acts of distancing; nor is the aesthetic attitude identical with the state of being psychologically distanced. If it were, aesthetics would be reducible to psychology and, as we have seen, Wittgenstein was against any form of psychologism in logic, aesthetics or ethics.

These qualifications bring up the tricky question of the status of Wittgenstein's aesthetic attitude in the *Tractatus*. Is the view from eternity a philosophical *theory*, a part of the ladder that we need to climb "to see the world aright" and then throw away? If so, we have a problem on our hands, since Wittgenstein also holds that the propositions and questions of philosophers arise from our failure to understand the logic of our language, and thus amount to nonsense. For the same reason his theory of the aesthetic attitude would go by the board as well. But how can this be? If the view from eternity is a necessary condition "to see the world aright" and we get rid of it, we are stuck in the lumber yard of the world. To dissolve this tension, we need to distinguish between holding a theory of the aesthetic attitude and adopting an aesthetic

---

36   Wittgenstein, *Notebooks*, 83.
37   Wittgenstein, *Culture*, 64.

attitude. One could adopt an aesthetic attitude and nevertheless think that spelling out a theory of it is impossible or pointless. And this seems to be Wittgenstein's view about ethics and aesthetics in the *Tractatus*: There is a transcendent point of view that does not involve holding a theory.

By the end of 1930 there was a sea-change in Wittgenstein's perspective. He was no longer interested in ladder-climbing:

> I might say: if the place I want to reach could only be climbed up to by a ladder, I would give up trying to get there. For the place to which I really have to go is one that I must actually be already. Anything that can be reached with a ladder does not interest me.[38]

This remark came at a time when Wittgenstein was in transit from the *Tractatus* to the radically new perspective of the *Philosophical Investigations*. A month prior to this entry, Wittgenstein recorded a conversation with Paul Engelmann that suggests a line of thinking similar to that of the aesthetic attitude, but without the vestments of the mystical and "transcendental". The human gaze seems to replace the divine gaze: "The human gaze", he writes, has the power of making things precious [conferring value on things]; though it is true that they become more costly too".[39] He writes:

> Engelmann told me that when he rummages around at home in a drawer full of his own manuscripts and letters from his dead relations, they strike him as so splendid that he thinks it would be worth making them available to other people. But when he imagines publishing a selection of them, the whole business loses its charm and value, and becomes impossible.[40]

Why is this? Why would the material look and feel different when transferred from the private to the public sphere? In response, Wittgenstein compares Engelmann's reaction with another case. He says:

---

38   *Ibid.*, 10.
39   *Ibid.*, 3.
40   *Ibid.*, 6.

Nothing could be more remarkable than seeing a man who thinks he is unobserved performing some quite simple everyday activity. Let us imagine a theatre; the curtain goes up and we see a man alone in a room, walking up and down, lighting a cigarette, sitting down, etc. so that suddenly we are observing a human being from outside in a way that ordinarily we can never observe ourselves; it would be like watching a chapter of biography with our own eyes,—surely that would be uncanny and wonderful at the same time. We should be observing something more wonderful than anything a playwright could arrange to be acted or spoken on the stage: life itself. But then we do see this every day without its making the slightest impression on us![41]

Wittgenstein's solution to the problem of how something can shift from the remarkable to the impossible involves an idea reminiscent of the aesthetic attitude. After pointing out that "[w]e see this every day without its making the slightest impression on us", he adds, "[b]ut we do not see it from *that* point of view". The implicit suggestion is that there is a change in the point of view for the purposes of aesthetic appreciation. He declares that "[o]nly the artist can represent the individual thing so that it appears to us as a work of art" and adds that "those manuscripts *rightly* lose their value if we contemplate them singly & in any case without *prejudice*, i.e. by someone who doesn't feel enthusiastic about them in advance". The crucial point is that

[t]he work of art compels us—as one might say—to see it in the *right* perspective but without art, the object is just a piece of nature like any other & the fact that *we* may exalt it through our enthusiasm does not give anyone the right to display it to us.[42]

Pictures of ordinary scenes do not collapse into sentimental snapshots because the artist forces us to see them "in the right perspective". His representations mean that even though we were not present and have no personal interest before viewing them, we sense the special mood, the aura of felt expression that they create in the context of the artwork. Moreover, given Wittgenstein's remarks, it is tempting to invoke the apparatus of the theory of the aesthetic attitude and regard the artist as

---

41 *Ibid.*
42 *Ibid.*,7.

putting the scene in the right perspective by "disinterestedly" looking at them. This is, of course, not to suggest that the artist is uninterested in the found material itself but rather that he filters out "feeling enthusiastic in advance", i.e. eliminates personal bias and prejudice, economic investment, ulterior motives and political posturing. It is in this sense that the first person point of view drops out since the material is presented and contemplated *sub specie aeterni*.

Since Engelmann's private manuscripts remain the same when transferred to the public sphere, what change accounts for the loss of charm and value? Wittgenstein notes that Engelmann is "enthusiastic in advance" about his letters and manuscripts because of "vested interests"—his affection for and personal connections to relatives and so on—and when he imagines the letters and manuscripts in the public sphere, he imagines viewers who do not share his enthusiasm, viewers for whom they are nothing special. For such viewers to appreciate them, his letters have to be presented in a different—artistic—way. A found-object must be shown so that it is seen for and in itself without the crutch of vested interests and knowledge of its original surroundings and context.

From this example we can tease out what Wittgenstein's dismantling of the traditional, sharp, dichotomy between "a fragment of nature" and "a work of art" comes to in practice. The perspective the artist supplies turns "[a] fragment of nature" into a work of art. Wittgenstein's remark here sounds somewhat like materials for an institutional theory of art. For when he says that "a work of art forces us to see the fragment of nature in the right perspective" or that "only the artist can supply the right perspective so that we can see the fragment of nature as a work of art", he seems to imply that the perspective is supplied by a wider context of historical and cultural practices in which we and the artist participate and are heir to. There is a development here that seems similar to the critical transformation of the theory of the aesthetic attitude into an institutional theory that occurred later in the history of twentieth century aesthetics.[43] Such theories privilege the institutional backdrop (museum, art gallery, concert hall etc) as supplying the right perspective for understanding and appreciating the work, thus neglecting the artist and the work of art. Wittgenstein's

---

43   See the works of Arthur Danto and George Dickie listed in the bibliography.

perspective is different from such theories in that for him the artist and the work of art is still at the centre with the cultural/institutional setting as backdrop. For Wittgenstein, the role of the artist as supplying the right perspective for understanding and appreciating the work of art is not lost from sight. Looking at things this way leaves room for the many ways an object can become a work of art without the "my way or no way" of institutionalization. As well, space is left open for the many ways and levels of appreciating art. For Wittgenstein there is no one way whereby a thing or a succession of sounds becomes art, nor a single way whereby they are appreciated.

At the end of the conversation with Engelmann, Wittgenstein returns to philosophy, almost as an after-thought: "But it seems to me that there is a way of capturing the world *sub specie aeterni* other than through the work of the artist. Thought has such a way—so I believe— it is as though it flies above the world and leaves it as it is—observing it from above, in flight". Here we see aspects of the relationship of the work of art to philosophy: In the spirit of Wittgenstein's philosophy, both the artist and the philosopher set things in front of us, as seen from "the right perspective"—without any mediating theoretical veil. However, the "transcendental", the *sub specie aeterni* view is still there in the Engelmann passage, lingering, if not full-blown. The eggshells of the *Tractatus* are still sticking to Wittgenstein's reflections.

Does this line of interpretation do justice to Wittgenstein's efforts at "ladder disposal"? When Wittgenstein speaks of "the right perspective" he is not proposing a theory of the aesthetic attitude or distance reminiscent of Arthur Schopenhauer's or Edward Bullough's theories; indeed he is not proposing a theory at all. He dissolves the problem and suggests that this notion be construed in a way that does not put philosophical weight on the "right perspective". He is noting that the *objet trouvé* when looked at as "a piece of nature like any other" and without artistic treatment, loses its value. His view is that we need the artist so that we look at or hear the thing without prejudice but *not* in a cold, "distanced" way. Although this is the right direction, it is plain that Wittgenstein's new perspective is fully enacted only in the work of the later philosophy.

4. Appreciating Music Naturally

In his later writings Wittgenstein cautioned against looking or going beyond the phenomenon. In both the arts and in philosophy, theorizing and looking beyond distract us from what is right in front of our eyes; they intrude on the job of carefully attending to the phenomenon and its features. He effectively invokes Grillparzer—one of his favourite authors—to drive the point home: "How easy it is to move about in broad distant regions, how hard to grasp what is individual & near at hand".[44] This signals a new attitude of attention to the particular case and a conception of philosophy that is more like a kind of aesthetics, albeit not aesthetics as conventionally construed as a branch of philosophy in text books.

This fresh "Look and see" approach helps with establishing a kind of balance. The theory of the aesthetic attitude as a general method for the appreciation of works of art and scenes of nature mainly feeds on a one-sided diet of examples drawn from the "contented arts": from representational painting, sculpture, and theatre. Works of music tend to be missing from such discussions, prompting the question: how is this theory to be applied to the understanding and appreciation of music?

The theory of the aesthetic attitude appears to be a non-starter for music, since it suggests that the best way to listen is dispassionately and "disinterestedly". If we apply "distance" literally, if we listen to it *sub specie aeterni*, we won't hear the music at all or hear it only faintly. And if we read 'distance' metaphorically, then we put the music "out of gear" from our ordinary life, sever it from our selves, from emotional and imaginative associations, and thus, our experience of the music is likely to lack depth. To appreciate music, we must enter its world, and if we are not moved, then its value is diminished. In contrast to theories of aesthetic attitude, Wittgenstein encourages emotional and personal involvement. If we listen to music with understanding we resonate with it. If we follow it with understanding, it engages us emotionally, since feelings accompany our listening to music much like they accompany events in our lives. What is more, our emotional responses to music provide access to what is in the music. What is in the music is inaccessible

---

44   Wittgenstein, *Culture*, 15.

to someone who has no emotional or imaginative involvement with it even if such a person may have a technical understanding of the work.

One important theme in Wittgenstein's remarks about music is that understanding and appreciating music does not consist in an aesthetic experience or process to which the subject has introspective access as supposed by the tradition. Writing in his notebooks in the 1940s, he asked: "What does it consist in: following a musical phrase with understanding?" He tends to put this question side by side with "What is it to hear a sentence or a word with understanding?" Could it consist in explaining meaning through inner experience? As he considers the issue, he steers away from the inner and leans toward what is outward:

> Don't look inside yourself. Ask yourself rather, what makes you say that's *what someone* else is doing. And *what* prompts you to say *he* has a particular experience? Indeed, do we actually say that? Wouldn't I be more likely to say of someone else that he's having a whole host of experiences?[45]

Wittgenstein continues to probe the ideas of aesthetic experience and attention. Perhaps we can say that "He is experiencing the theme intensely", means that something is happening in him when he hears it. Well, what? The interlocutor's voice kicks in and suggests that intensively experiencing the theme might consist in the sensations of the movements etc. with which we accompany it. But do we actually recall such an experience? The proposal, says Wittgenstein, is a mere theory, a picture to link up the expressive movements with an experience. The upshot of these remarks is thus far negative: to demythologize the traditional picture of situating meaning inside us and thus to destroy philosophical illusions about what it is to listen with understanding.

After this, Wittgenstein repeats the question and considers it further:

> What does it consist in following a musical phrase with understanding? Observing a face with a feeling for its expression? Drinking in the expression on the face? Think of the demeanor of someone who draws the face with an understanding for its

---

45   *Ibid.*, 58.

> expression. Think of the sketcher's face, his movements;—what
> shows that every stroke he makes is dictated by the face, that
> nothing in his sketch is arbitrary, that he is a delicate instrument?[46]

One implication is that it is not a matter of having a describable sort
of experience but of concentrating on the face, not allowing oneself to
be distracted, not being governed by one's own predilections. We are
not to "look inside ourselves" for doing so would just distract us from
the music and involve us in the idle exercise of grubbing about in the
soul. Rather than being passive witnesses to some internal happening,
understanding according to Wittgenstein involves attentive listening
with the music as the object of our focus, and we are to filter bias or
predilections that distract us from it. An implication is that whether one
is doing this or not is more evident to the careful observer than it is to
the artist.

Does this reading not trivialize "experiencing the theme
intensely"? For now the theme loses its significance, since it points to
nothing beyond itself, to no inner or outer experience that matters to us!
Wittgenstein responds:

> If you ask: how I experienced the theme, I shall perhaps say:
> As a question, or something of the sort, or I shall whistle it
> with expression etc. 'He is experiencing the theme intensely.
> Something is happening in him when he hears it.' Well, *what*?[47]

So far Wittgenstein's remarks on musical appreciation
underscore his claim that musical understanding/appreciation does not
consist in one thing—in a private inner aesthetic experience—but is
expressed through various public ways such as indications of attentive
and sympathetic focus on the music without such distractions as bias,
prejudice or inner gazing; appropriate gestures, movements, or facial
expressions. Nor is the musical object of our listening, he suggests,
disconnected from language and culture.

What then does Wittgenstein's practice of music criticism tell us
about his changing attitude to the "aesthetic attitude"? What he says
seems to have striking affinities with features of the aesthetic attitude

---

46   *Ibid.*
47   *Ibid.*, 59.

characterized by Jerome Stolnitz as disinterested and sympathetic attention to and contemplation of [the music] for its own sake alone. How then does the later Wittgenstein's perspective differ from a theory of the aesthetic attitude cleansed of its metaphysical pretensions and psychological props? There are observations and comments in the *Nachlass* about the music of various composers that indicate such differences, as well as a broad practice of music appreciation and criticism.

The first thing to notice is that for Wittgenstein, unlike for (strong) formalists, there are cultural resonances in a work of art. "I think", he remarks, "that in order to enjoy a poet, you have to like the culture to which he belongs as well. If you are indifferent to it or repelled by it, your admiration cools off". One might say, you have reached the limits of your appreciation. Wittgenstein's remarks are sometimes about the "intrinsic" features of the music, and at other times he makes allusions to the different European and ethnic cultures in which the works of music he discusses are embedded. Consider for instance his remarks about Austrian work: "I think good Austrian work (Grillparzer, Lenau, Bruckner, Labor) is particularly hard to understand. There is a sense in which it is subtler than anything else and its truth never leans towards plausibility".[48] This is followed by an analogy between Austrian composers' faces and their music, and in the case of Bruckner a comparison between his music and alpine scenery. "In Bruckner's music nothing is left of the long & slender (Nordic?) face of Nestroy, Grillparzer, Haydn, etc. but it has in full measure a round (alpine?) face even purer than was Schubert's".[49] An aesthetic attitude theorist would not only balk at such allusions but insist they just prove his point about the need to invoke the aesthetic attitude to filter bias and predilection.

In other remarks Wittgenstein makes specific comparisons between different musical figures in the history of music and draws analogies to works of literature:

> A Bruckner symphony can be said to have two beginnings: the beginning of the first idea & the beginning of the second idea. These two ideas stand to each other not as blood relations but as man & wife. His *Ninth* is a sort of protest against Beethoven's,

48   *Ibid.*, 5.
49   *Ibid.*, 19.

> & because of this becomes bearable, which as a sort of imitation
> it would not be. It stands to Beethoven's Ninth very much as
> Lenau's Faust to Goethe's, which means as the Catholic to the
> Enlightenment Faust, etc. etc.[50]

There are also other important analogies Wittgenstein draws between (some) music and language: "Schubert's melodies can be said to be full of *climaxes*, & this cannot be said of Mozart's; Schubert is baroque. You can point to particular places in a Schubert melody & say: look, that is the point of this melody, this is where the idea comes to a head".[51] With the introduction of expressions such as "the point of a melody" or "a musical idea coming to a head", there is room for imagining and speaking of musical arguments and conclusions. Wittgenstein juxtaposes musical and linguistic communications for our attention as if to say: there are musical acts that resonate with speech acts in that both are accompanied by similar gestures, facial expressions and movements. Thus, his perspective on musical appreciation invites broad as well as narrow appreciation; for music alone, but also for music's expressive gestures and cultural connections. As he connects music to language, gesture, argument and the human face, the intractable traditional problems seem to melt away.

There is also a characteristic emphasis on context: "Only in a quite particular musical context is there such a thing as three part counterpoint". Again, "One and the same theme has a different character in the minor than in the major, but it is quite wrong to speak generally of a character belonging to the minor. In Schubert the major often sounds sadder than the minor. And similarly, I think, it's idle and futile for the understanding of painting to speak of the characters of the individual colours. In doing so one really thinks only of special applications. The fact that green has one effect as the colour of a table cloth, red another, licenses no conclusion about their effect in a picture". For Wittgenstein the understanding and appreciation of music is not one thing: there may be narrow and broad appreciations of a work of music. Formalists consider the music alone and focus on the intrinsic features of a piece of music; this constitutes one sort of appreciation. There is, however, a

---

50   *Ibid.*, 39.
51   *Ibid.*, 54.

broader appreciation which resonates with the culture and history of a work, its technical aspects, and other works of art of the period.

Suppose we grant that these are relevant and often insightful considerations in the appreciation of a work of music. But what if a person is distracted by ideology or personal bias—the baggage imposed on the music—and is thus disabled from appreciating it? If this is so, then there is a point to adopting the aesthetic attitude when listening to such music. In this connection, think of listening to Shostakovich's *Fifth Symphony*. In this case the historical and political associations of the music may intrude on the informed listener's appreciation, while the aesthetic attitude may serve as bias remover. But is this right? Surely we hear and appreciate the music differently, if we believe that Shostakovich was a Stalinist peon or a subtle critic of the regime. In the latter case, we hear his *Fifth Symphony* not as a genuine tribute to Stalin, but as a parody or bitter irony. This makes for a crucial difference in our critical assessments. What then is the object of one's appreciation? Is it the music alone or is it the politics? Or is it not possible, in a case like this, to separate them? Wittgenstein's approach, unlike (strong) Formalism, offers us a way to make sense of these different reactions.

I have argued for the presence of an aesthetic attitude throughout Wittgenstein's works, albeit in different forms. He adopted an aesthetic attitude or transcendent gaze in his early work of the *Tractatus* with an implicit theory despite his disavowal of philosophical theory. This is a tension analogous to his Tractarian views about 'meaning': he jettisons "theory" yet holds a picture theory of meaning. The "middle Wittgenstein" starts his journey of descent from the ladder of the "transcendent" gaze to the human gaze, apparently without a theory or psychological accoutrements, and starts moving toward the significance of the everyday and the ordinary, yet he retains the view of the artist and the philosopher as *sub specie aeterni*. The later Wittgenstein embraced the human gaze with all its implications as he turned to the rough ground of social practice, culture and history to embed the appreciation of art. He provided, I argue, a deep critique of traditional ideas of aesthetic experience and attitude, a critique strikingly similar to George Dickie's more than twenty five years later. My central purpose has been to trace the 'secularization' of the aesthetic attitude Wittgenstein adopted in the *Tractatus* in the later works and in his notes on music. This development is somewhat parallel to the transformation of the theory of the aesthetic attitude into the institutional theory of art, since Wittgenstein's practice of musical understanding and appreciation is informed by the world of art and music. The history of analytical aesthetics in the second half of the twentieth century is anticipated in the later Wittgenstein's remarks about art and aesthetics, especially in his remarks about music.

Given this critical evaluation of the aesthetic tradition, I now turn to two related the questions: Did Wittgenstein hold on to musical formalism throughout his life, or was there, as in his philosophy of language, a break from his early views? Did he cease to be a musical formalist in his later period?

Chapter IV
Later Views: A New Era

1. Was the Later Wittgenstein a Musical Formalist?
A Shift in Perspective

I now revisit Wittgenstein's relation to musical formalism and argue that the later Wittgenstein was no musical formalist. It's a short step from the claim that the early Wittgenstein was a musical formalist to the claim that he was a formalist throughout his life. In fact such a large claim is immediately suspect, as it neglects the radical shift in philosophical perspective between the Wittgenstein of the *Tractatus* and the Wittgenstein of the *Philosophical Investigations*. In the early 1930s Wittgenstein was moving away from a formalistic approach to meaning and music. Concerning the latter: His diary entries at that time indicate a turning away from such formal concerns as unity and essence in music toward plurality and contingency. The importance of contingency came to the fore as he was reading Oswald's Spengler's *The Decline of the West*:

> Reading Spengler's Decline etc. & in spite many irresponsibilities in the particulars, [I] find many real, significant thoughts. Much, perhaps most of it, is completely in touch with what I have often thought myself. The possibility of a number of closed systems which, once one has them, look as if one is a continuation of another. And all this has to do with the thought that we do not know (consider) how much can be taken away from—or given to—the human being... That is, we consider all we have as self-evident & do not even know that we could be complete even without this & that, which we don't even recognize as some special capacity since to us it seems to belong to the completeness of our intellect. It's a shame that Spengler did not stick with his Good Thoughts & went further than what he can answer for. Greater cleanliness, however, would have made his

> thought more difficult to understand, but only this would really
> have made it lastingly effective, too. Thus is the thought that
> the string instruments assumed their Definitive Shape between
> 1500 and 1600 of enormous magnitude (& symbolism). Only
> most people see nothing in such a thought if one gives it to them
> without much ado. It is as if someone believed that a human
> being keeps on developing without limit & one told him: look,
> the cranial sutures of a child close at... years & that shows
> already that development comes everywhere to an end, that what
> is developing here is a self-contained whole which at some point
> will be completely present & not a sausage which can run on
> indefinitely.[1]

Music, in particular changes in music toward modern forms, continues
to fuel his reflections on the unrecognized or barely recognized role and
importance of contingency. Recall the prescient remarks Wittgenstein
made in 1930 about "the music of the future" being in unison and that the
old large forms (string quartet, symphony, oratorio etc.) will disappear
from compositional practice. Other remarks from the late 1940s are
characteristic of an anti-essentialist family resemblance stance about
melodic form:

> The melodies of different composers can be approached by
> applying the principle: Every species of tree is a 'tree' in a
> different sense of the word. I.e. Don't let yourself be misled by
> our saying that they are all melodies. They are steps along a
> path that leads from something you would not call a melody
> to something else that you again would not call one. If you
> simply look at the sequences of notes & the changes of key
> all these structures no doubt appear on the same level. But if
> you look at the field of force in which they stand (and hence
> their significance), you will be inclined to say: here the melody
> is something quite different than there (here it has a different
> origin, plays a different role, inter alia.[2]

These passages not only raise doubts about musical formalism—since
they highlight what is possible in composition and orchestration given
the contingency of the "definitive shape" of the string instruments—

---

1   Wittgenstein, *Public and Private*, 25, 27, 29.
2   Wittgenstein, *Culture*, 54.

but also envisage different conceptions of music. In the last passage Wittgenstein rejects the very idea of an essentialist melodic form and thinks of melody through the idea of family resemblance—an idea that has great potential for experiments in music.

Concerning meaning: this turning away from musical formalism runs parallel with the turning away from a formalistic and essentialist approach to language toward an anti-essentialist and an anti-reductionist orientation. The later Wittgenstein leaves behind the idea of musical formalism that music is self-contained and only about itself—along with the idea of "the form of the proposition" and "the picture theory" of meaning. No deep digging beneath the surface is therefore necessary, for nothing is hidden: everything is in the open. Questions of meaning are explored through investigating use in context, through considering examples *in situ*, by looking and seeing, listening and hearing, putting things side by side for appreciation. This sort of approach helps to explain how Wittgenstein's reflections on music played a role in the development of his philosophy of language, since it connects the shift in his musical thinking with the shift in his reflections about language. The attribution of a lifetime of uniform musical formalism denies such parallel developments between music and language, and thus trivializes the analogy between the two. To sentence Wittgenstein to a lifetime of musical formalism obscures rather than clarifies the role music played in the development of his philosophy of language. Thus it is right and wrong to regard Wittgenstein as a musical formalist: right if we mean the early Wittgenstein, wrong if we mean the later.

Another reason to maintain that the later Wittgenstein was no musical formalist is that it does not square with the consistent "anti-theory" thrust of his later philosophy. The Tractarian Wittgenstein was a full-blooded theorist in that he adopted a theory of meaning and of the proposition, while the Wittgenstein of the *Philosophical Investigations* regarded the inclination to theorize as a deep source of philosophical error. Since musical formalism is a philosophical theory, holding such a theory is consistent with the philosophical orientation of the early, but not the later Wittgenstein. In the *Philosophical Investigations* Wittgenstein explicitly stated that he is not interested in putting forth any sort of philosophical theory—about music or anything else: "And we may not advance any kind of theory.... We must do away with all

explanation and description alone must take its place".[3] He repudiates
the very idea of a philosophical theory of music in particular:

> If someone were to ask: What is valuable in a Beethoven sonata?
> The sequence of notes? The feelings Beethoven had when he
> was composing it? The state of mind produced when listening
> to it? I would reply, that whatever I was told, I would reject, and
> that not because the explanation was false but because it was an
> explanation: If I were told anything that was a theory, I would
> say, No, no! That does not interest me—it would not be the exact
> thing I was looking for.[4]

This passage makes it clear that the attribution of life-long formalism to
Wittgenstein is a falsetto.

At this point it might be asked: Was the early Wittgenstein a full-
blooded theorist? Did he not explicitly reject philosophical propositions
and theories as "pernicious nonsense"? Consider *Tractatus* 6.522:
"The correct method in philosophy would really be the following: to
say nothing except what can be said, i.e. the propositions of natural
science—i.e. something that has nothing to do with philosophy—and
then, whenever someone else wanted to say something metaphysical,
to demonstrate to him that he failed to give a meaning to certain signs
in his propositions. Although it would not be satisfying to the other
person—he would not have the feeling that we were teaching him
philosophy—*this* method would be the only strictly correct one". This
does not sound like a remark made by a philosophical theorist, yet, as
he acknowledged later, the author of the *Tractatus* was still a theorist, in
particular a Platonist about meaning or beauty in music and language.
Consider what he said later on in life when asked:

> whether he still held views expressed in the *Tractatus*. No. It's
> like this. If you find your way out of a wood you may think that
> it is the only way out. Then you find another way out. But you
> might never have found it unless you had gone the other way
> first. I should not be where I am now if I had not passed through
> what is expressed in the *Tractatus*. When I wrote that, I had
> Plato's idea of finding the general idea lying behind all particular

---

3   Wittgenstein, *Investigations*, §109.
4   Wittgenstein, *Wittgenstein and the Vienna Circle*, 116-117.

> meanings of a word. Now I think of the meanings as like fibres
> of a rope. One may run the whole way through, but none may.[5]

In a subsequent conversation, when asked about the *Tractatus*, he said: "There is a lot that is very fishy about that book".[6] While it is unclear how to reconcile Wittgenstein the theorist with Wittgenstein the anti-theorist in the *Tractatus*, what is clear is that in the *Tractatus* he did hold a theory about meaning, about the general form of the proposition, about what is transcendent, etc. Thus, attributing to him at that time a formalist theory of music falls into place and should no longer strike us as strange or inconsistent even though in the *Tractatus* the anti-theory theme is admittedly full of tension while it is consistently adopted and applied in the *Philosophical Investigations* and other later work in general.

We are left then with the problem of how to read those remarks by the later Wittgenstein that seem to support musical formalism. In particular, how can we disarm passages like the following of the impression of formalism: "It has sometimes been said that what music conveys to us are feelings of joyfulness, melancholy, triumph, etc., etc. and what repels us in this account is that it seems to say that music is an instrument for producing in us sequences of feelings. And from this one might gather that any other means of producing such feelings would do for us instead of music. To such an account we are tempted to reply 'Music conveys to us itself!'" To gloss such passages as Wittgenstein's endorsement of musical formalism betrays an insufficient awareness of the later Wittgenstein as a dialectical thinker. "Philosophical theories", he wrote, "need to be treated carefully, since they contain much truth". To preserve truths theories exploit, as well as to retrieve truths theories neglect, Wittgenstein conducts conversations with philosophical theorists.

Looking at it this way, the passage above ending with "[m]usic conveys to us itself" falls in place as part of a conversation in which Wittgenstein uses the important truth that motivates formalism to show that expressivist theorists of music err by leaving a central element out of their account of music and our understanding of it. He plays off the

---

5 Wittgenstein, *Public and Private*, 387.
6 *Ibid.*, 396.

truth formalism "contains" against theories of musical expressivism. Ironically, expressivist theories lose the music as they attempt to identify musical meaning with its emotional and causal effects. This is not to say Wittgenstein in turn embraces musical formalism, rather, he wants to hold fast to the truths musical theories such as formalism and expressivism "contain" and build on, and at the same time, throw overboard the theories themselves.

Reading Wittgenstein this way provides us with a fresh way of seeing his recurring comparisons of understanding a sentence with understanding a musical theme or phrase. In the early works the unveiled form—logical or musical—is the paradigm for understanding both language and music. It is noteworthy that he draws the analogy from music to logic—the assumption is that the understanding of logic will clarify the understanding of music. In the later works the analogy sometimes works the other way around—our understanding of music is supposed to shed light on our understanding of the workings of language—or better still, since there is no paradigm, the comparisons illuminate our understanding of both music and language. The idea is to put things side by side for comparison and contrast, hence for better understanding and appreciation. [Absolute] music is not representational, it is not about something 'out there', nor is it reducible to a notational sequence, yet we have a strong impression we understand it. Taking this fact seriously may help to liberate us from representational and formalistic biases in accounts of linguistic meaning.

Analogy, of course, is not assimilation. Granted that a musical phrase cannot be paraphrased, i.e. it cannot be translated into another medium like a sentence can be translated from one language into another to clarify its meaning. However, sometimes we can come to have a better understanding of the music by putting it side by side with another work of art—a dance, a poem, a painting. The musical phrase is not about something—it does not picture some slice of the world—but it is borne out of a cultural tradition and can best be understood in its connections with the forms of life and associated language games of that tradition. Music is not alone, as formalists suggest; it resonates with the whole field of our language games—with our other musical and cultural practices.

It is crucial to understand that music for the later Wittgenstein was not merely, if at all, a pleasing pattern of sounds; for him, music connects with the ways we speak and with human forms of life:

> If you ask: how I experience the theme, I shall perhaps say 'As a question' or something of the sort, or I shall whistle it with expression etc.... Does the theme point to nothing beyond itself? Oh yes! But that means:—The impression it makes on me is connected with things in its surroundings—e.g. with the existence of the German language & its intonation, but that means with the whole field of our language games. If I say e.g.: it's as if here a conclusion were being drawn, or, as if here something were being confirmed, or, as if this were a reply to what came earlier,—then the way I understand it clearly presupposes familiarity with conclusions, confirmations, replies, etc.[7]

Suppose that music were alone and isolated from the culture, as a strict formalist insistence on its radical autonomy suggests. It would then follow that deterioration in music could not be seen plausibly as a symptom of cultural malaise, yet this is precisely how the later Wittgenstein sees it, and this is borne out by his practice of music criticism. For instance, Wittgenstein's judgment that Mahler's music as worthless makes no sense—regardless of whether it is justified or unjustified—unless Mahler's music is *heard as* a symptom of cultural decline. To understand Mahler you need to know a lot about the history of music and Mahler's times. Again, to Donald Tovey's assertion that fate or tragedy had no role in Mozart's music because Mozart had no access to literature of that sort, Wittgenstein replied: "Naturally books & music are connected. But if Mozart found no great tragedy in his reading, does that mean that he did not find it in his *life?*"[8] These observations presuppose a connectedness between understanding music and other aspects of culture it is embedded in, even though narrow and one-sided ways of construing such connections are rejected. Musical formalism separates the two and impoverishes our resources for understanding music. Imagining and understanding music, like imagining and understanding language, is to understand a form of life. If a lion could sing or make music, we could not understand him.

---

7 Wittgenstein, *Culture*, 59.
8 *Ibid.*, 93.

2. Wittgenstein and Hanslick: A Kinship with Expressive Difference

We are now in a position to revisit and explore further the relation between Wittgenstein and Hanslick. As mentioned before, the fact that Hanslick's name is not on Wittgenstein's list of influences does not undermine the usefulness of proposing such a relationship. What matters most are the striking textual similarities in substance and vocabulary. Instead of a wholesale assimilation of Wittgenstein's views on music to Hanslick's, however, it's best to continue by putting side by side snapshots of Hanslick, the young and the mature Wittgenstein—and to note family resemblances and differences. Prominent resemblances emerge in comparing the later Wittgenstein and Hanslick on the question of musical understanding. Consider this key passage from Hanslick:

> The most significant factor in the mental process which accompanies the comprehending of a musical work and makes it enjoyable will most frequently be overlooked. It is the mental satisfaction which the listener finds in continuously following and anticipating the composer's designs, here to be confirmed in his expectations, there to be agreeably led astray. It goes without saying that the mental streaming this way and that, this continual give and take, occurs unconsciously and at the speed of lightning. Only such music as brings about and rewards this mental pursuing, which could quite properly be called a musing of the imagination, will provide fully artistic satisfaction.... Music is characteristically this type of activity par excellence, for the reason that its achievements are not static; they do not come into being all at once but spin themselves out sequentially before the hearer; hence they demand from him not an arbitrarily granted, lingering, and intermittent inspection, but an unflagging attendance in keenest vigilance. This attendance can, in the case of intricate compositions, become intensified to the level of spiritual achievement.[9]

Apart from describing attentive and appreciative listening to music as a "spiritual achievement", other important features of this memorable passage resonate with the later Wittgenstein. First, there is the connecting

---

9 Hanslick, *On the Musically Beautiful*, 64.

of questions about musical meaning and musical understanding which involve the retrieval of agency in musical understanding: listeners imaginatively and attentively follow a melody as a composer takes them on a journey of the familiar and the strange so they in turn anticipate but are also surprised, and so on. Meaning, whether in music or language, is not there all at once but unfolds—emerges through a consideration of context, what comes before and after. Furthermore, aesthetic enjoyment and appreciation of music does not merely consist in a passive inner experience of disengaged rapture. For Wittgenstein, appreciation "is shown by the way a person hums a tune, or his knowing when the bass comes in; or by certain questions such as 'Does this harmonize? No. The bass is not quite loud enough. Here I just want something different…'". This chimes with Hanslick's insistence that "an aesthetic reception of the music… occurs only when the listener notices [the music] entirely, when he listens to it attentively and is aware of its beauties". Hanslick's point has an anti-Cartesian thrust and offers an instructive parallel to Wittgenstein's line of thinking about meaning and understanding in language and music. Thus the requirement for understanding the meaning of a word or sentence, or following a theme with understanding cannot be some special, private inner musical experience; if it were then only the listener could know whether he or she got it right.

Now to family differences: a striking difference is that the later Wittgenstein threw overboard Hanslick's musical formalism for the reason that it isolated music from the rest of the culture and left it alone and bereft of significance. Hanslick's polemic against the "music of the future", as embodied in Franz Liszt's "programme symphonies" and Richard Wagner's *Tristan and Isolde* and *The Ring of the Nibelungen*, is concerned about protecting music's integrity against attempts to reduce it to "nothing but a means for the generation of musical configurations".[10] The trouble is Hanslick goes to the other extreme by isolating music from the other arts: poetry and painting, and he speaks as if music has nothing to do with ideas, language, thought, argument, emotions and feelings. In particular he asserts that

> an aesthetics of musical art must take as its most important task to
> set forth unrelentingly the basic distinction between the essence

---

10   *Ibid.*, xxiii.

of music and that of language and in all deductions hold fast to the principle that, where the specifically musical is concerned, the analogy with language does not apply.[11]

This highlights a crucial difference between the later Wittgenstein and Hanslick: while Hanslick denied that music has anything to do with expression of emotions/feelings and claimed that such talk about music is simply figurative or metaphorical, Wittgenstein thought it can be apt and descriptive. For Hanslick, "The music is sad" is a figure of speech, since music is not a sentient creature capable of feeling, nor does it necessarily have the effect of sadness on its listeners. For Wittgenstein, music may have a "soulful or tender expression" that is *not* to be described in terms of degrees of loudness and of tempo. Since "the human body is the best picture of the human soul and the face is the soul of the body", he goes on to compare music's soulful expression to a "soulful facial expression", and points to the absurdity of "describing the latter it in terms of the distribution of matter in space".[12] Also, it is idle and futile to speak in general of the minor key as sounding sad while the major does not; Wittgenstein points to Schubert as a counter-example since in Schubert the major occasionally sounds *sadder* than the minor.[13] Even if a piece of music is played on a music box, its gestures would still be expressive gestures for him, and he might even be surprised if he notices a fresh aspect in the music despite the fact that he knew what was coming next.[14] Nor is it to be thought that temporality of the clock and temporality in music are equivalent concepts:

> Playing in strict tempo is not necessarily playing according to the metronome. This is not to deny that to achieve a particular effect a certain sort of music should be played according to the metronome. The opening theme of the second movement of Beethoven's *Eighth Symphony* may be of this sort.[15]

In these passages the salient resistance to any sort of physical reductionism in music is reminiscent of Wittgenstein's opposition to

---

11   *Ibid.*, 44.
12   Wittgenstein, *Culture*, 96.
13   *Ibid.*, 96.
14   *Ibid.*, 83-84.
15   *Ibid.*, 80.

reductionism without remainder in the realm of our psychological vocabulary in general.

For Wittgenstein then the music is sad *like* a person is sad: it speaks and moves slowly, chokes up, falters, and stoops, wails with its face distorted. Commenting on structure and feeling in music, he observed that "feelings accompany our grasp of a piece of music as they accompany events in our lives".[16] Feelings are expressive of our humanity, of the human form of life. We tend to feel as if we were sad as we listen to the dirge; elated when listening to *Ode to Joy*, calm and orderly when listening to Mozart's *Jupiter Symphony*.

Of course, this is not to say Wittgenstein held an Expressivist theory about music. Rather, he wanted to do justice to music's expressive features—without distorting them under any kind of theory. As we have seen, music for the later Wittgenstein has a connection to our forms of life and associated language games that reverberate in the culture in which it is grounded. To understand a theme in music is to understand the ways in which it expresses complaint or a cry of despair, draws a conclusion, lodges a protest, nods agreement and so on.

A development in music, perhaps beginning with Haydn and certainly with Beethoven, was the appearance of irony. How to make sense of and understand irony in music? Wittgenstein's early formalist perspective could not achieve that, but his later perspective, I shall now argue, is more congenial to the endeavour of understanding and appreciation musical irony.

3. Irony In Music and Language: Face, Gesture, Tone

The idea that Wittgenstein was interested in musical irony may initially strike readers as unpromising at best and a non-starter at worst. The "non-starter" objection—that Wittgenstein could not be invoked as a source of reflection on musical irony, since even though he admitted music was an important part of his life, he could not or at any rate did not write on music at all—has already been surmounted. Such a view, as we have seen, no longer stands the test of reading the *Nachlass*, in particular the remarks that have been printed in *Culture and Value*

---

16   *Ibid.*, 20.

and *Public and Private Occasions* where there are many remarks on
music, including scattered remarks on the topic of irony in music. The
"unpromising" objection is that Wittgenstein did not have an ironical
bone in his body: the univocal and aphoristic style of his *Tractatus* is
a form of communication *sub specie aeterni*, designed to eliminate
any kind of double-speak, does not readily lend itself to irony. What
is more, although the later Wittgenstein of the *Investigations* is multi-
vocal and conducts conversations, he still heads for the concrete and
aims to put "things right before our eyes, not covered by any veil".
None of this, of course, precludes Wittgenstein having a sense of irony
or that he did make ironic remarks. I claim only that Wittgenstein was
no philosophical ironist: he did not say things he did not mean, nor did
he play with his reader through provocative teasing.

But is this not going too fast? Even if Wittgenstein's philosophical
style was not disposed to irony, it is noteworthy that he was interested in
the concept since he made remarks about Socratic irony as well as irony
in Kierkegaard. Note these passages from Wittgenstein's diaries and
O.K. Bouwsma's conversations with Wittgenstein: "About this time",
writes Bouwsma in 1950:

> we sat on a bench and he began talking about reading Plato.
> Plato's arguments! His pretence of discussion! The Socratic
> Irony! [...] The arguments were bad, the pretence of discussion
> too obvious, the Socratic irony distasteful—why can't a man be
> forthright and say what's on his mind?[17]

And in 1931, Wittgenstein comments:

> Dealing with authors like Kierkegaard [...] makes their editors
> presumptuous. The editors of [...] Augustine's *Confessions*
> or of a work by Luther would never feel this temptation. It is
> probably the irony of an author that inclines the reader to become
> presumptuous.[18]

In the same year the reference to irony is autobiographical:

---

17   O.K. Bouwsma, *Wittgenstein Conversations, 1949-1951,* Indianapolis: Hackett,
     1986, 60.
18   Wittgenstein, *Public and Private*, 77.

Last night I awoke with dread from a dream [...]. In the dream someone had died, it was sad & I conducted myself well & then as if upon returning home someone, a strong rural person (of the sort of our Rosalie) (I am also thinking of the Cumaean Sybil) gave me a word of praise & something like: 'You are someone after all.' This image disappeared & I was alone in the dark & said to myself—with irony ['mir ironische'] 'You are someone after all....' [19]

These quotations show that the *later* Wittgenstein not only reflected on the concept of irony in the work of others, but had a sense of self-irony. But what is most important, especially in view of what I argue for later, is that the word 'irony' characterizes a kind of tone of voice with which the words are spoken, as in, for instance, "Watch your tone" as an admonition against insolence). In this sense it may serve as an expressive marker, much like annotations composers add to a score to help musicians interpret the music. In light of all this, my aim to gather and interpret Wittgenstein's scattered remarks about irony in music may prove to be more promising than it has initially appeared. So I will now sketch the background required to appreciate the problem of musical irony and then attempt resolve it.

A natural approach to understanding musical irony is to take irony in its verbal or literary sense, analyze its meaning, and see if the analysis can be extended to music. Irony, we may say, is at home in everyday discourse and literature where there is reference to something said or an allusion is made to some situation. A central feature of verbal irony is the incongruity between what a person says and means in that the intended meaning is the opposite of that expressed by the conventional meaning of the sentence. What is more, the ironist typically deflates, pokes fun at or mocks what is said or alluded to, and intends the ironic meaning to be penetrated by an audience. Unless the latter condition obtains, verbal irony is perceived to collapse into lying or outright deception.

Now then: since in pure or absolute music nothing is said or referred to; since there is no distinction between sentence meaning and speaker's meaning analogous to verbal/literary irony; and since speech acts such as 'mocking' are content-dependent, absolute music apparently cannot accomplish the complex communicative and expressive acts

---

19 *Ibid.*, 101.

involved in irony. Hence, the possibility that a tune, a melody, a style, or even a whole musical tradition may be musically undercut in a "purely" musical composition is ruled out. This is not to say that according to the literary paradigm musical irony is impossible in general. Rather, musical irony makes sense, but only if the medium of music is aptly combined with language, as in song or program music, where the accompanying text provides the required additional conditions—where the theme interacts with language.

Examples of this sort of irony may be heard in the *lieder* of Robert Schumann. Working with such an example is appropriate since it is instructive and since Wittgenstein thought that his cultural ideal may come from the time of Schumann:

> I often wonder whether my cultural ideal is a new one, i.e. contemporary, or whether it comes from the time of Schumann. At least it strikes me as a continuation of that ideal, though not the continuation that actually followed it then. That is to say, the second half of the 19th century has been left out. [20]

Without pre-judging the import of this passage which clearly stands in need of careful interpretation, it is worth noting there is a parallel between the interdependence in Schumann's activities as reader, diarist, critic and musician and Wittgenstein's as reader, diarist, critic, music devotee and philosopher. Also noteworthy in this connection is Schumann's setting Heine's verses to music wherein Heine's often sneering irony is softened to reflect 'the truth' of the poems "in a beautiful garb". In so doing, Schumann appropriates for himself the role of a musical-poetic sensibility and this resonates with Wittgenstein's stand in relation to philosophy: "[...] really one should write philosophy only as *one writes a poem;*"[21] and his self-described style: "My style is like bad musical composition".[22]

Schumann's *lied Die beiden Grenadiere* is a useful aid to our understanding of *one* form irony can take in music: it is instructive of musical irony as understood through the literary paradigm. The last part of the song is properly characterized as ironical, because the meaning of

---

20   Wittgenstein, *Culture*, 4.
21   *Ibid.*, 28.
22   *Ibid.*, 45.

its words and the *Marseillaise* accompanying those words on piano are a counterpoint to each other. A noted Schumann scholar remarks: "The resolve of the patriotic soldier's closing speech, supported by the strains of the *Marsellaise*, is expunged by the piano's intoning of a solemn Requiem hymn as the French soldier sinks, lifeless, to the ground". It is the Requiem hymn that undercuts and musically mocks the words "Then my Emperor will be passing right over my grave / Each sword clashing and flashing/ And I, fully armed, will rise up from that grave/ The Emperor's, the Emperor's protector", as the *Marseillaise* extols the Emperor Napoleon. Perhaps 'irony' by itself is not strong enough to describe what is going on here, and needs to be qualified as '*bitter irony*'.

This explains certain comments by music critics: "The mock seriousness in the *Marseillaise* heightens the impact of the final ironic statement". "Gerald Finley's [Schumann *lieder* specialist] rendition has an uncanny ability to conjure up a state of mind that is instantly recognizable in purely auditory terms as he expresses a note of bitterness in the tale of a soldier who dreams of violence and glory". These critical observations suggest that the ironic effect may be accomplished in purely musical terms and therefore an account of musical irony based on the literary paradigm is one-sided, being based on "a narrow diet of examples". The literary account also runs counter to the practices of composers, music critics and informed listeners. So, we might push the envelope and regard the idea of irony accomplished through musical means as a fresh problem for philosophers of music.

Let's frame this new problem the following way: On the one hand, music critics describe some pieces of absolute music as ironic. On the other hand, what could it mean to describe a musical passage this way? Instead of an *a priori* rejection of the idea, let's attend to pieces of instrumental music described and heard as ironical. It might be said that perhaps we need to go no further than to another piece by Schumann, namely, *Carnival Jest* from Vienna which employs the *Marseillaise* in a similar way, but this time in a "purely" musical context. There is a subtle contrast between the jolly atmosphere sketched in the fourth episode of the first movement (Rondo) of the composition and the disguised musical quotation of the *Marseillaise*. As a reminder of the destruction and suffering incurred in the name of equality and fraternity during the Napoleonic wars, Schumann subtly employs echoes of the (then disallowed) *Marseillaise* to mock the artificially cheerful atmosphere of Vienna. The discrepancy in the music, however, cannot be just any lack of fit, since the ironic is different from mere conflict. To hear the conflict as musical irony, we need to recognize that the expectations expressed in the quotation of the *Marseillaise—equality and fraternity*—clash with the then Viennese status quo and deflate the artificially cheerful atmosphere of the piece. Thus, we have a counter-example to the standard view that there can be no irony in absolute music.

This counter-example may be less than compelling for two related reasons. First, the title *Carnival Jest from Vienna* suggests Schumann had a subject matter in mind; namely, a Viennese carnival. Second, the musical quotation of the *Marseillaise* and the grasp of its significance involve extra-musical references, so the irony cannot be appreciated by those unaware of the historical and cultural context. Schumann's piano piece can therefore be an instance of irony only if the musical quotation of the *Marseillaise* is *heard and understood as* a more or less critical comment on Viennese light-heartedness under Metternich. So there is a presupposition the audience understands at some level "the cultural/conversational implicature" of that tune. This point goes beyond music and reaches literary irony too, since Jonathan Swift's *A Modest Proposal* could not have the impact of irony or satire, were the extra-literary historical conditions of starvation in Ireland not presupposed as background.

In general, the standard account of musical irony gives the impression that compared with the resources of language and literature, music, for all its affective power, is sparse in its clothing and minimal in its resources, a poor cousin on the margins of the rich family of fine arts. Wittgenstein, by contrast, offers a rather different take on music's resources. A striking feature of Wittgenstein's approach is that he does not privilege literature over music, but puts music on equal footing with the other arts:

> Music, with its few notes & rhythms, seems to some people a primitive art [...] but only its surface is simple, while the body which makes possible the interpretation of this manifest content

has all the infinite complexity that is suggested in the external
forms of other arts & which music conceals.[23]

One way to read this important remark is to liken the idea of notation
to surface grammar. We might say that music notation is comparable to
words in a dictionary where, despite the vast variations in the workings
of language, everything looks the same. Since what we do with language
can be concealed by surface grammar, so can the workings of music be
concealed by its notation; thus, music's handicaps compared with the
other arts are more apparent than real.

This reading does not go far enough, however, to do justice to
the significance of Wittgenstein's remark. A more substantial reading
would bring attention to the wide range of expressive gestures made
possible by the use of different modulation and tone of voice. This more
substantial reading goes a long way to explain why Wittgenstein adds
that, despite music's primitive appearance, "[i]n a certain sense, it is the
most sophisticated art of all".[24] Although this apparent privileging of
music serves as an antidote to the conventional valorizing of literature
among the arts, it counters the spirit of Wittgenstein's remarks that puts
music on par with the other arts. The suggestion cannot be that we make
music paradigmatic over literature, for such an inversion, instead of
re-orienting our ways of thinking, would shift rather than decline the
privileged paradigm.

So, unlike the conventional view, Wittgenstein puts music side
by side with the other fine arts. For him music and books are connected
and teaching someone to appreciate poetry or painting can be part of an
explanation of what music is.[25] We are to juxtapose music and language
and explore similarities and differences between them to see how they
may illuminate each other. One significant parallel is that listening to
some music leaves an impression that it speaks, that the composer and
performer communicate:

> Think about how it was said of [Josef] Labor's playing 'He is
> speaking'. What was it about this playing that was so reminiscent
> of speaking? And how remarkable that this similarity with

---

23 *Ibid.*, 11.
24 *Ibid.*
25 *Ibid.*, 81.

> speaking is not something we find incidental, but an important
> & big matter!—We should like to call music, and certainly *some*
> music, a 'language'; but no doubt not *some* [other] music. Not
> that this need involve a judgment of value. [26]

The impression that some music is like speech cuts deep because with
speech comes a connection with understanding, meaning and expression.
We can follow it, have expectations about its turns, be moved by it and
surprised how a movement develops, as well as discuss it as if it were
communication. This leads to the thought that comparisons between
pieces of music and their performance may shed light on understanding
language and vice versa.

What are the indications of music's speech-like affinities? One
indication is music's "significant irregularity" suggesting inflection and
modulation of voice:

> Phenomena akin to language in music and architecture.
> Significant irregularity—in Gothic for instance (I am thinking
> too of the towers of St. Basil's Cathedral.) Bach's music is more
> like language than Mozart's or Haydn's. The recitatives on the
> double basses in the fourth movement of Beethoven's *Ninth
> Symphony.*[27]

The remark that "understanding a sentence is much more akin to
understanding a theme in music than one may think"[28] is important
because in the analogy it is understanding music that, as it were, wears
the trousers.

Wittgenstein thinks comparisons with music throw into relief the
shortcomings of exclusively referential or representational theories of
meaning and language learning. This is because a theme in absolute
music is a felt communication and can be followed with understanding,
yet it has no external reference. Thus the analogy helps us to resist over-
simple models of understanding language on the model of referential
or representational theories.[29] The point is that music is expressive
communication, yet absolute music does not refer, represent or describe.

---

26   *Ibid.*, 71.
27   *Ibid.*, 40.
28   Wittgenstein, *Investigations*, § 527.
29   Wittgenstein, *Investigations*, § 1.

This is not to say, as some robust formalists would assert, that there is no place in absolute music for allusion, reference, or representation. Consider the delightful example of Camille Saint-Saëns's *Le Carnaval des Animaux* (*Carnival of the Animals*) where it is plain that there is reference and representation. Hear The Elephant and The Swan introduced, 'named', and sketched as musical characters. So, even though absolute music rarely names, refers, or represents, sometimes it does. It is noteworthy that the piece was written for children and it resonates with the role of pointing in language learning sketched in *Philosophical Investigations* §6, §8, §9: In Saint-Saëns's "narrowly circumscribed region" of music, there is a kind of musical ostension, but it would be absurd to think that all music is like that.

Again, Olivier Messiaen's *Chants d'Oiseaux* (*Birdsongs*) is a striking piece of representational instrumental music. The composer describes it this way:

> As it coincides with the return of the songs of birds, the piece can be played at Eastertide. The piece was written in the middle of the forest of Saint-Germain-en-Laye; there appear also several songs of birds found in the Perin Meadow of Fuligny (Aube) and in the Gardépé (Charente). In these places one hears the whimsical stanzas of the blackbird, the sweet virtuosity of the (European) robin, and the powerful and clear calls [...] of the song thrush. The piece begins in the afternoon, about four o'clock. Then the night comes. In the growing darkness, the nightingale begins a long solo: mysterious and tender notes, mingled with a celebrated refrain on a battery of two jointed sounds—ti-ko-ti-ki-ti-co —the attack, joined and plucked, the timbre of a damp harpsichord haloed with gongs..... [30]

What we have here are two examples of instrumental music that refer and represent and the piece by Messiaen is clearly not program music. There is a strong resonance here with Wittgenstein's critique of Augustine's picture of the essence of language as naming or reference: "Augustine, we might say, does describe a system of communication; only not everything that we call language is this system. And one has to say this in many cases where the question arises 'Is this an appropriate

---

30   Jon Gillock, *Performing Messiaen's Organ Music,* Bloomington: Indiana University Press, 2009, 74-78.

description or not?' The answer is: 'Yes, it is appropriate, but only for this narrowly circumscribed region, not for the whole of what you were claiming to describe.'"[31] So, it is a balanced view we are after, rather than a one-sided view skewed by a philosophical theory of music or language that stipulates an exclusively descriptive or expressive function as the essence of music or language.

How to do things with music? If external reference is not a major use or gesture of absolute music, what are the other things we do with music? What are our varied reactions to music? In a striking passage Wittgenstein goes on to draw useful comparisons between music and language. "Does the theme point to nothing beyond itself?" Wittgenstein or his imagined conversation partner plaintively asks, as if the theme were robbed of significance if it had no external reference. Wittgenstein continues:

> Oh, yes! But that means:—The impression it makes on me is connected with things in its surroundings—e.g. with the existence of the German language & of its intonation, but that means with the whole field of our language games. If I say e.g.: it's as if here a conclusion were being drawn, or, as if here something were being confirmed, or, as if this were a reply to what came earlier,—then the way I understand it clearly presupposes familiarity with conclusions, confirmations, replies, etc.[32]

Noticing the "as ifs" is crucial here to prevent misunderstanding in interpretation. There is no claim made to equate the meaning of a theme with the meaning of a statement or assertion. Although the theme does not refer to an object or a slice of reality, it still has meaning for us in that it resonates with our language, ways of life and social practices, as well as the conventions and history of music itself.

Following this line of thought, we can put music and language side by side and listen *for* how themes and tones resonate with assertions, commands, questions, and conclusions in speech. Wittgenstein points us in this direction when he remarks: "If you ask how I experienced the theme, I shall perhaps say "As a question" or something of the sort, or I

---

31   Wittgenstein, *Investigations*, §3.
32   Wittgenstein, *Culture,* 59e.

shall whistle it with expression etc".[33] The positive force of the analogy between music and language then is that attentive listening to music brings into focus embodied gestures or "acts" that we tend to forget when reflecting on meaning and communication. A central concern in such comparisons pertains to the kind of acts the composer, player, or speaker is performing when they use a musical phrase in a certain context. We may not only ask for the meaning of a phrase, but also what the speaker meant by a particular *gesture* or *tone* of voice. Here the distinction between sentence meaning and speaker's meaning kicks in.[34] Even though much of "absolute music" may be empty of, or thin on, semantic content in the sense of specific experiential or referential content, it still resonates with the inflection of a question, the sound of an answer, the tone of a complaint ("I heard a plaintive melody"), the shrillness of a command, or leave an impression of conversation, conflict or disagreement, or of coming from a great distance.

The question of what a musical phrase means then is *partly* a question of what the composer or the performer intended by using that musical expression or phrase. The tone of voice, the way it is performed, or the musical or extra-musical context may suggest that the expression is not to be taken at face value. We may, as it were, understand what is said, but may be puzzled or taken aback by the tone used in saying it. There are, "musical gestures or acts" with which the theme or phrase is performed that are analogous to speech acts that we perform with sentences and words. In some cases then musical meaning is usefully explored through the treatment a phrase, theme or melody receive. This may help to unpack Wittgenstein's remark that absolute music looks simple only on the surface but its body has all the complexity of the other arts. If a body of music is open to interpretations that are as deep as those of the other arts, there may be room for *hearing* irony in it.

In thinking about understanding music, we are tempted by the picture that understanding here as elsewhere consists in some sort of inner experience to be introspectively identified and described. Wittgenstein deflates such expectations: "If I now ask 'What do I actually experience then, if I hear the theme & hear it with understanding?—Nothing but

---

33   *Ibid.*, 59.
34   H.P. Grice, "Utterer's Meaning, Sentence Meaning, and Word Meaning", *Foundations of Language* 4 (1968), 225-242.

inanities occur to me by way of a reply. Such as images, kinaesthetic sensations, thoughts and the like".[35] Reducing the idea of understanding music to such private experiences threatens the stability of understanding music as a social practice by suggesting that the vocabulary of musical understanding is analogous to a private language. In any event, to speak of understanding music as an experience may be "passable" as long as "no experiential content" is asked for or provided. So, on occasion it might be insightful to say: that sounds like an answer to a question that came before, but it would be nonsense to ask what the question or what the answer was—apart from repeating, perhaps with emphasis, the musical phrases in context.

So, to get a grip on the question what does it consist in, following a musical phrase with understanding or playing it with understanding, we are not to proceed by way of introspection. "Don't look inside yourself. Ask yourself rather, *what* makes you say that's what *someone else* is doing. And what prompts you to say he has a particular experience? Indeed, do we ever actually say that? Wouldn't it be more likely to say of someone else that he is having a whole host of experiences? Thus understanding music does not consist in any one thing, be it experiencing some specific experiential content, kinaesthetic sensations or a cluster of images or associations. I would perhaps say: 'He is experiencing the theme intensely'; but ask yourself, what the expression of this is?'"[36]

If understanding a musical phrase is not some unique inner experience, how is it expressed then?

> *More likely*, by pointing out the expressive movements of one who understands. [...] Appreciation of music is *expressed* in a certain way, both in the course of hearing & playing and at other times too. This expression sometimes includes movements, but sometimes only the way the one who understands plays, or hums, occasionally too parallels he draws & images which, as it were illustrate the music. Someone who understands music will listen differently (with a different facial expression, e.g.), play differently, hum differently, talk differently about the piece than someone who does not understand. His appreciation of a theme will not however be shown only in phenomena that accompany

---

35   Wittgenstein, *Culture*, 80.
36   *Ibid.*, 58.

the hearing or playing of the theme, but also in an appreciation
for music in general.[37]

Our explanations resonate with these signs of understanding insofar as
they include a gesture, sometimes a dance step or words describing
a dance. Again, other signs of understanding are the sorts of poems,
paintings, pictures of scenes of nature, or other pieces of music we put
side by side with the work in question. Such parallels would bring out
family resemblances between the looks or expressive features of the
two works of art. The parallels do not serve as explanations that give
compelling reasons for acceptance, but rather have the form: "It's as
though…; then he [to whom we give the explanation] says 'Yes' now I
understand it.'"[38] Unlike for strong formalists, music in Wittgenstein's
view, is not alone and isolated, but is intimately involved in the culture
in which it originates and derives its importance from connections with
our lives.

Wittgenstein was interested in the ways music is expressive and
he connected "sad music" with "sad person". His friend O.K. Bouwsma
followed up this approach to musical meaning[39] and suggested that we
ask: in what ways is sad music like a sad person? With a sad person,
we look for sadness in the face, in the eyes, in the sound of voice, in
bodily posture and other movements. We can hear sadness as well as
see it. This is a move in the right direction but expressivists, no matter
how subtle they are, take what Wittgenstein sees as a helpful analogy
and turn it into a *theory* about musical meaning or understanding. The
theory provides a ready to hand answer to a problem we come across in
aesthetics. say, we listen to a piece of music and wonder why the tune
is so dull and then we suddenly play it properly, with a certain accent
or gesture, and so on, and suddenly something clicks and we express
appreciation. What happens?

We saw that invoking an "inner experience" to account for
appreciation won't do. Wittgenstein wants to steer us away from the
question of 'what happens': the question of what happens when we
click is simply a pseudo-question, like the question what happens when

---

37 *Ibid.*, 80.

38 *Ibid.*, 79.

39 O.K. Bouwsma, "The Expression Theory of Art" in *Philosophical Analysis: A Collection of Essays,* ed. Max Black, Ithaca: Cornell University Press, 1950.

we think. If we ask such a question, we must continue by asking what happens when, in what circumstances, and what happens in and then the mentalistic picture recedes and the important the role of expressive behaviour as criteria for aesthetic appreciation comes to the foreground. Indeed he went on to say: "The behaviouristic approach is in a way good for these problems".[40] Was Wittgenstein a behaviourist then? Did he translate sentences, say, about appreciating music into sentences about patterns of behaviour? Hardly. He would have rejected such moves as exercises in reductionism. "Am I saying something like, 'and the soul itself is merely something about the body'? No. I am not that hard up for categories".[41]

"A theme", Wittgenstein remarks, "no less than a face, wears an expression".[42] It's noteworthy that in his music criticism Wittgenstein speaks of the face of individual composer's music. Consider: "In Bruckner's music nothing is left of the long & slender (Nordic) face of Nestroy, Grillparzer, Haydn, etc. but it has in full measure a round full (alpine) face even purer than was Schubert's". Of course Wittgenstein is not talking about the faces of these people as such but the face of their music or dramatic or comic language. The English translation seems to hover ambiguously between the two, while the German original makes it clear it is the face of the music that is at issue. Again, Wittgenstein can imagine "an exciting scene in a silent film accompanied with music by Beethoven or Schubert & might gain some sort of understanding of the music from the film. But not an understanding of music by Brahms [... because he is too abstract]. Bruckner on the other hand does go with a film".[43] How does this perspective on musical expressiveness allow for the discernment of irony in music? If face and tone play a role in hearing irony in music, how so?

If sad music is to be put side by side with a sad face or a sad voice, then ironic music is to be juxtaposed with an ironic face or an ironic voice. What face does an ironical musical expression wear then and what is the sound of its voice? Irony cannot be discerned by inspecting a line in the musical score, just as an isolated remark in a

40   Wittgenstein, *Public and Private*, 403.
41   Wittgenstein, *Remarks on the Philosophy of Psychology*, Volume II, Oxford: Basil Blackwell, 1988, 690.
42   Wittgenstein, *Culture*, 59.
43   *Ibid.*, 29.

text cannot be read as ironical unless we are provided with context, background or the writer's intentions. If the text is a script for a play, we may hear it in the actor's tone of voice or see it in his facial expression and gestures. In the musical score the composer may have written notes for the performer, giving directions for the musical treatment of the phrase. Or the performer may interpret the score as ironic in light of what hits off the music best or information he may possess about the life and times of the composer. If the piece is well performed, there is likely "uptake" on the part of an attentive audience as they hear a tone of humorous playfulness, deflation, mocking or ridicule in the way the phrase is played in response to the theme.

Wittgenstein addresses these issues explicitly in two passages in the left-over manuscript material included by G.H. Von Wright in *Culture and Value*. The first aligns musical irony with a face that is distorted: "I could equally have said: the distorted in music. In the sense in which we speak of features distorted by grief". The second passage invites us to listen to various pieces of music and hear irony's various tones, in order to compare and contrast them. This "Listen and hear" approach is analogous to the "Look and see" approach of the *Investigations*.[44] Wittgenstein cites and compares instances of irony in the music of Wagner and Beethoven, and makes explicit observations about the ironical tone of voice through analogy: "Irony in music: E.g. Wagner in the *Mastersingers*. Incomparably deeper in the Fugato in the first movement of the *Ninth*. Here is something that corresponds to the expression of bitter irony in speech".[45] (Here a confession is in order: sometimes I can hear the irony in the movement, sometimes not. Perhaps this variation depends on how a particular conductor treats the movement or it may be due to my less than refined musical ear.)

These remarks highlight the importance of the history of music as background and the need for further exploration into the affinities between the irony in the Fugato of Beethoven's *Ninth Symphony* and the expression of bitter irony in speech. Wittgenstein underscores this train of thought by making observations about the origins and contingency of irony in the history of classical music:

---

44   Wittgenstein, *Investigations*, §66.
45   Wittgenstein, *Culture*, 63.

> In Beethoven's music what one might call the expression of
> irony is to be found for the first time. E.g. in the first movement
> of the *Ninth*. With him, moreover, it is a terrible irony, that of fate
> perhaps.—In Wagner irony reappears, but turned into something
> bourgeois. You could no doubt say that Wagner & Brahms, each
> in his own way, imitated Beethoven; but what with him was
> cosmic, is mundane with them. The same expressions are to be
> found in him, but they follow different laws.[46]

One might take issue with Wittgenstein's claim that irony in music first
appears in Beethoven, unless one means the irony of fate, for Haydn's
quartet "The Joke", as musicians refer to it, is a fine example of playful
irony and predates Beethoven's *Ninth*. This piece, if it is ironic, also
shows that Wittgenstein was factually wrong in thinking that irony in
music first appears in Beethoven.

How can a piece of music, we might ask, be expressive of "the
irony of fate"? Perhaps we may begin such a discussion by saying that a
listener can hear the irony of fate only if he is acquainted with situations
where there is an outcome of events contrary to what was expected or
is fitting. The listener senses the development of the theme, expects a
certain conclusion, and is startled and unsettled when what emerges is
contrary to what he anticipated. But is that not simply *a surprise*? To
differentiate the two we need to hear the musical treatment not only as
jolting but as destructive of the struggling motif. This is, to be sure, an
auditory experience, but it must be situated in a musical environment
which makes it possible to hear the comment to belie or otherwise make
futile the motif commented on. I.e. it is hearing an aspect. In the Fugato,
we may say, a motif previously introduced has the audible effect of
making the second motif break down, despite its palpable struggle to
advance. This is the expression of cosmic or bitter irony. The passage in
the Fugato is like a blizzard on the Canadian prairies where, despite our
best efforts to make headway in a momentary lull, we are beaten down
by the resurging elements of wind and snow.

Other questions: How are we to discern that irony in Wagner
is transposed into the civic mode, and what is cosmic in Beethoven
becomes mundane with Brahms and Wagner? We are perhaps to listen
for "cosmic" qualities in Beethoven's music—themes that allude

---

46   *Ibid.*, 93.

to tremendous strength and power in nature. Brahms and Wagner domesticate these qualities by bringing them down from sublime cosmic heights to human interaction, so that they no longer overwhelm—thus making them "mundane".

But *how* is this manifest in their music? "The same expressions occur in [Beethoven's] music, but obeying different laws. In Mozart's or Haydn's music again, fate plays no role of any sort. That is not the *concern* of this music".[47] If the expressions are the same, then their context, surroundings, their treatment and the uses they are put to are significant factors making for differences in meaning. Fate, cosmos, and nature: these will have an iron-clad inevitability about them. The argument will be characterized by an overwhelming necessity and force, as if the conclusion had the force of a logical "must", a kind of tsunami of deduction that destroys the plans of the heroic protagonist. Mundane irony, in contrast, is a gentler and more sociable thing which requires an audience, a peculiar dialogue that mocks or deflates instead of annihilating: it disconcerts, embarrasses, or punctures, as it calls us, through musical conversations, to moments of self-understanding.

Wittgenstein returns to and dismisses an explanation of the alleged fact that tragic irony is never a concern in Mozart's music. In doing so, he makes a rare and surprising allusion to his British contemporary, the music critic and conductor Donald Tovey, "That ass Tovey", he offensively condescends, "says somewhere that this, or something similar, is connected with the fact that Mozart had no access to literature of a certain sort. As though it were established, that only books had made the music of the masters what it was. Naturally, books and & music are connected. But if Mozart had found no great *tragedy* in his reading, does that mean he did not find it in his *life*? And do composers always see solely through the spectacles of poets?[48] Here Wittgenstein issues reminders that Tovey's explanation suffers from a one-sided diet of examples preventing him from recognizing possible alternatives. Thus we have a move characteristic of Wittgenstein's later philosophy, but what is perhaps uncharacteristic is the "name-calling". We might, in all fairness, balance Tovey's error Wittgenstein identifies, by citing a striking passage from Tovey that is very much in the spirit

---

47 *Ibid.*
48 *Ibid.*, 93e.

of Wittgenstein's proposal of juxtaposition: putting music, text, and picture side by side so that they can mutually illuminate one another. Here is Tovey's amazed and amazing reaction to the first movement of Beethoven's *Ninth*: "The catastrophic return reveals fresh evidence of the gigantic size of the opening. Now we are brought into the midst of it and instead of a distant nebula we see the heavens on fire. There is something terrible about this triumphant major tonic".[49]

A few concluding remarks on irony: "[T]o enjoy a poet", Wittgenstein remarks, "you have to like the culture to which he belongs as well. If you are indifferent to or are repelled by it, your admiration cools off".[50] Wittgenstein did *not* identify with the culture of his own time, the spirit of which was manifest in modern music, architecture and so on. He lived, as Henrik von Wright remarked, the decline of the West (*Untergang des Abendlandes*).[51] However, a Spenglerian emphasis on how changes in the culture shape our judgment and appreciation has implications for the evaluation of composers. For instance, we have come to recognize our own face and gestures—our own condition—in Mahler's musical gestures and face. The situation is like that with Post-Impressionist painters in England in the early twentieth century. It took an authoritative artist and painter such as Roger Fry who organized an exhibition that made Londoners aware of the virtues of Cézanne and other Post-Impressionists. Through this exhibition the London public realized that the Post-Impressionists were not incompetent draughts men, but were interested in making us see differently through painterly studies of light and how it affects our perception of objects.

In light of this, consider an astute comment by Francis Sparshott about *hearing* aspects: "There are ambiguous situations: if an imaginative musician takes Handel's *Hallelujah Chorus* and adds a steady and mechanical drum beat to it, is he being ironic, or just having a friendly conversation with an admired predecessor?"[52] This remark gives us a direction for listening to Mahler rather differently than Wittgenstein did when he complained of Mahler's "shameless musical

49   Donald Francis Tovey, *Essays in Musical Analysis,* London, 1935, vol. II, 18.
50   Wittgenstein, *Culture,* 96.
51   G.H. von Wright, *Wittgenstein,* Oxford: Basil Blackwell, 1982, 212.
52   Francis Sparshott, "Aesthetics of Music: Limits and Grounds" in *What is Music?,* ed. Philip Alperson, University Park, PA: The Pennsylvania State University Press, 1987, 92.

thefts".[53] A greater appreciation of irony and quotation has made Mahler, after a long period of neglect, more appealing from the 1970s onwards. We have learned to listen to Mahler in a way that some of his music is heard as a friendly or perhaps ironical conversation with admired predecessors. The treatment of *Frère Jacques* as a funeral march in the third movement of his *First Symphony* (*The Titan*) is a striking example of musical irony as it reminds us of joyful security and at the same time deflates it with a reminder of loss and grief. Hence, the double aspect perception involved on the part of the listener. What a difference a minor key makes in this context!

If a theme in music may thus become a fresh part of our expressive repertoire and provide us with a new gesture, then it also lends itself to the possibility of ironic treatment. Consider national anthems: they are usually performed at public events to express allegiance and reverence for one's country. If "patriotism", as Wittgenstein said, "is the love of an idea"[54] and collective action contravenes this idea, the possibility of ironic treatment in performing the anthem arises. For instance, in Jimi Hendrix's *Zeitgeist* send up of *The Star-Spangled Banner* at the Woodstock Festival in 1969 the musical gestures are more complicated than in conventional renditions. As the electric guitar boldly articulates the melody of the national anthem as baseline, the gesture of allegiance and reverence are musically evident. However, as Hendrix uses sustained amplifier feed back to create distortion and mimics the sounds of explosions and machine guns firing, his screeching guitar undercuts the lyrical baseline. The conflicting gestures of allegiance and of protest and resistance are musically felt in the gap between melody and extreme dissonance. When challenged that his rendition of the anthem was unpatriotic, Hendrix replied "To me it was beautiful". Later on he said: "We play it the way the air is in America today. The air is slightly static, see".[55]

Moving back to Beethoven and to the present. In a joyous mood of human solidarity, I can hum or whistle Beethoven's *Ode to Joy*; in another mood, I can whistle it with irony. Again, in a concert hall setting, the *Ode* is usually heard as joyful, but in a radically different situation

---

53 Wittgenstein, *Public and Private*, 93.
54 *Ibid.*, 63.
55 Charles Cross, *Room Full of Mirrors: A Biography of Jimi Hendrix*, New York: Hyperion, 2005, 271.

it can be *heard* as bitter irony: imagine a physician in Afghanistan, listening to the *Ode* as she sets out to care for the wounded after a suicide attack. Might she not, however—if resolute—also hear in the *Ode* a source of hope?

In any event, encouraged by Wittgenstein's close identification with composers, I now examine remarks he made about particular composers, including Franz Schubert, Johannes Brahms, Richard Wagner, Gustav Mahler, Josef Labor and others.

Chapter V
Wittgenstein and the Composers

1. Not Only Science But Art Also Teaches

Writing about the influences on Ludwig Wittgenstein's work, Georg Henrik von Wright remarks that Wittgenstein received deeper impressions from some writers in the borderlands between philosophy, religion, and poetry than from professional philosophers.[1] Surprisingly, von Wright does not mention composers of music despite the fact that Wittgenstein also criss-crossed the borderlands between music and philosophy and received nourishing ideas for his line of thinking from composers. The question that recurs, and that I now address from a different angle, is: who are these composers and tone poets whom Wittgenstein took up for his own work and why?

What motivates this question is an unexamined assumption in the modern culture of the West about a division of labour: scientists instruct us and artists entertain us. This assumption, as we have seen already in our discussion of Hanslick, is a prominent feature of the *scientistic* culture that developed in the second half of the nineteenth century, became pervasive in the twentieth century and is now part of the prevailing cultural ideology. Wittgenstein rejected this complacent dichotomy between scientists and artists: "People nowadays think, scientists are there to instruct them, poets, musicians etc. to entertain them. *That the latter have something to teach them; that never occurs to them*".[2] Examining this assumption in light of Wittgenstein's remarks about the composers he engages in his writings—Bach, Mozart, Haydn, Beethoven, Mendelssohn, Schumann, Schubert, Wagner, Mahler and Labor—may help us to understand why he read and listened to composers and how the allusions to music and "tone poets" have

---

1 Von Wright, *Wittgenstein*, 33.
2 Wittgenstein, *Culture*, 42.

implications for his philosophical perspective, style and even for his work ethic. Johann Sebastian Bach, for instance, is admired and aspired to partly because of his immense capacity for work:

> Bach said that everything he achieved was the result of industry. But industry like that presupposes humility & an enormous capacity for suffering, strength then. And anyone who in addition can express himself perfectly simply addresses us in the language of a great human being.[3]

To begin, let's consider composers' names. As paradigms for referential theories of meaning, the essence of naming has been taken to consist in rigid designation or strict reference. Strange to say, the word 'this' has been called, by no less a philosopher than Bertrand Russell, the only genuine name. The paradigm of naming then would be applying the word 'this' to a simple object directly in the centre of my visual field. A complex object won't do, since its complexity would give rise to ambiguity of reference. Applying this to proper names: A proper name means whom it stands for and thus it has meaning only if it has a bearer. But what died when Robert Schubert died was not a name but a person. Alternatively, we might say, as Russell did, that an ordinary proper name can be defined as a *fixed* definite description that uniquely picks out the person named. I do not have, however, a fixed description that I am prepared to substitute for Robert Schubert, only a whole series of props I am ready to lean on should the one I am leaning on be taken from under me. Wittgenstein provides a classic discussion of this issue in *Investigations* §39–47 where he shows in detail why such theories falter and ultimately fail. He uses Moses as an example to make his points, rather than, as we did, Schubert.

In a remark in his diary for 1934, Wittgenstein takes up a different dimension than simply reference of our use of proper names. How is it, he wonders, that we have the impression that the great masters [in music or painting] have just the names that suit their work? Sometimes we wonder what name would hit off the character of a particular piece of music much like we wonder what name would hit off a particular person's character. In such instances, Wittgenstein says, we project an appropriate name on the person or music, taking the method of

---

3   *Ibid.*, 81.

projection as given. At other times we project the character of the person or music into the name & treat the name as given. As we have already seen, he speaks of composers in a manner keeping with these remarks. Thus Schubert is melancholy and irreligious, has an alpine face and his melodies are full of climaxes like mountain peaks. "You can point to a particular place in a Schubert melody & say: look, that is the point of this melody, this is where the idea comes to a head".[4] Schubert's name is also mentioned with regard to counterpoint:

> Counterpoint might represent an extraordinarily difficult problem for a composer; the problem namely: given *my* propensities what should be *my* relation to counterpoint. He may have found a conventional relation, yet feel perhaps that it is not *his*. That it is not clear what the importance of counterpoint to him *ought* to be.[5]

Then Wittgenstein adds that he was thinking of Schubert in this connection who still wanted to take lessons in counterpoint at the end of his life. Wittgenstein thought that "his aim may have been not simply learning more counterpoint, but rather determining where he stood in relation to it".[6] Crudely put, one might say that counterpoint basically involves the interweaving of independent voices or melodic lines that contribute to the emerging polyphony which, in turn, enhances and comments on the individual voices. If so, then counterpoint offers us a key to understanding the structure and style of the *Investigations* as a matter of different voices within a dialogue sketching conflicting philosophical views and aiming at their dissolution by doing justice to each. We can discern, in many passages, various voices arguing: the voice of the tradition or temptation, crisply proposing a philosophical theory; the voice of the everyday arguing against it, the voice of the narrator bringing about a sort of balance. In the case of the analysis of proper names: there is the *subliming* voice of the tradition (the ostensive 'this' as the only genuine name), the crisp clear voice of correctness (Russell with his theory of definite description), and then the voice

---

4   *Ibid.*, 54.
5   *Ibid.*, 46-47.
6   *Ibid.*

of the everyday pointing to the fluidity in our use of proper names in keeping with our ordinary practices.

I am inclined to think Wittgenstein was in the same sort of predicament with respect to dialogue that Schubert was in with respect to counterpoint: he wanted to determine how he stood in relation to these dissonant voices. Such a musical parallel, we may be tempted to think, lends support to reading the *Investigations* as a genuinely conflicted dialogue of dissonant voices where justice is done to each voice yet none is singly or whole heartedly embraced, for that would lead to another philosophical theory and thus to a dogmatic tone.[7] We are, however, given indications in a remark about Schubert, that the voice of the everyday, of the ordinary—and these are not to be taken as necessarily equivalent to the sense of ordinary as the conventionally accepted—is the preferred voice: "The last two bars of the Death & the Maiden theme; you may think first that this figure is conventional, ordinary, until you understand its deeper expression. I.e. until you understand that here the ordinary is filled with significance".[8] The voice of the everyday is the voice that gives the philosopher what he longs for: "thoughts that are at peace".[9]

Now to Brahms, Bruckner and Wagner: A year after his return to Cambridge in 1929, Wittgenstein's notebook entries indicated his close identification with composers:

> I feel well only when I am enthusiastic. Then again I fear the collapse of this enthusiasm. Today Mrs. Moore [wife of the moral philosopher G.E. Moore] showed me a stupid review of a performance of Bruckner's 4th symphony where the reviewer complains about Bruckner & also talks disrespectfully of Brahms & Wagner. At first it didn't make an impression on me since it is natural that everything—great and small—is barked at by dogs. Then it pained me after all. In a certain sense I feel touched (strangely) when I think that the mind is never understood.[10]

Two things stand out in this passage: one is the intensity of identification

---

7   David Stern, *Wittgenstein's Philosophical Investigations: An Introduction,* New
     York and Oxford: Oxford University Press, 2004.
8   Wittgenstein, *Culture,* 60.
9   *Ibid.,* 50.
10   Wittgenstein, *Public and Private,*19.

with the composers Brahms, Bruckner, and Wagner; the other is the sharp contrast with modern philosophy's attitude toward enthusiasm: Wittgenstein endorsed its value for his happiness and work despite the philosophical tradition's entrenched distrust of the passions. What is more, he embraced enthusiasm and spirit as sources of vitality and creativity: "The best state of mind for me is the state of enthusiasm (*Begeisterung*) because it consumes the ridiculous thoughts at least partially & renders them useless".[11] Next day's entry reveals he is still outraged about the critics tirade against the composers:

> On yesterday's matter: did these great ones suffer so unspeakably so that some buttface (*Arschgesicht*) can come today & deliver his opinion about them? This thought fills me with a sort of hopelessness.—Yesterday I sat for a while in the garden at Trinity & there I thought, strange how the well-developed physique of all these people goes together with complete unspiritedness (I don't mean lack of intellect.) And how on the other hand a theme by Brahms is full of vigor, grace, & drive & he himself had a potbelly. In contrast the spirit of our contemporaries has no springs under its feet.[12]

Since Wittgenstein rarely invoked a vulgarity in his writing to express how he felt about an issue, the fact that he does so in this context by calling shallow critics "buttface" indicates intense moral indignation. But not only that; palpable is the thought: If Brahms, Bruckner and Wagner are spoken of disrespectfully and rejected, how can Wittgenstein hope to be understood?

Wittgenstein, as we have seen, was passionate about Brahms's music and speaks of "the strength of musical thinking", of "the overwhelming skill", of the "complete rigour" in Brahms who is "too abstract" to go with a film, hence pictorial representation cannot do justice to his music despite its "earthiness". Such features, Wittgenstein imagines, are connected with Brahms "thinking with the pen" when composing music, and in this respect he likens himself to Brahms: "I [too] really do think with my pen, for my head often knows nothing of

---

11 *Ibid.*, 23.
12 *Ibid.*, 19-21.

what my hand is doing".[13] Brahms stands as a paradigm, an "object of comparison", as Wittgenstein takes stock and assesses himself: "I never more than half succeed in expressing what I want to express. Indeed not even so much, but perhaps only one tenth…. My writing is often nothing but 'stammering.'"[14]

Admired though he is, not even Brahms is above criticism. First, the objection is made that Brahms' instrumentation is lacking a sense of colour and this does not sit well with his colourful themes. Wittgenstein responds to the objection by pointing out that colourlessness is already in Brahms' themes, so there is no inconsistency between theme and instrumentation. Then follows a comparison between Brahms and Bruckner: "The themes [in Brahms] are already in black and white, just as Bruckner's are already colourful; even if Bruckner had for some reason written them down in one system only so that we knew nothing of a Brucknerian instrumentation. One could say now: well then everything is okay for to the black and white themes belongs a black and white (colourless) instrumentation". But, after all, Wittgenstein admits, the initial objection contains a measure of truth even though it misses its target: now the discrepancy consists in that Brahms colourless themes are not consistently followed up in his instrumentation since patches of colour permeate the instrumentation. Unexpectedly, what we miss, Wittgenstein suggests, is colourlessness:

> I believe that precisely in this lies the weakness of Brahms' instrumentation, namely in that it is frequently not decidedly black and white after all. Thus arises the impression that often makes us believe that we are missing colours because the colours that are there don't have a pleasing effect. In reality, I think, we are missing colourlessness. And often this shows itself distinctly, for example in the last movement of the *Violin Concerto* [*Concerto for Violin and Orchestra*, D Major, opus 77] where there are very peculiar sound effects (once as if the sounds were peeling like dry leaves from the violins & where yet one senses this as an isolated sound effect, while one senses Bruckner's sounds as the natural clothing of the bones of these themes. (It's quite different for Brahms' choral sound which takes root in the themes just as Bruckner's orchestral sound does

---

13   Wittgenstein, *Culture*, 24.
14   *Ibid.*, 16.

in Bruckner's themes.) (The harp at the end of the first part of the *German Requiem*.)[15]

There is then, in Wittgenstein's view, a better fit between Bruckner's orchestration and his themes than we find in the case of Brahms—with the exception of the latter's choral sound. The discussion indicates the importance Wittgenstein attached to the alignment between what you say and how you say it—whether in music or philosophy. The aesthetic/ethical import is one of integrity: there has to be harmony between the substance of expression as it were and the ways/means we express that substance. To get this right, like Bruckner with his compositions, Wittgenstein kept on revising his remarks.

Bruckner's music is subtle, its truth implausible and difficult to understand, yet his symphonies, even though they are like "daisies" compared to the "trees" of Mozart, Haydn and Beethoven. Although it seems odd to speak of Bruckner's monumental symphonic memorializing of his spiritual struggle as a "daisy", we can see Wittgenstein's point. In his view, Bruckner's symphonies are "infinitely more closely related to a symphony from the heroic period than any by Mahler" whose symphonies are "abstract musical *pictures*" rather than living, breathing things. In his own way Bruckner still speaks the old language while Mahler speaks a new one. There are further interesting observations: Bruckner's music has a round full alpine face and might go with a silent film in the sense that a film could throw light on the music and vice versa; "A Bruckner symphony can be said to have *two* beginnings: the beginning of the first idea & the beginning of the second idea. These two ideas stand to each other not as blood relations, but as man & wife".[16] We are to hear in the sustained spiritual searching of a Bruckner symphony the origins, development and recapitulation of each of the two ideas, including the "clash" between the two—witness the long tortured dissonance before the transcendent peace at the end of the *Ninth*.

Another observation brings to the fore Wittgenstein's preferred methods of gaining deeper appreciation of a work of music, namely,

---

15 Wittgenstein, *Public and Private*, 115.
16 Wittgenstein, *Culture*, 39.

putting appropriate musical works side by side and looking for musical/ speech acts in the works:

> Bruckner's Ninth is a sort of *protest* against Beethoven's, & because of this it becomes bearable, which as a sort of imitation it would not be. It stands to Beethoven's Ninth very much like Lenau's Faust to Goethe's, which means as the Catholic to the Enlightenment Faust, etc.[17]

Goethe's Enlightenment Faust, despite his pact with Mephistopheles, is redeemed on the merit of his struggle for wisdom and science, but the Catholic/Lenau Faust is damned: wisdom and *scientia* are not enough. Faith in the Resurrection and redemption are a *must*. Beethoven's *Ninth Symphony* as redemptive revolution with its affirmation of faith in humanity stands in contrast with the dark timbres of Bruckner's *Ninth* and its affirmation of transcendent value. If Beethoven believed only in heaven and nothingness, then Bruckner's musical/spiritual journey is a reminder of both heaven and hell. In Beethoven, we might say, "you can experience the horrors of hell in one day; that is plenty of time".[18] In Bruckner, "If I am really to be saved, what I need is certainty, not wisdom, dreams or speculation, and this certainty is faith… holding fast to redemption".[19]

2. Wittgenstein's Reception of Wagner

Among the other composers whom Wittgenstein read and whose music he listened to is, perhaps surprisingly, the figure of Richard Wagner. Wittgenstein, I claim, read and engaged Wagner's writings on music and culture, thereby developing in some measure his own habits of cultural criticism. In particular, I argue that traces of Wagner's cultural critique are evident in Wittgenstein's practice of music criticism, especially in his remarks about Felix Mendelssohn and Gustav Mahler. Moreover, Wittgenstein not only read Wagner but listened to and made remarks about Wagner's music and, as he considered such specific topics as

---

17   *Ibid.*
18   *Ibid.*, 30.
19   *Ibid.*, 38.

melody, motif and irony, he provided a series of remarks towards a critique of Wagner himself. Also, I contend that Wittgenstein's analogy between music and language, one of the main axes of the *Philosophical Investigations*, relates to the interplay between language and music in Wagner. Finally, I take up the question of "internal critique" and suggest that, if philosophical confusion owes its existence to language being turned/turning against itself, Wittgenstein finds a similar inclination to turn against oneself in Wagner. However, by the time Wittgenstein gets through with Wagner, what is of value in Wagner is made anew, and a trenchant critique of Wagner himself—Wagner turned against Wagner—emerges.

Looking at the available biographical details, we can identify an early and a later attitude to Wagner. The early attitude is one of enthusiastic admiration for and absorption in Wagner's *Die Meistersinger von Nürnberg*. Wittgenstein is reported to have said that he watched thirty performances of the opera over one and a half years during his days as an engineering student in Berlin.[20] About a decade on, when on leave in Olmütz, Moravia, during the First World War, he enjoyed musical soirées in the company of Jewish friends including the architect Paul Engelmann and the pianist/organist Fritz Zweig who eventually became the first conductor at the Berlin State Opera House. "In our conversations", recalls Engelmann, "we execrated Richard Wagner, that destroyer of music and culture, who at the time was still considered the pope of music and above all criticism. Wittgenstein did not join in these execrations, but he did not much object either".[21] The fact that Wittgenstein "did not *much* object either" suggests that he *did* take exception to the execrations but muted his objections out of friendship, or better still, he distinguished between Wagner's music and Wagner the unpleasant person as he did later in a conversation with Drury.

What is so striking about Wagner's *The Mastersingers* that explains Wittgenstein attending thirty of its performances in the course of a year and a half? Even if he exaggerated, the question stands: What did he see or hear in the opera that his intense interest, by ordinary standards, bordered on an obsession? Among other possible reasons,

20   McGuinness, *Wittgenstein: A Life*, 55.
21   Engelmann, *Letters from Ludwig*, 64.

McGuinness mentions the fact that *The Mastersingers* "was a treatment of problems of music and life at the same time—and its solution lay in the need for rules that can be discovered even within spontaneity but only when a note of reverence has been introduced".[22] At this point a set of reminders about what Wagner does in *The Mastersingers* is needed. Against the then current operatic vogue and conventions, he asserts that works of art need to engage important human problems, takes up the issue of the role individual artists should play in their community, and shows how creation works and to what purpose. The solution lies in the need for rules and tradition, but without rule worship, since it leads to mechanical reactions and a lack of spontaneity. By helping the Knight Walther to write his prize winning song, Hans Sachs, through socially responsible artistic innovation, renews a community facing decadence. Steering the "vain deceits" and unacknowledged illusions of his community into socially positive as well as artistically creative achievements, Walther uses the power of artistic illusion to create the experience of order and meaning. As Wagner elaborates the theme of illusion (*Wahn*) in his opera, Schopenhauer's negative evaluation is turned on its head as Sachs transfigures the creation of illusions into positive value. In his humble role as village shoemaker, Sachs embodies the metaphor of the "craftsman" in his approach to art and society. He invokes the accepted standards of composition that inform his tradition and urges others to understand their own traditions and use them to create something new. In this process the distinction between illusion and delusion emerges: illusions are constructive in that they enhance society, delusions, on the other hand, are socially harmful and destructive.

If the young Wittgenstein was a Wagnerite, what does that have to do with his philosophical/aesthetic practice and perspective? How did the impressions and concerns of *The Mastersingers* spill over, if at all, into the early work of the *Tractatus* and the later work of the *Investigations*? Addressing these questions requires some stage setting; namely, sketching the Romantic conception of how music and culture are related. As Yuval Lurie pointed out, this Romantic background (shared by Wagner and Wittgenstein) regards a musical tradition as a cultural achievement developed organically by joint human effort. This

---

22   McGuinness, *Wittgenstein: A Life*, 55.

includes past practices of expression connecting us with human beings who came before us. It is a living reminder of the spiritual bond with them and of our nature as cultural beings.[23] In music you can still hear the primitive, the organic, the longing for the eternal or inexpressible, what cannot be said but must be shown. Music shows us our shared forms of life, the grounds and origins of associated language games which are their refinement: musical gestures of dirge, of mourning, of prayer, of worship, of celebration, of violence and war, of coronation, of contemplation and so on, are expressive of basic central moments of our lives as human beings. These tend to disappear in much of "modern music" where there is only a fading resonance with shared forms of life: we can no longer hear the primitive, the organic, the longing for the eternal, for what is "otherwise inexpressible". Music's "inexpressive", cosmopolitan "modern tongue" erodes the connection with life-forms, obliterates background and spirit, precisely those elements that make for the possibility of meaning.

Wittgenstein had a deep aversion to "modern music", did not understand its language, and argued against it several times in debates when at Cambridge.[24] What he meant by 'modern music' is not clear, but probably the music of Mahler and Strauss in whom he heard the incipient undercutting of tonality, the baseline which makes musical meaning possible, a tendency that later emerged as principle in Arnold Schönberg and Béla Bartók. I propose we look at Wagner's musical and Wittgenstein's philosophical concerns and put them side by side with their Romantic inheritance as backdrop. A central feature of Wagner's destructive critique of conventional opera is that its language lost connection with important human problems and concerns; its rules of composition have become mechanical. Opera, he concluded, is a dead genre, and he goes on to argue this thesis in a critical review of the history of opera (18th and early 19th century) with particular reference to Italian and French opera. The latter he saw as an "excuse" for conviviality and conversation among the audience with the occasional aria thrown in to provide pause and relief. In the former he saw the tyranny of melody: "As Metternich... could not conceive the state

---

23   Yuval Lurie, "Culture as a Human Form of Life: A Romantic Reading of Witt-
     genstein", *International Philosophical Quarterly* 32 (1992), 193-195.
24   Pinsent, *A Portrait*, 42, 46.

under any form but that of *absolute monarchy*, so Rossini, with no less force of argument, could not conceive the opera under any other form than that of *absolute melody*. Both men said: Do you ask for opera and state? Here you have them—there are no others!"[25]

Grand opera, exemplified in the works of Meyerbeer, receives some of Wagner's bitterest polemic: Meyerbeer's operas are primarily concerned with "effect"—"a working without a cause". He severed the operatic text from the music, "having razed the poet to the ground, and upon the ruins of poetry the musician was crowned the only authentic poet".[26] If we reduce "life-portraying poetry... to meaningless wretched rubbish", the only thing that could give the musical expression "its being, warranty, and measure, then the musical expression itself becomes void of any real expression".[27] It might be thought that Wagner's aim is to re-conceive opera, but that is not so since he regards opera at an end. He wants to create something new that he calls "music drama", and the name is intended to mark a discontinuity from opera as well as forge a musical form that restores "life-portraying" poetry to its proper place and connects the music with life and its problems—so that it is not mere idle entertainment but existentially instructive.

Wittgenstein's *Tractatus,* like Wagner's essays on opera, mounts a destructive critique of the western philosophical tradition and re-conceives the task of philosophy. Traditional philosophy—that idling, decadent "nonsense", "language gone on holiday" as he later described it—fails to engage genuine human problems and thus should be thrown overboard; its problems are to be dissolved through the logical analysis of language: through unearthing the depth grammar behind the veneer of deceptive surface grammar. As Wagner re-conceives something new in his music dramas, so Wittgenstein re-conceives philosophical activity in the *Tractatus*: For God's sake", he said to students, "don't do that [philosophy in the traditional style]; do something different". To call what he was doing 'philosophy' is all right as long as we realize that "it was not the same kind of thing as Plato or Berkeley had done, but that we may feel that what he was doing 'takes the place' of what Plato

---

25   Richard Wagner, *Wagner on Music and Drama*, eds Albert Goldman and Evert Sprinchorn, tr. H. Ashton Ellis, New York: E.P. Dutton, 1964, 106.

26   *Ibid.*, 118.

27   *Ibid.*, 118-119.

and Berkeley did, but that it is really a different kind of thing".[28] What he did was something different from what used to be called philosophy, but is related to it by family resemblance, and hence "a legitimate heir". Since traditional philosophy and opera lost touch with human problems and instincts, they were both at an end and in need of foundational critique to be born again.

Another dominant theme, both in Wagner and Wittgenstein, is the theme of the propositionally inexpressible: what "cannot be said with sense" by means of language, something that, to adopt and invert Ramsey's vocabulary, you can perhaps whistle but cannot say. Wagner also speaks of the necessity in music for a clear and accurate expression of the "otherwise unspeakable".[29] Notice that music's expression of the otherwise inexpressible is not to be thought of as second best or murky, but as "clear and accurate". What we have here is the striking idea of music as philosophy's other, as expressing the transcendent in its own *sui generis* way.[30] The early Wittgenstein puts the lumberhouse of the world—the realm of empirical fact and science—in its place. This leaves the realm of value in a special sphere of its own, of which we must be silent. What can be said is circumscribed by a rule for meaningful propositions, and the limits of language, hence the limits of meaningfulness, is delineated precisely from the inside. This leaves the "inexpressible", the transcendent, i.e. value and spirit, in a totally different realm. [Absolute] value can be musically expressed, artistically performed or ethically enacted, but cannot be linguistically captured.

Wagner's *The Mastersingers* was an important work for several reasons: not only because it presented a whole world and an aesthetic perspective on life, but more importantly because it was iconic of the *how and what* of creative artistic endeavour. *The Mastersingers* proposed that creativity must emerge from traditional practices, and this resonates both with the *Tractatus* and the *Investigations*. Trying to do more with less, the *Tractatus* is a modernist work with a craftsman-as-poet-like approach to philosophy. Having laid down a rule for what counts as

---

28 G.E. Moore, "Wittgenstein's Lectures in 1930-1933" in *Wittgenstein: Philosophical Occasions*, eds Klagge and Nordmann, 96.

29 Wagner, *Music and Drama*, 217-218.

30 Lydia Goehr, *The Quest for Voice: Music, Politics, and the Limits of Philosophy* (Berkeley: University of California Press, 1998).

a meaningful proposition, Wittgenstein argued that the philosophical tradition is defunct, since its assertions lack sense. Wittgenstein throws away the ladder and puts an end to philosophy. What remains is an activity of clarification with formal logic as a critical tool for the detection and exposure of "plain nonsense". However, the "important nonsense" we employ in our attempts to transcend our linguistic cage is nevertheless shown. So, there is good nonsense and bad nonsense.[31] The good "nonsense" is unspeakable, yet Wittgenstein cannot but respect it deeply for it points to insights that cannot be propositionally articulated. It is the mystical whose expression may be found in artistic/ musical and ethical gestures.

For Wagner too, "music was demoniacal, a mystically exalted enormity: everything concerned with rules seemed only to distance it".[32] There is, then, in Wagner an attack on formalism and abstraction— witness *The Mastersingers* mocking Beckmesser's rule-obsessed behaviour. Wagner rejects formalist attempts to create or capture musical meaning *via* formulating or following explicit rules, since such attempts always leave something essential out. Similarly, the later Wittgenstein rejects the formalist approach in the philosophy of language: formalist attempts to grasp the meaning of words and propositions fail, for a rule itself requires interpretation, which in turn requires other interpretations and so on. The attempt to capture meaning through a rule is reminiscent of Beckmesserish behaviour. An obsessive preoccupation with rules not only fails to do justice to the musical tradition but leads to lifeless, mechanical repetition, making a mockery of music and composition. This resonates with the "conventionalism" of the *Investigations* that the norms and rules are contingent and implicit in our practices. Their apparent necessity corresponds to our deep need for convention.

How does this explain the sharp difference between the approach to philosophy in the *Tractatus* and the *Investigations*? If the Tractarian distinction between the sayable and the unsayable goes by the board as a piece of untenable metaphysics, then music as philosophy's other, as expressing what cannot be propositionally expressed, does not survive in the later work either. I contend that it does survive, but with a difference:

---

31   David Stern, *Wittgenstein on Mind and Language,* New York and Oxford: Oxford University Press, 1995, 70.
32   Goehr, *Quest for Voice,* 39.

in the early work the unsayable is the domain of the transcendent, and in the later work what is unsayable is the background of practices. "The inexpressible (what I find enigmatic & cannot express)", Wittgenstein remarked, "perhaps provides the background, against which whatever I was able to express acquires meaning.[33] So, critical modernism shows one face in the *Tractatus*: metaphysics is replaced by science—by what can be said—and ethics, aesthetics and the mystical are relegated to the realm of the inexpressible, what has to be shown. The domain of the unsayable is really a strategy of resistance to scientism and the modernist tendency to level and reduce—to eliminate spirit. The face of the later philosophy is different, since the transcendent is incarnated in the immanent and meaning is explored through the various language games we play: "But if we had to name anything which is the life of the sign, we should have to say that it was its use".[34]

A remark, in early 1930, from a conversation with his Cambridge student and friend Maurice Drury, in which Wittgenstein calls Wagner "the first of the great composers who had an unpleasant character",[35] indicates his changing attitude to Wagner. This assessment did not blind him to a fact no serious musician or music lover can deny, namely, Wagner's greatness as a composer. This acknowledgement, however, is followed by a critique of Wagner that signals a shift in Wittgenstein's attitude from youthful and enthusiastic admiration to mature and balanced critical appreciation. The particular texts where he later engages themes from Wagner support this claim and provide us with materials for a better understanding of Wittgenstein's musical aesthetics and cultural perspective. There are more than seven explicit entries about Wagner in the *Nachlass*. Of particular significance are the remarks on Wagner's ways of composing: his motifs and melodies, his phrasing and dramatic texts, the relation in his operas between words and music, and Wagner's use of irony compared with its use in Beethoven and Brahms. I propose to tease out of each what can shed light on Wittgenstein's philosophical and aesthetic concerns.

One theme is about the relationship between content and form:

---

33 Wittgenstein, *Culture*, 23.
34 Ludwig Wittgenstein, *The Blue and Brown Books,* Oxford: Basil and Blackwell, 1964, 4.
35 *Ludwig Wittgenstein Personal Recollections,* ed. Rhees, 126.

> Strange to see how a material resists a form. How the material of the Nibelung-legends resists dramatic form. It does not want to become drama & won't become one & it surrenders only where the poet or composer decides to treat it epically. Thus the only lasting & authentic passages of the *Ring* are the epic ones in which text or music narrate. And therefore the most impressive *words* of the *Ring* are the stage directions.[36]

How are we to read these trenchant remarks? Is to say that the stage directions are the most impressive words of the *Ring* to belittle the text of the *Ring Cycle*? Rather than that—which would really trivialize and thus sabotage Wagner's perspective on the relation between text and music—a more appreciative way of looking at the remark would be as drawing attention to the importance of stage directions for ways of world-making, for providing the setting and scenario for action. While tragedy makes use of actors, the epic narrates, it tells a story; tragedy is poetry, while the epic is prose; tragedy is Greek, where a highborn person, within an established community, meets a terrible end; the epic deals with a hero who founds a nation or a community. Thus the lasting and authentic passages of the *Ring* are those which have the features of the epic. Wagner himself is inauthentic as he tries to force his epic/mythical material into the tragic mode of the Greeks. The music dramas of the *Ring Cycle* are less like classic Greek tragedy and more like epic Homer. So, Wagner is misguided, for although he is doing something different, he does not know it. The theme of a failure of self-understanding raises its ugly head and casts a shadow on Wagner's greatness, or so Wittgenstein may think.

Wittgenstein also makes astute, albeit plaintive, observations about form, style, and expression in Wagner:

> Wagner's motifs might be called musical prose sentences. And just as there is such a thing as 'rhyming prose', so too these motifs can certainly be put together into melodic form, but without their constituting *one* melody. Wagnerian drama too is not drama, but a stringing together of situations as if on a thread, which for its part is only cleverly spun but not, like the motifs & situations, inspired.[37]

---

36 Wittgenstein, *Public and Private Occasions*, 109.
37 Wittgenstein, *Culture*, 47.

If the melodic form and the drama are merely cleverly spun together, then they are exercises of mere skill. This is evident, we are told, in the Overture to *The Mastersingers*: "Where genius wears thin, skill may show through".[38] There is no essence that unifies the Wagnerian motifs into an identifiable melody, as there is no essence to meaning or language in Wittgenstein's later philosophy. What is struck here is the important theme of anti-essentialism, and in a 1946 diary entry we sense that Wittgenstein thinks about melody through the lens of family resemblance. Consider again:

> The melodies of different composers can be approached by applying the principle: every species of tree is a 'tree' in a different sense of the word. I.e. Don't let yourself be misled by our saying they are all melodies. They are steps along a path that leads from something you would not call a melody to something else that you again would not call one. If you simply look at the sequences of notes & the changes of key, all these structures no doubt appear on the same level. But if you look at the field of force in which they stand (and hence their significance), you will be inclined to say: Here melody is something quite different than there (here it has a different origin, plays a different role, inter alia.)[39]

3. Wagner As Hearing Aid: Wittgenstein's Remarks on Mendelssohn and Mahler

So far I have eavesdropped on Wittgenstein listening to Wagner's music. However, Wittgenstein's remarks on other composers and their music also show earmarks of the vocabulary and perspective Wagner used in his writings on music and culture. Wagner's essays have sometimes been regarded as futile reflections or special pleadings which were for him necessary to get down to his real work: composing *The Mastersingers*, the *Ring Cycle* and so on. The impression we are given is that Wagner had to clear his mind of rubbish, before turning to

---

38   *Ibid.*, 49.
39   *Ibid.*, 54.

what was really important, namely, his compositions. The strategy is to rescue Wagner from Wagner, his "beautiful" music from the "ugly" man. In this context, the influential essay *Judaism in Music* is as contentious as it is informative. Wagner constructs a conception of the Jewish artist as deficient in originality, lacking primordial force and instinctive expression, and speaking the musical idiom with a distracting foreign accent. There is, he averred, an intimate connection between speech/ language and music; song, he held, is not only speech intensified to the level of passion, but the prototype of music. To compose poetry or music, one needs to have a native speaker's knowledge of the language in which one composes.[40]

Language, with its modes of expression and development, is not the work of scattered individuals, but the joint emanation of an ancient community, and only the person, Wagner asserted, whose life has been fostered in that community can expect to participate fully in its creations. To express something positive requires that the artist draw his inspiration from the loving contemplation of that instinctive life to be found among the community within which he dwells. Jews, declared Wagner, were aliens to European culture, and therefore, lacked the required instinct and passion for fluent expression and creative work— they were onlookers who merely echo and imitate. As Jewish composers approached the community looking for creative nourishment, everything appeared "strange and unintelligible".[41] Therefore, what they had to say could only be superficial and trivial, dealing with questions of 'how to speak' rather than with 'what to say'.[42]

This conception of Jewishness was then applied by Wagner to the history of European music, singling out Felix Mendelssohn—an obvious counter-example to his generalizations—for criticism: "whom Nature had endowed with specific musical gifts as very few before him... who had the amplest score of specific talents, the finest and most varied culture... the highest sense of honour, yet he was incapable of calling forth in us that deep, heart searching effect which we await from art...". Nor could this help him "to develop further the things which had sprung from our soil".[43] Mendelssohn, according to Wagner,

---

40   Wagner, *Music and Drama*, 51-52.
41   *Ibid.*, 54.
42   *Ibid.*, 53, 54.
43   *Ibid.*, 57.

was incapable of the musical expression of deep, powerful, instinctive emotions; his music is akin to a kaleidoscope, presenting us with pleasing figures through lenses coloured by diverse, polite moods; he is derivative, appropriating any individual feature which he could gather from his predecessors. Mendelssohn poaches from Bach as he imitates Bach's speech, and is chiefly concerned with good manners, about being as agreeable as possible, about the 'how' rather than about the 'what'.[44] Wagner contrasts Mendelssohn with Beethoven. Whereas Beethoven's musical language is anchored in instinct and passion, marked by "a clear and accurate expression of the otherwise unspeakable", Mendelssohn, dwindles these trophies, reducing their effect to dissolving views and fantastic shadow pictures. "Mendelssohn is credible only when giving expression to a soft melancholy resignation, making a confession of his own impotence. This would be tragic, were it not for the fact that Mendelssohn is incapable of the strong feelings required by tragedy".[45]

Between 1930 and 1950 Wittgenstein made a series of remarks about composers, especially about Mendelssohn and Mahler, that repeatedly resonate with Wagner's musical/cultural criticism, in particular with his essay on *Judaism in Music*. The connection with Wagner seems supported by Wittgenstein's allusion to Mendelssohn's Jewishness and gathers density and momentum as Wittgenstein continues to use Wagner's anti-Semitic cultural vocabulary to characterize works of art, but with a difference: in his sense works of Gentiles as well as Jews may be "Jewish", judging by the remark "There is something Jewish about Rousseau's character".[46] Consider then Wittgenstein's apparent complaints about Mendelssohn: "[He] is perhaps the most untragic of composers",[47] conforming to his surroundings[48]; he is deficient in musical thought since he does not tackle significant human problems, nor does he engage or pose a challenge to the understanding: "If one wanted to characterize the essence of Mendelssohn's music one could do it by saying that there is perhaps no music by Mendelssohn that is hard to

---

44 *Ibid.*, 58.
45 Richard Wagner, *Judaism in Music*, tr. Edwin Evans, London: W. Reeves, 1910, 38-39.
46 Wittgenstein, *Culture*, 1.
47 *Ibid.*, 3.
48 *Ibid.*, 4.

understand".[49] Again, even though one expects rigour from Mendelssohn's short imaginative, ornamental melodies, he is only half-rigorous,
while Brahms in contrast is consistently rigorous;[50] and he neither con-
fronts life's dark side, nor does he look death in the face.

It is almost as if for a time Wagner was Wittgenstein's hearing
aid, especially since at the time Wittgenstein adopted and put to use
Wagner's vocabulary of Jewishness as a cultural category. The above
remarks on Mendelssohn seem to have an anti-modern gist with a
conservative if not a fascist upshot. To boot, in another characteristic
passage Mendelssohn is described as a reproductive rather than an
original artist, ornamenting other people's ideas:

> Within all great art there is a WILD animal: tamed. Not, e.g.,
> in Mendelssohn. All great art has primitive human drives as
> its ground bass. They are not the melody (as they are, perhaps,
> in Wagner), but they are what gives the melody its depth &
> power. In this sense one may call Mendelssohn a 'reproductive'
> artist. In the same sense: my house for Gretl is the product of a
> decidedly sensitive ear, good manners, the expression of great
> understanding (for a culture etc.). But primordial life, wild life
> striving to erupt into the open—is lacking. And so you might
> say, health is lacking. (Kierkegaard). (Hothouse plant.)[51]

There are several interesting points here: Wagner is credited with
melody as the ground bass of his art, but more importantly, the motif
of "taming instincts" Wittgenstein ascribed to "all great art" does not
coincide with Wagner's idea of the culture-specific sensitivity of the
artist; as well, and between the lines, Mendelssohn's music is great but
in a different sense than "taming the wild beast within". To elaborate
the second point: Wagner linked musical production to specific cultural
forms of life, while Wittgenstein links it to "the taming of *universal*
human instincts". This suggests that music for Wittgenstein is broadly
connected to the human form of life while for Wagner it is connected to
specific cultural modes. The distinction allows Wittgenstein to escape
from "the ugly" nationalist aspects of Wagner's music criticism and

---

49   *Ibid.*, 27.
50   *Ibid.*,18.
51   *Ibid.*, 43.

makes room for an appreciation of Mendelssohn for what he is/what his music is. Mendelssohn is concerned with human identity, while Wagner is concerned with national/cultural identity. Mendelssohn is civil and civilizing, concerned with "Let's be human", while Wagner is concerned almost exclusively with German identity.

This distinction cannot however be a sharp dichotomy, since the culture-specific comes into play on the level of available means of expression used to "tame primitive human drives"—the wild animal. So, Wittgenstein's approach offers a kind of balance between two extremes. Mendelssohn's melodies transform the culture-specific, and, through skill and style, renders them universally accessible. He accepts the given forms of life, while Wagner is attempting to break through to new forms. Two different senses of greatness: one tries to work within a musical tradition, speak its language but in a way suitable to the times, while the other rejects it and struggles to give birth to new forms. If this is right, then Wittgenstein's remarks are not updated echoes of Wagner's sentiments, but rather, as I claim, they have an anti-modern gist with critical potential.

The Wagnerian resonance, however, seems reinforced by Wittgenstein's surprising comments in which he speaks of his older Viennese contemporary Gustav Mahler, of his music and style as self-deceived and inauthentic, lacking in courage and originality. Mahler's ways of incorporating his predecessors' themes or melodies are singled out for critical attention:

> When for a change the later ones of the great composers write in simple harmonic progressions, they are showing allegiance to their ancestral mother. Especially in these moments (where the others are most moving) Mahler seems especially unbearable to me [Wittgenstein]. I always want to say then: but you have only heard this from the others, that isn't (really) yours.[52]

We are given the impression that Mahler's lack of originality borders on being a copy-cat or a mere improviser. But since the other composers in the tradition do the same sort of thing, why are *they* not thieves as well? Why is it that they can express allegiance or piety to "the ancestral mother", while Mahler is not permitted to do so?

---

52 Wittgenstein, *Public and Private Occasions*, 93.

Wittgenstein's remarks about Mahler are valuable partly because they provide us with a different perspective on Mahler's music from our current adulatory hagiography. Thus we are better able to appreciate— though not necessarily agree with—the reception of Mahler's music by some of his contemporaries, critics who were ambivalent and sometimes negative about Mahler the composer, although they thought highly of him as a conductor. For instance, Brahms, Hanslick, Hans von Bülow, Victor von Herzfeld and Robert Hirschfeld number among these critics. The fact that some of these critics were Jewish or friends of Mahler or among the musical cognoscente refutes the claim that the criticism was necessarily motivated by anti-Semitism. Von Bülow's reaction to Mahler's *Todtenfeier*, on which Mahler's *Second Symphony* is based, seems similar to Wittgenstein's awareness of Mahler's music as "totally different", of its radical discontinuities from the tradition: "Well, if that's music then I have misunderstood all I know about music".[53] And Brahms, having seen the score of the *Second*, remarked: "Up to now I thought Richard Strauss was the chief of the iconoclasts, but now I see that Mahler is the king of the revolutionaries".[54] Again, Felix Weingartner, a conductor, composer as well as a friend of Mahler, heard the *Second Symphony* remarked: "Just as in his compositions there is valuable material mixed with banalities that are hard to bear, so also in his interpretations his intellectual enthusiasm seemed to kindle incomprehensible extravagancies".[55]

Wittgenstein hints of Mahler's abuse of the expressive phrases and devices that he borrows from the tradition. Repetitions of a musical phrase or theme, we might say, need not offend, but do so when they pretend to an emotional punch they no longer have—when we have the impression that the composer is simply pushing our emotional buttons. Through such use of derivative expressive devices Mahler, so it seems to Wittgenstein, makes complacent compositional gestures. These are the ways Wittgenstein hears Mahler as deceiving himself:

> Lying to oneself about oneself, deceiving yourself about the pretence in your own state of will, must have a harmful influence

---

53   Kurt and Herta Blaukopf, *Mahler: His Life and Work*, tr. Paul Baker, London: Thames and Hudson, 1976, 94.

54   *Ibid.*, 117.

55   *Ibid.*, 114.

on one's style; for the result will be that you cannot tell what is genuine in the style and what is false. This may explain the inauthenticity of Mahler's style; and it is the same danger that I run myself. If one is acting a part to oneself, then it's this that the style expresses. And then the style cannot be one's own. Whoever is unwilling to know himself is writing a kind of deceit.[56]

This passage links Mahler the self-deceptive person to Mahler's musical self-deception: he is composing a kind of deceit. But Wittgenstein is not only concerned that he himself is at risk of writing a kind of deceit, but he may also concerned that the obscurity that befell Mahler and his music for decades after his death may also happen to him. The passage quoted above was written in 1938 when Wittgenstein looked back and attempted to come to grips with what happened to a once celebrated fellow Viennese whose music suffered a long period of neglect before it was eventually revived and became established as part of the classical concert repertoire in the 1960s and early 70s. It is as if Wittgenstein, thinking about and identifying with Mahler, experienced a moment of status anxiety.

Another passage, from the late 1940s, invokes again the theme of self-deception and seems to assert not only that Mahler's music is worthless but that Mahler could not have realized that it was worthless:

If it is true, as I believe, that Mahler's music is worthless, then the question is what I think he should have done with his talent. For quite obviously it took a string of very rare talents to produce this bad music. Should he, say, have written his symphonies & burnt them? Or should he have done violence to himself & not have written them? Should he have written them & realized that they were worthless?

But how could he have realized that? I can see it because I can compare his music with that of the great composers. But he could not do that; for someone to whom that has occurred may have misgivings about the value of his production, because he no doubt sees that he does not, so to speak, have the nature of the other great composers,—but that does not mean that he will grasp the worthlessness; because he can always tell himself that he is, it is true, different from the rest (whom however he admires)

56　*Ludwig Wittgenstein Personal Recollections*, ed. Rhees, 193.

but excellent in another way. We could perhaps say: If nobody whom you admire is like you, then presumably you believe in your own value only because you are you.—Even someone who struggles against vanity, but not entirely successfully, will always deceive himself about the value of what he produces.[57]

What this passage makes explicit is the assumption on which rest Wittgenstein's reasons for dismissing Mahler; namely, the assumption of a shared background of genres, paradigms and norms on which the possibility of making comparisons between Mahler and the musical tradition depend. His symphonies are to be listened to with ears tuned to the past which gives us the paradigms of musical worth. Such a method of comparison enables Wittgenstein to use Brahms to assess Mendelssohn, or Bruckner to judge Mahler, and Beethoven to judge both. If this assumption is called into question, then those evaluative comparisons as to worth and genre are themselves called into question. What is more, there is the absurd charge that Mahler, who was deeply steeped in the musical tradition having studied and conducted the music of the great composers throughout his life, was incapable of making the relevant comparisons.

But the deeper trouble with Mahler, as Wittgenstein sees it, is that in addition to being prone to self-deception, his music invites and perpetuates self-deception, encouraging escape from the human condition, thus failing to connect with music's capacity to instruct and cultivate our humanity. As Roger Scruton remarks: "Those sweet Ländler melodies, those distant trumpets and faux-naïf effects [in Mahler]: do they not invite us into self-deceived and unsubstantiated dreams?"[58] Again, the collapse into comforting popular melodies and children's lullabies at crucial junctures in his symphonies shows Mahler's difficulty in resolving conflict; for instance, *Frère Jacques* arranged as a funeral march in Mahler's *First Symphony*. Mahler is heard by Wittgenstein as an aid to self-deception and wishful thinking, to futile longing and transcendence—think of the effective use of the *Adagio* from his *Fifth Symphony* in Lucchino Visconti's film adaptation of Thomas Mann's *Death in Venice*. Mahler, according to Wittgenstein,

---

57   Wittgenstein, *Culture*, 99.
58   Roger Scruton, "Wittgenstein and the Understanding of Music", *British Journal of Aesthetics*, XLVI/1 (2004), 7.

falls short of the integrity and discipline of aesthetic greatness, as he undercuts the Socratic feature of the dialogue between music and philosophy in the great European tradition from Bach, through Mozart, to Beethoven and Brahms—which aims at truth, clarity of expression and self-understanding. If it sounds strange to attribute such a critical vocabulary to Wittgenstein, recall what he says of Beethoven: "Beethoven is a realist through & through; I mean his music is totally true, I want to say: he sees life totally as it is & then exalts it".[59]

To regard such assessments as two sides of the same prejudice, namely, that music has a fixed referential nature that late Beethoven reflects, while Mahler covers up the fractured nature of bourgeois life, seems not only too narrow a reading, but it is also at odds with the character and drift of Wittgenstein's many other remarks about music. Striking and characteristic is the following: "Does the theme point to nothing beyond itself?" asks Wittgenstein's plaintive conversation partner, as if the absence of fixed external reference robs the theme of significance:

> Oh, yes! But that means: The impression it makes on me is connected with things in its surroundings—e.g. with the existence of the German language & its intonation, but that means with the whole field of our language games. If I say e.g.: it's as if here a conclusion were being drawn, or, as if here something were being confirmed, or, as if this were a reply to what came earlier,—then the way I understand it clearly presupposes familiarity with conclusions, confirmations, replies, etc.[60]

Again: "If you ask: how I experienced the theme, I shall perhaps say 'As a question' or something of the sort, or I shall whistle it with expression etc".[61] Although the theme does not have a fixed reference to a slice of reality, it still has meaning for us in that it resonates with the multiplicity of our language games, ways of life and social practices, as well as the conventions and history of music itself. So perhaps it is better to see the comparative assessments of Beethoven and Mahler as attempts at appreciation from different angles—juxtaposing the composition with the composer, his musical predecessors and his times.

---

59 Wittgenstein, *Public and Private*, 81.
60 Wittgenstein, *Culture*, 59.
61 *Ibid.*

4. A Different Reading: Wittgenstein's Self-Understanding As Music Critic

So far, to bring out Wagner's influence on Wittgenstein, I have emphasized affinities between them. Now I point to crucial differences and propose a different reading sensitive to Wittgenstein's self-identification, more attentive to context, and taking into consideration related textual evidence. One important thing to notice about Wittgenstein's remarks on Mendelssohn and Mahler is the background: it is taken for granted that both Mendelssohn and Mahler are great musical figures and he, as a Jewish thinker", identifies with them.[62] After describing Mendelssohn as "perhaps the most untragic composers", Wittgenstein immediately identifies with him: "Tragically holding on, defiantly holding on to a tragic situation in love always seems to me quite alien to my [cultural] ideal. Does that mean that my ideal is feeble?... I believe that fundamentally I have a gentle & calm ideal. But may God protect my ideal from feebleness & mawkishness".[63] And when he speaks of Mendelssohn being dependent on his surroundings and not being "self-sufficient like a tree that stands firmly in its place", he immediately associates himself with Mendelssohn: "I too am like that & tend to be so".[64] Again, when he says that in a sense Mendelssohn is a reproductive artist, he recognizes and embraces this feature in both his artistic and philosophical works: "In the same sense: my house for Gretl [his sister] is the product of a decidedly sensitive ear, *good* manners, the expression of a great *understanding* (for a culture, etc.)".[65] These are prized qualities in any artist or philosopher, even though, unlike Wagner, Mendelssohn and Wittgenstein are *not* disposed to walk on the "wild" side. Again, Mendelssohn's great achievement is acknowledged: [his] *Violin Concerto* is remarkable in being the last great concerto for the violin written. There is a passage in the second movement which is one of the great moments in music".[66]

But what about the apparent objection that Mendelssohn's music is not deep enough and hence does not challenge our understanding?

---

62   *Ibid.*, 16.
63   *Ibid.*, 4.
64   *Ibid.*
65   *Ibid.*, 43.
66   *Ludwig Wittgenstein Personal Recollections*, ed. Rhees, 127.

This sounds like a devastating criticism if looked at in isolation. However, a completely different light is thrown on the remark if read it in the larger context of Wittgenstein's cultural perspective. Consider what he says when he reflects on Tolstoy's connecting the *importance of the work of art with what everyone can understand:*

> Tolstoy: the meaning (importance) of something lies in its being something everyone can understand. That's both true & false. What makes the object hard to understand—if it's significant, important—is not that you have to be instructed in abstruse matters in order to understand it, but the antithesis between understanding the object & what most people *want* to see. Because of this precisely what is most obvious may be what is most difficult to understand. It is not a difficulty for the intellect but one for the will that has to be overcome.[67]

If this is so, then the fact that there is no music by Mendelssohn that is hard to understand—in the sense that it requires technical musical training or places intellectual demands on the listener—is a positive remark, and the idea is that Mendelssohn's music attends to the significance of the ordinary. Thus, what formerly sounded like a criticism turns out to be a recommendation about how to appreciate Mendelssohn and an indirect refutation of Wagner and like-minded critics. The same approach, with qualifications, may be usefully adopted to better understand Wittgenstein's remarks on Mahler.

A careful reading shows Wittgenstein identifying with Mahler. What sounds like devastating criticism of Mahler is actually of a piece with Wittgenstein's attitude to philosophy as an exercise in avoiding self-misunderstanding due to misunderstanding one's cultural historical moment and what it allows one to do. Consider:

> But what seems most dangerous is to put your work into this position of being compared, first by yourself & then by others, with the great works of former times. You shouldn't entertain such a comparison at all. For if today's circumstances are so different, from what they once were, that you cannot compare your work with earlier works with respect of its genre, then you equally cannot compare its value with that of the earlier work.

---

67   Wittgenstein, *Culture*, 25.

> I myself am constantly making the mistake under discussion.
> Incorruptibility is everything.[68]

In this passage Wittgenstein reduces to absurdity his previous rationale for assessing Mahler's music as worthless, since past paradigms and norms can no longer be legitimately invoked to support such evaluations. If a Mahler symphony is a work of art "it is one of a totally different sort from a symphony from in the heroic period".[69] Similarly, Wittgenstein's philosophy is "a different kind of thing from what Plato and Berkeley did".[70] His philosophy is in a way like Mahler's music: while Mahler improvises on borrowed themes and melodies, Wittgenstein issues reminders, observations and critical clarifications on traditional theories. There is also a parallel Wittgenstein draws between his own teaching activities and Mahler's training musicians: "When Mahler was himself conducting, his training performances were excellent; the orchestra seemed to collapse at once if he was not conducting himself. Perhaps this holds for me too. I have thought about it".[71]

Another significant departure from Wagner is the way Wittgenstein handled the distinction between *what is said* and *how it is said*—between substance versus skill and style. Wittgenstein was disposed to praise an author for having something to say or dismiss them as having nothing to say—so this distinction mattered. Yet unlike Wagner's narrow emphasis on the "what" in his comments about Mendelssohn's music, Wittgenstein was insistent on both the "what" and the "how"—how we say things and in what context. This naturally leads to Wittgenstein's and Wagner's different attitudes to originality. As we have seen, Wagner took originality to be mostly originality of content—a possession some artists have and others don't—and used this alleged deficiency as a weapon to clobber Meyerbeer and Mendelssohn—composers whom he judged as un-rooted in German soil. When discussing originality the mature Wittgenstein made relevant distinctions, since criticism— whether aesthetic or moral— is importantly about making distinctions. One may be derivative in content yet original in the formulation of that

---

68   *Ibid.*, 77.
69   *Ibid.*, 17.
70   Moore, "Wittgenstein's Lectures", 96.
71   Wittgenstein, *Culture*, 43.

content, or have an original style of presentation. "It is possible", he remarks:

> to write in a style that is unoriginal in form—like mine—but with well chosen words; or on the other hand in one that is original in form, freshly grown from within oneself. (And also of course in one which is botched together just anyhow out of old furnishings).[72]

Then Wittgenstein marks off taste from originality: "[Taste] cannot create a new organism, only rectify what is already there; it loosens screws & tightens screws, it doesn't create a new original work. Taste rectifies, it doesn't give birth".[73] The most refined taste has nothing to do with creative power. Hence, "a great creator needs no taste: the child is born into the world well formed". Taste Wittgenstein characterized as a refinement of sensibility that does not act but merely assimilates. Then his remarks take a Socratic turn as he wondered if he has only taste or originality as well. He saw clearly that he has taste, since we can see what we *have*, but not what we *are*. Originality is not a possession, it is a state: we are or are not original. He then made a striking remark relating originality to self-expression: "Someone who does not lie is original enough.... In fact it is already a seed of good originality not to want to be what you are not".[74] This may relate to his complaints about Mahler and, to a lesser extent, Mendelssohn. The former he saw as wanting to be what he was not; the latter as being too polite and not having sufficient courage for genuine self-expression.

How does this discussion connect with Wittgenstein's philosophical practice? If "a philosopher is not a citizen of a community of ideas", then the question of originality of content does not arise. Indeed, the emphasis is on skillful philosophers who are engaged in a struggle with language that in some way is misused in philosophical theorizing. Through returning language to its everyday uses and contexts, Wittgenstein sets it against the language of theory and thus resolves the "problems that trouble us". The philosopher's aim is not the construction of new or original theories: there are enough

---

72 *Ibid.*, 60.
73 *Ibid.*, 68.
74 *Ibid.*, 68.

of those already. They are not interested in erecting a building or in the construction of new theories, but "in having the foundations of possible buildings transparently before [them]".[75] Does this leave room for creativity in philosophy? It does and does not. Philosophy, in the *Tractatus* as well as in the *Investigations,* is neither continuous with, nor on the same level as, science; it is an under-laborer or an overseer of science. Philosophy does not give us new information, nor does it provide new hypotheses, theories or explanations; rather, it aims to clarify:

> And we must not advance any kind of theory. There must not be anything hypothetical in our considerations. We must do away with all *explanation,* and description alone must take its place. And this description gets its light, that is to say, it purpose, from the philosophical problems.[76]

Nevertheless, there is room for creativity in philosophy, and here Wittgenstein turns Plato's attack on poetry in the *Republic* on its head. Like Wagner with music, he connects philosophy with "life-giving poetry". The poet-philosopher provides fresh similes and metaphors, different ways of seeing, and thereby unearths and removes problems brought about by the stranglehold conventional grammatical analogies exercise on our thinking. Remember that a "simile that has been absorbed into the forms of our language produces a false appearance, and this disquiets us. 'But *this* isn't how it is!'—we say. 'Yet *this* is how it has to *be*!'".[77]

Such a simile conjures up a "*picture* that holds us captive. And we could not get outside it, for it lay in our language and language seemed to repeat it to us inexorably".[78] It is in this sense that "[a] preference for certain similes underlies far more disagreements than we might think... and that a good simile refreshes the intellect".[79] To identify one sort of philosophical error, we point to a false analogy that has been taken up into language and shaped our conception but which

---

75   *Ibid.,* 9.
76   Wittgenstein, *Investigations,* §109.
77   *Ibid.,* §112.
78   *Ibid.,* §115.
79   Wittgenstein, *Culture,* 17-18.

we did not recognize as an analogy. Its effect is a constant battle and uneasiness—a constant stimulus.

So, the raw material of philosophy is actually second-hand consisting of hand-me-downs: clusters of misleading similes and grammatical analogies that theories feed on. Philosophy partly involves rummaging through the Sally Ann stores of culture and science, picking and choosing with a view to use and function. And perhaps in this task skill, taste and sensibility are more in demand than originality:

> You can as it were restore an old style in a new (or newer) language; perform it afresh so to speak in a manner that suits our times. In doing so you really only reproduce.... What I mean is *not* however giving an old style a new trim. You don't take the old forms & fix them up to suit today's taste. No, you are really speaking, maybe unconsciously, the old language, but speaking it in a manner that belongs to the newer world, though not on that account necessarily one that is to its taste.[80]

If philosophy is in this sense second-hand, then a philosopher is like an immigrant coming into a new country and learning its language. In §32 of the *Investigations* Wittgenstein suggests such an analogy when he considers Augustine's picture of language learning: "And now, I think, we can say: Augustine describes the learning of human language as if the child came into a strange county and did not understand the language of the country; that is, as if it already had a language, only not this one. Or again: as if the child could already *think*, only not yet speak. And 'think' here would mean something like 'talk to itself'".[81] Perhaps an immigrant is a better fit with this picture than a child. And if "learning philosophy is really recollecting, remembering that we really used words in this way",[82] then philosophy as "second-hand" is a compelling analogy. Philosophers, like strangers, may notice some things with new eyes that natives do not, precisely because natives take the most important things for granted. Here Wittgenstein's distinction between 'learning' and 'training' may be instructive. Since both already have a language, Augustine's child (the philosopher) is more like an immigrant

---

80   *Ibid.*, 68-69.
81   Wittgenstein, *Investigations*, §32.
82   Wittgenstein, *Philosophical Occasions*, 179.

who is learning English as a second language and thus they contrast with children who are *trained* (*Abrichtung*) in the linguistic practices of their mother tongue. Perhaps this difference has an inadvertent affinity to Wagner's point that in an important sense a cultural idiom cannot be learned through explanation but only through training.

Ironically enough, Wagner makes room for the talents of Jewish philosophers: "The Jew's greatest contribution is in intellectual life since he depends on his understanding of his adopted community and other people for his survival".[83] Since we are all similarly dependent, going with this line of thinking suggests Wagner's "Jew" is best seen as a figure for the philosopher in all of us. Not so, however, with composers, since original composers, for "authentic creative" musical communication and expression, need to be grounded in the cultural ways of life of their communities. Philosophical creativity, for Wagner, is then an oxymoron. There is a residual whiff of this Wagnerian attitude in Wittgenstein. Recall the remark we began with:

> I often think that the highest I wish to achieve would be to compose a melody. Or it mystifies me that in the desire for this, none ever occurred to me. But then I must tell myself that it's quite impossible that one will occur to me, because for that I am missing something essential or *the* essential. That is why I am thinking of it as such a high ideal because I could then in a way sum up my life; and set it down crystallized. And even if it were but a small, shabby crystal, yet a crystal.[84]

Other important differences between Wagner and Wittgenstein have to do with the way they regard the prototype and their conception of the work of art. Wagner treats the prototype as the standard to which every-thing *must* conform. In this respect there is, as Thomas Mann remarked, a lot of Hitler in Wagner: "[t]here is, in Wagner's bragging, in his end-less holding forth, his passion for monologue, his insistence on having a say in everything, an unspeakable arrogance that prefigures Hitler".[85] Anything that does not fit Wagner's "Idea" is found—as we have seen

---

83   Wagner , *Music and Drama*, 18; 53.

84   Wittgenstein, *Public and Private*, 17-19.

85   Thomas Mann, "Letter to Emil Preetorius" in *Pro and Contra Wagner*, tr. Allan Blunden, Chicago: University of Chicago Press, 1985, 210.

in his music criticism—intolerable, and hence dismissed or expunged. Polyphony, even a different voice that goes against this "Idea", is anathema to him. This is in sharp contrast with one of the leitmotifs of Wittgenstein's later philosophy; namely, the emphasis on various voices present in the conversations and arguments of the *Investigations*. For a time he even contemplated "Let me teach you differences" as a motto for his *Investigations*. As Wittgenstein exposes the philosophical roots of dogmatism and prejudice in Wagner's conceptual 'hearing aid'—the essentialist prototype is recognized as a symptom of our craving for generality. Wagner is contemptuous of, while Wittgenstein is attentive to, the particular case; he takes composers one by one, and through comparisons highlights their differences. Their conception of the work of art also diverged. Wagner had a *theory of art*—the total-work-of-art—for which he argued in his essays and which he endeavoured to instantiate in his music-dramas. Wittgenstein, on the other hand, refused "the artwork of the future" as an aesthetic monstrosity demanding identity and commonality that in turn erase differences among the forms of music.

Based on his treatment of Mendelssohn, Mahler and other composers, what can we say about the sort of music critic Wittgenstein was? This question might be seen as presumptuous, since it rules out the possibility that Wittgenstein could hold, with Tolstoy, that there is no need for critics and criticism, for in genuine art there is nothing to explain.[86] We are reminded of the measure of truth in this objection by Wittgenstein himself who remarked: "In art it is hard to say anything that is as good as: saying nothing".[87] However, such an abolitionist stance toward criticism is unsatisfactory, since it does not square with Wittgenstein's practice. The abolitionist's conception of the critic as providing explanations, however, chimes with Wittgenstein's aversion to causal and theoretical explanation in philosophy: "We must avoid all explanation and stick to description". This suggests Wittgenstein's conception of the task of the critic is closer to Clive Bell's: "The function of the critic is to make us see; to be continually pointing out those parts [of the work] whose combination produce significant

---

86   Leo Tolstoy, *What Is Art?*, London: Penguin, 1995, 94-95.
87   Wittgenstein, *Culture*, 26.

form".[88] The formalist approach, according to which the job of the critic is to scrutinize the work, is more promising in that it captures part of Wittgenstein's practice of bringing attention to aesthetically relevant features of a musical work. However, as we have seen, the formalist critic excludes anything considered external to the work, such as the cultural, biographical/historical, or social context, while Wittgenstein's practice often includes them. Consider:

> For how can it be explained what 'expressive playing' is? Certainly not by anything that accompanies the playing.—What is needed for an explanation? One might say: a culture.—If someone is brought up in a particular culture—then reacts to the music in such-and-such a way, you can teach him the use of the phrase 'expressive playing'. [89]

To describe music as self-deceptive or lacking authenticity involves abandoning a strictly formalist approach to music criticism, because it presupposes a sense of the history of the western musical tradition and an understanding of the culture in which the music is embedded.

Nor did Wittgenstein believe, as Beardsley and Wimsatt[90] did, that the composer's intentions are irrelevant to the evaluation of the piece of music. So, it cannot be correctly claimed that Wittgenstein falls into the class of formalist critics who assert that all critical consideration of the music (or work of art) has to be internal to the work. His remarks on Mendelssohn and Mahler, reveal that he does not fall into this school of criticism, by virtue of his including historical, cultural, biographical and ethical factors to bear on a piece of music, including such issues as authenticity and alienation. Was he then a historicist critic who conceived of his job as being concerned with re-visioning the work, with how to make it relevant to one's times? Well, sometimes he does that; for instance, he said that to give the same deep effect, Brahms has to be played differently in our times than he was played in his own times. Again, this is not only too narrow a conception of the work, but also neglects the task of understanding it the way the artist intended

---

88   Clive Bell, *Art,* London: Chatto and Windus, 1931, 4.
89   Wittgenstein, *Remarks,* 468.
90   W.K. Wimsatt and Monroe C. Beardsley, "The Intentional Fallacy", *Sewanee Review,* LIV (1946), 468-488.

us to understand it, along with trying to understand it as it would have been understood in its time. Perhaps Wittgenstein view of criticism is closest to the idea of criticism as retrieval where the critic reconstructs the creative process which terminates in the illumination of the work of music under consideration. This view allows composer's intentions, as well as cultural, biographical and social context to play a role in critical inquiry, *with the work of music remaining the primary focus of interest*, rather than getting lost in the morass of detail.[91]

However, even this comprehensive approach does not do justice to Wittgenstein's practice of music criticism, since for him musical works and artistic products in general are embedded in a culture and express that culture's spirit and values. Hence music wears a *face* and has a certain physiognomy. Thus Mendelssohn's music wears Mendelssohn's face and is expressive of the European-Jewish spirit. Music is not cut off from the culture but is intimately connected with its language-games and associated forms of life. Thus, understanding music, like understanding speech/language, provides an answer to why Wittgenstein bothers with music: for its own sake, to be sure, because he loves it; but also because as a cultural barometer, it sheds light on the ebb and tide of the culture, its language games and the human forms of life. It seems then that Wittgenstein's practice of music criticism is too complex to fit the neat and tidy conventional classificatory schemes. His advice to music critics, if they are to avoid being a buttface is: "Say what you want say, as long as it helps to shed light on the facts".

4. Why Was Wagner Absent from the Silents?

One way to shed light on works of art is by a method of juxtaposition. "All that aesthetics does", Wittgenstein said, is "to draw your attention to a thing, to place things side by side". If by giving "reasons" of this sort you make another person "see what you see" but it still does not appeal to him", that is "an end" of the discussion.[92] A fragment from 1934 mentions Wagner's music and suggests an application of Wittgenstein's

---

91 Richard Wollheim, "Criticism as Retrieval" in eds Alex Neill and Aaron Ridley, *The Philosophy of Art Readings Ancient and Modern,* New York: McGraw-Hill, 1980, 185-204.

92 Moore, "Wittgenstein's Lectures", 106.

method of juxtaposition to achieve or enhance musical understanding. In it he compares the music of several composers and speculates about how our understanding of their music would fare with this method of juxtaposition. The idea is to see how a scene in a film without words might enable us to better appreciate the music accompanying it: "In the days of silent films all the classics were played with the films, except Brahms & Wagner. Not Brahms because he is too abstract. I can imagine an exciting scene in a film accompanied with music by Beethoven or Schubert & might gain some sort of understanding of the music from the film. But not an understanding of music by Brahms. Bruckner on the other hand goes with a film".[93]

Several questions arise here. If a scene in a film cannot aid us in understanding Brahms because Brahms is too abstract, is this also the reason why Wagner cannot be understood this way? Is Wagner too abstract as well? Wittgenstein is mute about why Wagner's music was not used to accompany silent films. Judged to be too abstract, Brahms's music, presumably, cannot be visually represented either through the depiction of a scene from nature or through human actions. By contrast, perhaps Beethoven, Schubert and Bruckner can be so visualized. In Brahms, there is the strength and rigour of musical thought, which requires propositions and argument for understanding. I doubt this could hold for Wagner unless we stress the role of narrative and language in Wagner. To express what Wagner expresses stories must be narrated—words must be used. So the idea is to put silent film and music side by side, and see whether a scene can contribute to our musical understanding. What we need to notice is that Wittgenstein talks of silent films. What happens when the word comes into the picture, as it were? The big theme of philosophical interest here may be expressed this way: Can a picture, an image or visual representation in film— for that is what the silents were all about—throw light on music—on a language without content, without representation? Can these two be paired for reciprocal illumination? Apparently, but Brahms and Wagner, for different reasons, cannot be juxtaposed this way. I tried to suggest an answer to the 'Why not?' about Wagner.

Did Wagner have to wait for the 'talkies' to have his music illuminated by word and action in films? Consider the scene in Francis

---

93   Wittgenstein, *Culture*, 29.

Ford Coppola's *Apocalypse Now* where, to the tune of Wagner's *Valkyries*, attack-helicopters, like birds of prey, are swooping down to napalm a Vietnamese village and its inhabitants. The violence of the music—its jarring sounds signaling death and destruction descending—juxtaposed with the scene does increase our sense of sublime horror of mythical proportions and vice versa. When the actor Robert Duval, in the role of the American officer in charge of a squadron of helicopters, surveys the carnage and corpses intoning "I love the smell of napalm on Sunday morning"—we realize the Judaeo-Christian spiritual ritual of the Sabbath—the one thing regarded higher than nature—has been reduced to an orgiastic ritual of violence and destruction. Did Wagner's *Valkyries* have to wait for Francis Ford Coppola's helicopter scenes to receive cinematographic illumination? Perhaps the genre of motion pictures ended with the eclipse of the silents, and something different, a successor with sound, speech and new technology took its place, much like what happened to opera after Wagner or to philosophy after Wittgenstein. If you cite the recent silent film *The Artist* as a counter-example, think again: it feeds off the resources of the talkies as well.

Reading in general may have numbed Wittgenstein's soul, but as I argued, he not only listened to and commented on Wagner's music, he read Wagner's essays and adapted some of Wagner's ideas for his own use. A conventional reading may suggest Wittgenstein was a Wagnerian throughout his life and his music/cultural criticism suffered from Wagner's 'ugly' flaws. I offered a different reading on which we can describe Wittgenstein's development as an emancipation from the 'ugly' Wagner towards the mature Wittgenstein as philosopher of culture. This points to a new appreciation of Wittgenstein's remarks on Mendelssohn and Mahler as older brothers, as it were, with whom he shared a cultural ideal and from whom he learned about himself and his work as he discerned their family resemblances and differences. I argued that despite his negative assessment of Mahler's music—with which few would agree—Wittgenstein identified with Mahler in a qualified way and discerned striking similarities and differences between his own and Mahler's relation to the tradition.

So far I have been occupied primarily with Wittgenstein's provocative judgment that Mahler's music is bad. Instead of attributing this judgment to a curious lapse in Wittgenstein's musical/aesthetic sensibility, I have sketched out and situated possible reasons for his making such a judgment. Now I take up the theme of contingency, the full realization of which has important implications for both music and philosophy.

Chapter VI
Breakdown of Tradition

1. Composing Music and Doing Philosophy in a Time of Decline

How then does Mahler compose in an era of the breakdown of tradition? He not only admires the great figures of Beethoven and Wagner, but pays homage to them by weaving fragments of their music into his compositions. Such gestures of "allegiance to the ancestral mother" show that Mahler is still engaged in musical construction. He is musically Janus faced: he looks forward in his attempts to breathe new life into the form of the symphony by the introduction of choral/vocal music and of the massive scale, and at the same time, through musical quotations, looks back to the past. If the only value that remains for evaluation is authenticity or "incorruptibility", then Mahler, Wittgenstein seems to hold, falls short, for he misunderstands his own cultural/historical moment and, in this sense, lacks self-knowledge.

The trouble with Mahler then is that although he is aware of this, he is unable to come to grips with and fully resolve the ensuing emotional conflict. To do so, he sought Freud's help:

> In the course of the talk with Freud, Mahler suddenly said that now he understood why his music had always been prevented from achieving the highest rank through the noblest passages, those inspired by the most profound emotions, being spoiled by the intrusion of some commonplace melody. His father, apparently a brutal person, treated his wife very badly. It became unbearable to the boy, who rushed away from the house. At that moment, however, a hurdy-gurdy in the street was grinding out the popular Viennese air 'Ach du lieber Augustin'. In Mahler's opinion the conjunction of high tragedy and light amusement

was from then on inextricably fixed in his mind, and the one mood inevitably brought the other with it.[1]

Wittgenstein identified with Mahler as a tragic figure who cannot really do what he would like to do. Mahler lives in an age when his adopted means of musical expression—the symphonic form—is dead, yet he refuses to accept the fact that it can not be revived. In contrast, Wittgenstein accepts for his own work the import of cultural decline. Unlike Mahler, who embraced the symphonic form and continued to write symphonies, Wittgenstein disavowed the description of his own work as 'philosophy'. Like the *Tractatus*, Mahler's music still "draws a picture", still represents, while the later Wittgenstein, having rejected abstract representational theories of meaning, goes on to present concrete language-games. This turn away from essentialist theories of meaning runs parallel to a turn away from the idea of an essentialist melodic form to a shift toward a family resemblance, contextualist account of melody that stresses the role a particular melody plays in a particular context, in a musical field of force. Of course, thinking of melody through the lens of family resemblance does not mean rejection of melody as such:

> The melodies of different composers can be approached by applying the principle: Every species of tree is a 'tree' in a different sense of the word. I.e. Don't let yourself be misled by our saying that they are all melodies. They are steps along a path that leads from something you would not call a melody to something else that you again would not call one. If you simply look at the sequences of notes & the changes of key all these structures no doubt appear on the same level. But if you look at the field of force in which they stand (and hence at their significance), you will be inclined to say: here the melody is something quite different than there (here it has a different origin, plays a different role, inter alia. [2]

In contrast to Mahler, the later Wittgenstein does not employ traditional or modern forms or styles of philosophical discourse—such genres as

---

1   Alma Mahler, *Gustave Mahler, Memories and Letters,* ed. Donald Mitchell, Seattle and London: University of Washington Press, 1971, xiii, 175.

2   Wittgenstein, *Culture*, 54.

the conventional philosophical treatise, book or essay—which have been typically used to expound theories; nor does he intend to engage in metaphysics. Instead of system building, there is clarification by way of the incisive "remark" (*Bemerkung*), which is his distinctive mode of writing: "The work of the philosopher is to assemble reminders for a particular purpose".[3] Instead of a unified, essentialist vision of language, there is attention paid to the plurality of language games; instead of univocality, there is a gathering of diverse voices, a careful discernment of sense and usage. This, we might say, is a Loosian moment in Wittgenstein: for him, theory construction, system building, essentialist visions of meaning and language are culturally as inauthentic for "moderns" as ornament in architecture is for Adolf Loos who famously declared that ornament is crime.[4] Such decorative devices are fine for human beings of another age, or of another tradition, but not for European civilization of the late nineteenth and twentieth century.

So the later Wittgenstein's attitude is different from Mahler's in that Wittgenstein is fully aware of his cultural/historical moment: he bites the bullet and instantiates in his practice the Spenglerian diagnosis of cultural decline. It is characteristic of Wittgenstein's work in philosophy that there is no pretense to originality or grand theorizing, no false gestures to Plato the 'ancestral father' who is opposed, rather than deferred to, this way: "I cannot characterize my [later philosophical] standpoint better than by saying that it is opposed to that which Socrates represents in the Platonic dialogues".[5] Since the symphonic form is exhausted, Wittgenstein seems to have thought that Mahler should not have used it for expressive purposes and doing so engulfed him in a sort of inauthenticity, namely, a betrayal of who he is. Mahler as a composer puts on a false identity: he is of *this* time, *this* culture and *these* circumstances, yet by using another epoch's expressive robes, he pretends to be someone else of *another* time and culture. Wittgenstein is scrupulous about resisting this form of self-deception by disowning the characteristic vocabulary and genres of cultural epochs distinct from

---

3   Wittgenstein, *Investigations*, §127.
4   Adolf Loos. "Ornament and Crime" (1908) in *Crime and Ornament: The Arts and Popular Culture in the Shadow of Adolf Loos*, eds Bernie Miller and Melony Ward, Toronto: YYZ Books, 2006.
5   Friedrich Waismann, *Ludwig Wittgenstein and the Vienna Circle,* Oxford: Blackwell, 1976, 33.

his own. "Everything ritualistic (everything that, as it were, smacks of the high priest) is strictly to be avoided because it straightaway turns rotten". Therefore he will not use 'as if' and similar phrases or modes of expression. Nor can he invoke God, even though he is inclined to do so when speaking of the spirit of his work.[6]

Mahler's partial awareness of his predicament was evident in his reaction to Arnold Schoenberg's conception and practice of "the music of the future"—a music without architecture or build up, a music that challenges the harmonic tradition and employs small forms with economy of style and instrumentation. "Why am I still writing symphonies", Mahler exclaimed, "if *that* [referring to a piece of music Schoenberg sent him] is supposed to be the music of the future?" Schoenberg's musical weather forecast bears an uncanny resemblance to Wittgenstein's tentative thoughts about the music of the future more than two decades later:

> I shouldn't be surprised if the music of the future were in unison. Or is that only because I cannot clearly imagine several voices? Anyway, I can't imagine that the old large forms (string quartet, symphony, oratorio etc) will be able to play any role at all. If something comes it will have to be—I think—simple, transparent. In a certain sense, naked. Or will that hold only for a certain race, only for one kind of music?[7]

'Unison', as in "singing in unison", suggests people singing or playing the same tune without harmonizing. The affinity between Wittgenstein's and Schoenberg's forecasts about "the music of the future" calls for a more careful look at Wittgenstein's attitude to, and assessment of, modern music and musical experiments. I now turn to these tasks by first looking at real family resemblances and differences.

---

6   Wittgenstein, *Culture*, 10.

7   Wittgenstein, *Public and Private*, 49.

2. The Brothers Wittgenstein and the Musical Journey of the West

In 1930 Wittgenstein sketched a foreword to what is now published as *Philosophical Remarks* which is revelatory of his attitude to the then current European/American civilization of which music is a manifestation. Even though the Foreword is often quoted, its import for music is rarely noticed or explored in depth:

> This book is written for those who are in sympathy with the spirit (*Geist*) in which it is written. This spirit is, I believe, different from that of the prevailing European and American civilization. The spirit of this civilization the expression of which is the industry, architecture, music, of the present day fascism & socialism, is a spirit that is alien & uncongenial to the author. This is not a value judgement. It is not as though I did not know that what today represents itself as architecture is not architecture & not as though he did not approach what is called modern music with the greatest mistrust (without understanding its language), but the disappearance of the arts does not justify a disparaging judgment on a whole segment of humanity. For in these times genuine & strong characters simply turn away from the field of the arts & towards other things & somehow the value of the individual finds expression. Not, to be sure, in the way it would in a time of Great Culture. Culture is like a great organization which assigns to each of its members his place, at which he can work in the spirit of the whole, and his strength can with a certain justice be measured by his success as understood within that whole. In a time without culture, however, forces are fragmented and the strength of the individual is wasted through the overcoming of opposing forces & frictional resistances; it is not manifest in the distance traveled but rather perhaps in the heat generated through the overcoming of frictional resistances... the fact remains that I contemplate the current of European civilization without sympathy, without understanding its aims if any. So I am really writing for friends who are scattered throughout the corners of the globe.[8]

In this passage the tone and substance of Wittgenstein's reference to

---

8 Wittgenstein, *Culture*, 8-9.

twentieth century music is no longer the youthful and light tone of the early Cambridge days when Wittgenstein and David Pinsent had great fun arguing against modern music and dismissing it. "Heaven knows", remarks Brian McGuinness, "what they meant [by modern music], perhaps an amalgam of Richard Strauss and Gustav Mahler… certainly not the atonal music already burgeoning in Vienna".[9] McGuinness is right on the first count: Recall Pinsent's diary entry about Wittgenstein's refusal to hear selections from Strauss' *Salome* at a concert they attended together. Now we can see why: he heard in Strauss' music symptoms of cultural malaise—the end of a distinctive musical culture. Unlike Mahler's ambivalent attitude to the tradition, in turn reverent, in turn ironic, Strauss was undermining its language with his aggressive and triumphal use of dissonance. McGuinness seems to miss, however, the close connection between Strauss and Schoenberg and hence the continuity between the music of Strauss and Mahler on the one hand and that of Schoenberg on the other. The May 1906 performance of *Salome* in Graz was attended by Schoenberg and his students and Schoenberg's *First Chamber Symphony*, written in the summer of that year, "resonate with aspects of *Salome*'s fractured tonality".[10]

By the time Wittgenstein wrote the 1930 foreword, his youthful negative attitude was transformed into a deeply felt critical assessment of modern music as a symptom of the spiritual/cultural malaise of the West, it being implicit that he is acquainted with modern music, but does not understand its language and is mistrustful of it. Significantly, when Wittgenstein says that he does not understand the language of modern music, he is not confessing ignorance but rather a philosophical puzzlement about the possibility of modern musical communication, about its coherence and goals. Wittgenstein also sees the music of the twentieth century as an aspect of fascist and socialist ideologies that stifle meaningful creative expression, where "the strength of the individual is wasted through the overcoming of forces & frictional resistances". In such an ideologically fraught milieu there was a breakdown of meaningful musical communication and music's capacity to express "human value" in the arts was compromised. Hence Wittgenstein

---

9   McGuinness, *Wittgenstein: A Life*, 125.
10 Alex Ross, *The Rest Is Noise: Listening to the Twentieth Century,* New York: Picador, 52.

contemplates European/American civilization in the twentieth century, including its music, "without sympathy, without understanding its aims if any".

But what about Shostakovich and like-minded others? The suggestion that his music fails at meaningful human communication or creative expression is hardly credible. The fact is, however, that Wittgenstein is not far off the mark, since Shostakovich as a person, and in many cases his music, were compromised—on the surface serving the Soviet propaganda machine but on a deeper level undercutting it. How could a composer not be compromised when Stalin published a negative and threatening review, with all its consequences, of a major composition? Listening to the finale of his *Fifth Symphony* we might ask: Is this a paean to Stalinist communism or a musical satire of it? More likely, walking an ambiguous path—a parody of bitter rejoicing. It won't do to say it makes no difference how we hear it because it *does*—it enters into how we receive and react to it.

In any event, Wittgenstein's writing off a whole century of music is disconcerting and leads us to question the relevance of his remarks on music for us today. Disconcerting, since it seems to confine the possibilities for the development of music and discourage musical experimentation—the lifeblood of music—and thereby arrest the musical progress of the West. Irrelevant, since the concept of music has radically changed and he seems wedded to a particular concept and period of music, refusing to countenance anything different. Wittgenstein, it might be said, belonged to the old school of *beaux arts*, art with aesthetic values, a legacy of the Renaissance.[11] Shall we then write Wittgenstein off as yesterday's man, as a man of another cultural era who was left behind the musical journey of the West, as a backward thinker from whom there is little to learn? To do so, in my view, would be a grave error. I prefer to adopt Brian McGuinness approach: "To learn today from Wittgenstein's attitudes, we need to alter them—to mollify or intensify or more probably to refocus them".[12] Now I proceed in this

---

11   As Cyril Barrett notes in his essay "Changing the Rules in Art" in *Wittgenstein and Aesthetics*, ed. Kjell Johannessen, Bergen: University of Bergen, Institute of Philosophy, 1998, 1-17. But we have seen in Chapter III, section 1 that such privileging of "beautiful art" is at odds with Wittgenstein's critique of the dominant place allotted to the beautiful in traditional aesthetics.

12   Brian McGuinness, *Approaches to Wittgenstein,* London: Routledge, 2002, 124.

spirit and revisit the Wittgenstein family, in particular Ludwig's brother, Paul, drawing real family resemblances and differences that will throw light on Ludwig's attitude. I argue that implicit in the 1930 foreword is a cryptic assessment of atonal music which formed the basis of why he was mistrustful of it and did not understand its language.

Paul lost his right hand in the Great War, an event that presented a challenge to the meaning of his life as a concert pianist. Since there was scant piano music composed for the left hand in the repertoire, he proceeded to commission works for the left hand from modern composers. With the help of Richard Strauss, Sergei Prokofiev, Maurice Ravel, Paul Hindemith, Erich Korngold, Franz Schmidt and Josef Labor, he aimed to establish himself as a concert pianist on the international stage. The blind Labor was held in high regard as a composer by the entire Wittgenstein family—he was a regular guest at their home concerts and, during the First World War, Ludwig had spent several days of his military leave with him. The idea that at such meetings there was no discussion of the exciting current musical scene in Vienna to which they were both existentially connected is less than credible. It is noteworthy that in 1922 all the Wittgensteins attended celebratory concerts in honour of Labor in Vienna and a few days earlier Paul played the concerto Labor composed for him.

There was at least one modern composer then whom Ludwig held in high regard, namely, Labor, who, comparatively speaking, gets a surprising amount of attention in Wittgenstein's comments about composers. In a remark made in 1929, Labor is listed as a member of a family of Austrian artists whom Wittgenstein admired and often referred to in his remarks about art and culture: "I think good Austrian work (Grillparzer, Lenau, Bruckner, Labor) is particularly hard to understand. There is a sense in which it is *subtler* than anything else and its truth never leans to plausibility".[13] Might Wittgenstein have thought of his own work as belonging to this family? The following question and answer indicate a 'Yes' and at the same time responds with a 'No' to Tolstoy's assertion that it is always the fault of the artist if a work of art is not understood: "Are you a bad philosopher then, if what you say is hard to understand? If you were better, then you would make it

---

13   Wittgenstein, *Culture*, 5.

easy to understand what is difficult.—But who says that is possible?! [Tolstoy]".[14]

In 1931, another remark alludes to Labor's late style as an advanced musical thoughtfulness: "Labor's seriousness is a very late seriousness"[15] and, again, in the same year, an admiring reference to the absence of sentimentality in Labor's music: "Labor, when he writes good music, is absolutely unromantic. That is a very remarkable & significant indication".[16] What is more, Labor's observation about some musical ideas is invoked and applied, albeit it in a non-musical context:

> The idea is worn out by now & is no longer usable. (I once heard Labor make a similar remark about musical ideas.) In the way silver paper, once crumpled, can never be smoothed out again. Nearly all my ideas are a bit crumpled.[17]

Labor is mentioned, together with Mendelssohn, as "the grain of mustard that grows up to be a great tree. To the extent there is courage, there is connection with life & death. (I was thinking of Labor's & Mendelssohn's organ music.) One might say: 'Genius is courage in one's talent.'"[18] Finally, there is the important passage I already cited about Labor's playing as being reminiscent of *speaking* and how this similarity with speaking is not an incidental but an important and big matter.[19]

Wittgenstein also defended Labor from unjust deprecation. Because of his blindness, Labor was underestimated and insulted by Clara Schumann, so Ludwig and his sister Gretl defended him and rightly criticized Schumann:

> Labor told me that in his presence [Clara Schumann] stated her doubt that a blind person could do this & that in music. I (Ludwig) don't know anymore what it was. Labor was evidently outraged about this & told me 'but he can do so.' And I thought: how characteristic with all the tact she must have had to make

---

14　*Ibid.*, 87.
15　*Ibid.*, 20.
16　*Ibid.*, 21.
17　*Ibid.*, 24.
18　*Ibid.*, 44.
19　*Ibid.*, 71.

such a half pitying, half disparaging remark about a blind musician.—That's bad nineteenth century, Ebner Eschenbach would never have done this.[20]

Clara Schumann was lacking "genius" and "something human in her personality"—a deep humanity and a talent for precise judgement. Gretl added: "After all she was not what [the Austrian writer Marie von] Ebner Eschenbach was".[21] We can only imagine what Clara Schumann might have said about Paul Wittgenstein as a one-armed pianist!

It is also important for our purpose to see who were the composers *not* commissioned by Paul and why; and who were not played despite having been commissioned. Arnold Schoenberg was not commissioned, even though he and Paul were both students of Josef Labor and despite Schoenberg being an occasional guest at the Wittgenstein musical soirées.[22] There can be little doubt then that Paul knew Schoenberg's music and the aims of the Second Viennese School. Musically and politically conservative, he had reasons for *not* commissioning work from them. Schoenberg's rejection of tonality and of the musical language of the tradition as dysfunctional, as no longer having a logical and ethical basis, was precisely the sort of view Paul, and presumably Ludwig also, opposed. Pronouncements from Schoenberg to strive for complete liberation from all forms and symbols of cohesion, for the emancipation of dissonance and for direct self-expression without a shared backdrop of tonality[23]—engendered mistrust of the new music in the brothers Wittgenstein.

Perhaps this explains Paul's decision *not* to commission Schoenberg, although the more likely explanation may be that Schoenberg's music was controversial and thus would not have helped with Paul's goal to establish himself as a pianist on the international circuit. We may still be puzzled, however, why Ludwig thought so highly of Labor and apparently nothing at all of Schoenberg. There is a significant entry in Wittgenstein's diaries in early 1931 which make one sit up and ask the question again:

---

20   Wittgenstein, *Public and Private*, 71.
21   *Ibid.*, 37.
22   Waugh, 31.
23   Schoenberg, *Theory of Harmony*, 1-2.

The music of past times always corresponds to certain maxims of the good & right at that time. Thus we recognize in Brahms the principles of Keller etc etc. And that is why good music which is found today or recently, which is modern, must seem absurd, for if it corresponds to any of the maxims articulated today it must be dirt. This sentence is not easy to understand but it is so: Today no one is clever enough to formulate what is right & all formulas, maxims, which are articulated are [plain] nonsense. The truth would sound completely paradoxical to everyone. And the composer who feels it in him must stand with this feeling in opposition to everything that is nowadays articulated & according to present standards he must therefore appear absurd, stupid. But not engagingly absurd (for after all, this is basically what corresponds to the present attitude) but vacuous.[24]

Then Wittgenstein adds "Labor is an example of this where he created something really significant as in some few pieces".[25]

If Labor's genuine contributions *must* sound absurd and vacuous given that moral value is impossible to formulate and that the times are out of joint, how much more so must sound Schoenberg's striking compositions of new music. The difference Ludwig may have heard and that perhaps explains his neglect of Schoenberg is that Labor, unlike Schoenberg, really spoke the old language, perhaps unconsciously, but spoke it in a manner that belongs to the newer world, without on that account necessarily being in accordance with its taste. In some of his writings Schoenberg, unlike Labor, was rather shrill in repudiating the old language as he proposed a new language and a new "theory" for music. What we have in Schoenberg, or so the brothers may have thought, is a radical turn away from the then accepted conventions of music to an artificial, formal approach playing at language yet devoid of its characteristic associations.

Contrasted with the natural air of tonality and melody, atonal music smacked of an artificial language reminiscent of Esperanto to which Ludwig expressed intense aversion:

Esperanto. Our feeling of disgust, when we utter an invented word with invented derivative syllables. The word is cold, has

---

24 Wittgenstein, *Public and Private*, 68-69.
25 *Ibid.*

no associations & yet plays at 'language'. A system of purely
written signs would not disgust us like this.[26]

The aversion is significant for us in that it is reminiscent of the
turn away from the logico-philosophical disparagement of ordinary
language—a hallmark of the early philosophy of the *Tractatus*—to a
new attitude to the every day:

> When we talk about language (words, sentences, etc.) I must
> speak the language of every day. Is this language somehow
> too course and material for what we want to say? Then how
> is another one to be constructed?—And how strange that we
> should be able to do anything at all with the one we have![27]

Another, perhaps equally important, issue is connected to Ludwig's
later concerns with the possibility of a "private language" on the one
hand, and to Paul's strenuous attempts to understand and play the compositions he commissioned from contemporary composers on the other.
How could the new "language of atonality" be understood and "spoken"? How could meaningful self-expression take place under such
conditions? The language of atonality would have struck the brothers
so idiosyncratic as to border on the unintelligible—a private musical
language whose "speaker" contemptuously turned his back on the audience and possibly failed to understand even himself. Rather than adding
to a musical language that enlarges the terrain of shareable experience,
the modern musical avant-garde reduced that terrain—or so the brothers, especially Ludwig, may have thought, given his later remarks about
a "private language". [28]

It may seem that there is a whiff of the retreat to the "private
citadel" about Schoenberg, especially in light of his occasional polemical
pronouncements and behaviour: "I strive", he wrote, "for complete
liberation from all forms, from all symbols of cohesion and of logic".
In addition, he suggested, as an aid to understanding his composition
Erwartung, to listen for "colours, noises, lights, sounds, movements,

---

26   Wittgenstein, *Culture*, 60.
27   Wittgenstein, *Investigations*, §120.
28   *Ibid.*, §269 and §275.

glances, gestures".[29] The appeal to sensations suggests an appeal to the purely subjective in the understanding of his music: to an experience or series of experiences we have while hearing it. The later Wittgenstein opposed such a view: "What do I actually experience then if I hear the theme & hear it with understanding?" he asks. "Nothing but inanities occur to me by way of a reply. Such as images, kinaesthetic sensations, thoughts and the like".[30] This is also a reply to Schoenberg's instruction to "listen for colours, noises, lights and sound". You may listen for these and "hear" them, but doing so does not *suffice* for listening with understanding.

The more promising second string of Schoenberg's instructions appeal to "movement, glances and gesture" suggest public criteria for understanding. This is more in tune with Wittgenstein who adds that movement, glance, gesture have to be appropriate to the music and assume some understanding of music itself. Consider:

> Appreciation of music is *expressed* in a certain way, both in the course of hearing & playing and at other times too. This expression sometimes includes movements, but sometimes only the way the one who understands plays, or hums, occasionally too parallels he draws & images which, as it were, illustrate the music. Someone who understands music will listen differently (with a different facial expression, e.g.), play differently, hum differently, talk differently about the piece than someone who does not understand. His appreciation of a theme will not however be shown only in phenomena that accompany the hearing or playing of the theme, but also in an appreciation for music in general.[31]

There is also Schoenberg's strange behaviour turning his back on the applauding audience after the 1913 Vienna premiere of *Gurre-Lieder*— one of his older pieces composed when he was still under the influence of a late-Romantic style.[32] But who can blame him after the abuse he suffered at their hands on previous occasions. Nevertheless one wonders: why did he consent to the performance of a composition he

---

29　Ross, *The Rest Is Noise*, 62.
30　Wittgenstein, *Culture*, 79.
31　*Ibid.*, 80.
32　Ross, *The Rest Is Noise*, 59.

no longer believed in, and then express contempt for the enthusiastic audience? Was his contempt for the "philistines" and the "bourgeois" so intense that their favourable reaction to an old work simply confirmed his judgement that if "they" appreciated it, it must be flawed in the sense that the break from the "old language", from the old values, was insufficient for the new music he was pioneering? In any event, the language of atonal music—despite some resonance with what may have seemed to some as a private language—was not a logically private language inaccessible to all but the composer, since it was successfully taught and learned, its rules and principles mastered by Schoenberg's pupils and followers. What is more, Schoenberg had a healthy attitude ands considered an audience with a musical ear essential to the dissemination of music and art:

> Among laymen I have found people whose organs of perception were much more sensitive than those of most professionals... if there is any sense at all of disseminating art—the receptiveness, the sensitivity, the powers of discrimination of the layman are absolutely prerequisite.[33]

The brothers Wittgenstein had different political perspectives—Paul leaning to the Right and Ludwig, apparently apolitical, but 'in his heart' leaning to the Left. Despite the inclination to think that in general the Left is friendly while the Right is hostile to musical/artistic experimentation, the fact is that the Left can also be reactionary about art just as the politically right can accept the musically far out. Notwithstanding their different politics, the brothers shared a love of music, were responsive to each other's views, argued about the "right" interpretation of musical works, and discussed even trivial events about it. Here is a neglected fragment that gives an idea of the nature and extent of their interaction. Ludwig, Drury reports, was impressed by his brother's grasp of the classical repertoire: "Today he [Ludwig] talked to me about his brother Paul Wittgenstein, the pianist. On one occasion some friends played a few bars of music from any one of a number of composers from widely different periods, and his brother was able without a mistake to say who the composer was and from which work

---

33   Arnold Schoenberg, *Theory of Harmony,* tr. Roy E. Carter, Berkeley and Los Angeles: University of California Press, 1978, 414-415.

it was taken".[34] Ludwig was critical, however, of Paul's interpretation of the works and on one occasion, when Paul "was practicing the piano and Ludwig was in another room of the house, the music suddenly stopped [Paul] burst into the room saying: 'I can't play when you are in the house. I feel your scepticism seeping under the door".[35]

On a lighter note: On one occasion, Paul passed on to Ludwig a letter from a bad composer's wife who invited Paul to contribute his favourite recipe to a musician's cook book she was compiling. Ludwig wrote to the woman humorously offering to make a contribution as a philosopher:

> For is not philosophy music and music philosophy?... My favourite food is tomatoes in mayonnaise... If you should honour me with inclusion in your little book, please quote my full name as I do not wish to be confused with the pianist Paul Wittgenstein, who may well enter your Pantheon but with whom I have no connection whatsoever.[36]

If the brothers took up such musical trivia, then surely they discussed the substantive issue of a challenge to the very foundation of the musical tradition occurring at the time in Vienna. In that case the assumption that Ludwig was not aware of the sea change in music or familiar with current musical events in Vienna through his own experience, through Paul and Labor, or through reading newspaper clippings, does not cut it. The fact of the matter is that Ludwig was aware that the language of music has been extended to include increasing dissonance and new modulations, but his attitude was characteristic of his philosophical perspective: neither to commend, nor deplore it but "rather: that's how it is".[37]

As to the new music, Paul struggled to understand and play it, as shown in his encounters with Sergei Prokofiev and Maurice Ravel, two modern composers among half a dozen or so he commissioned to compose piano concertos. Prokofiev as well as Ravel knew Paul admired Mozart and Brahms above all. What Prokofiev wrote to Paul

---

34   *Ludwig Wittgenstein Personal Recollections*, ed. Rhees, 150.
35   *Ibid.*
36   Waugh, *The House of Wittgenstein*, 192.
37   Wittgenstein, *Culture*, 63.

when sending his *Concerto No. 4 in B-flat for the Left Hand* is revealing of Paul' sensibility: "You are a musician of the 19th century, I am of the 20th. Don't judge the piano part too hastily; if certain moments seem to be indigestible at first, don't press yourself to pronounce judgement, but wait a while".[38] Paul never played the piece and explained this in a way that is also instructive about Ludwig's attitude: "Even a concerto Prokofiev has written for me I have not played because the inner logic of the work is not clear to me, and of course I can't play it until it is". As a pianist Paul was an expert on the early Romantic and late Classical repertoire and in general had a mistrust of modern music. Ludwig, like Paul, understood the "inner logic" of 18th and 19th century music; however, since the inner logic or language of later music was opaque to him he left modern music alone. On this view, both Paul and Ludwig were left behind on the musical journey of the West because they were stuck in the past.[39]

This quick dismissal does not square with the facts since it is odd to suppose that by this time in the 1930s Ludwig would not realize that there is more than one kind of logic, and no hierarchy among logics. Nor does such a dismissal square with Paul's disciplined efforts to understand and play the modern works he commissioned. He spent many hours with Prokofiev studying his score but could not *fully* understand it. When Prokofiev wrote to him expressing regret that Paul was not pleased by the composition, Paul wrote back: "That's not fair. Your concerto, or at least a considerable part of it, is comprehensible to me, but there is an enormous difference between a poem that displeases me and one whose meaning I cannot fully grasp".[40] The encounter with Ravel followed the same trajectory to begin with, but eventually Paul's struggles with Ravel's *Concerto pour la main Gauche* paid off and are characteristic of his approach and attitude. When Ravel came to Vienna to play the Concerto, Paul's reactions were at first rather negative: "He (Ravel) was not an outstanding pianist, and I wasn't overwhelmed by the composition. It always takes me a while to grow into a difficult work. I suppose Ravel was disappointed, and I was sorry, but I had never learned to pretend. Only much later, after I'd studied the concerto

---

38   Waugh, *The House of Wittgenstein*, 180.
39   Yuval Lurie takes this approach in *Wittgenstein on the Human Spirit,* Amsterdam: Rodopi, 2012, 149-151.
40   Waugh, *The House of Wittgenstein*, 180.

for months, did I become fascinated by it and realize what "a great work it was". And then a surprising admission: "It is astonishing. Although averse to any so-called modern music, it is just the 6/8 part, the most dissonant of the whole, which I like best".[41]

There were quarrels with Ravel about the orchestration—Paul argued that a middle section of the concerto should be played by the piano rather than the orchestra as Ravel composed it. Eventually Paul realized that the change he wanted "would ruin the concerto". After a diligent study of the piece he mastered it and his efforts resulted in critically acclaimed performances. By 1933 Paul and Ravel have patched up their differences enough to allow Paul to play it in Paris with Ravel conducting. The Paris premiere of *Concerto for the Left Hand* performed by Paul, with Ravel conducting, took place in 1933. When asked about the quarrel in an interview at the time of the New York premiere in 1934 Paul said: My quarrel with Ravel has long been settled; he and I are on the best of terms".[42] Performances of the Korngold and the Schmidt commissions were enthusiastically received in Vienna, both by critics and audience.

The disagreements with Ravel and other commissioned composers indicate another affinity between Paul and Ludwig: they were both forthright about their reactions, and then if a mistake was made, admitted it and tried to set it right. Ludwig, like Paul, never learned to pretend. This trait is evident in Paul's exchange with Ravel about the role of the performer as interpretive artist. "Performers must not be slaves", Paul said to Ravel after making alterations to the *Concerto* by taking lines from the orchestral part, adding it to the piano part. Ravel was furious and insisted in turn that Paul plays the music as written, adding "Performers must be slaves". While it is unlikely that Ludwig would have approved of Paul's control freakish acts of interference with Ravel's orchestration, he would endorse Paul's line that performers must *not* be slaves. The stance resonates with Ludwig's remark that Brahms cannot be played today the way he was played in his own times; rather the pianist needs to imaginatively interpret the score in light of present circumstances and emotional sensibilities. More importantly, when Ludwig expressed mistrust of modern music

---

41 Waugh, 177.
42 Waugh, 177.

because he could not understand its language, he was raising a question about the intelligibility of that language rather than confessing to brute ignorance: he was voicing the objection that the conditions necessary for musical communication do not obtain and therefore the composer is composing musical nonsense.

The Berlin premiere of the commissioned piece from Strauss titled *Panathenäenzug* was a critical failure for Paul as well as for Strauss: "It is easy to understand", wrote the music critic for the *Berliner Zeitung am Mittag:*

> that this pianist who had the misfortune to lose his right arm in the war does everything to stay in the limelight. It is hard to understand however how Strauss could have produced such an absolute failure... that goes beyond the limits of our endurance.[43]

However, the Vienna premiere a few months later was a critical and public success, praising Paul for his "astonishing energy and skill as an artist who, if we close our eyes, deceives us into imagining a two-handed pianist". A similarly astonished critic elaborated a little after the New York premiere: '[A]fter a few moments of wondering how the devil he accomplished it, one almost forgot that one was listening to a player whose right sleeve hung empty at his side. One found oneself engrossed by the sensitivity of his phrasing and the extent to which his incredible technique was subordinated to the delivery of the musical thought".[44]

The critic who raised the questions that Ludwig would probably have seen as hitting the nail on the head was the English critic Ernest Newman who asked whether Paul and his composers tried to do the impossible and, if not, was what they were doing worth doing? After hearing Paul's performance of Ravel's Concerto at the Proms in London, Newman wrote:

> I have every sympathy with Paul Wittgenstein in a loss of an arm during the war, and the profoundest admiration for the courage that enabled him to work up a one-handed technique afterwards.... All the same I wish composers would stop writing

---

43 Waugh, 158.
44 Waugh, 185.

one-hand concertos for him, or at any rate inflicting them on us…. The thing simply cannot be done; the composer is not only hampered in the orchestral portion of his work by consideration of the limitations of the pianist but even in the purely pianistic portions he is driven to a series of make shifts and fakes that soon become tiresome. From another point of view, it is true, the regrettable physical disability of Herr Wittgenstein may have saved the work as a concerto, for only one hand can, in the nature of things, be at worst only half as bad as it might otherwise have been.[45]

Newman makes explicit the assumption underlying part of the critical admiration that what we have here is a kind of circus act: a disabled concert pianist heroically trying to approximate the standards set by two handed pianists. Regrettably, said the critics, no matter how gifted, dedicated and technically skilful anyone is, it cannot be done. The requisites for the "ideal" simply do not obtain. The moral support for Paul is palpable in Newman's remarks, but Paul and collaborative composers are discouraged from continuing this kind of musical experiment, for it is bound to fail.

Although Ludwig may have thought that Newman raised the right questions, he was not in full agreement. Ludwig is on record saying that he was concerned about his brother continuing his career as a one-handed concert pianist, since he may be perceived as "a freak". Nevertheless Ludwig identified with his brother as we can infer from his saying to friends that he [Ludwig] knew that he himself was "a freak". What is more, he often thought of what sort of philosophy would enable his brother to cope with and respond to such a loss—a loss that Ludwig thought analogous to incapacitating mental illness in a philosopher. We may, however, ask, in light of Ludwig's later philosophy that invites experiments in philosophy, why let such musical experiments be undercut by a rigid insistence on the same standards for all, presupposing some fixed archetype? Notice, the commissioned composers complained about Paul's willful interventions in their work, *not* about his disability which was taken for granted. Similarly, it would be a huge mistake to see Para-Olympians' performance as circus acts, rather than different Olympians in their own right yet members of

---

45   Waugh, 186.

the same family. Paul's composers approached their commission as a challenging musical experiment, as an occasion to write a different sort of concerto, not as a musical impossibility.

Suppose that, unlike Paul who struggled and partly succeeded to appreciate later developments in music, Ludwig did not make the required effort because he was unable, unwilling or indifferent. In that case Ludwig was left behind on the journey of the creative musical culture of the West and he had nothing to say, explicitly or implicitly, about modern music—he simply left it alone. I don't buy this conclusion because there is a better reading that does justice to what we know about him, to his life-long love of and interest in music, as well as being in alignment with his later philosophical perspective. A clue is provided in Wittgenstein's reflections on his cultural ideal for dissolving the tension:

> I often wonder whether my cultural ideal is a new one, i.e., contemporary, or whether it comes from the time of Schumann. At least it strikes me as a continuation of that ideal, though not the continuation that actually followed it then. That is to say, the second half of the 19th century has been left out. This, I ought to say, has happened quite instinctively & was not a result of reflection.[46]

There are two things that strike me as interesting and important about this passage. First, it opens up the possibility of diverse ways of meaning, valuing and living outside the dominant culture. This suggests that we are not compelled to adopt an either/or picture of being a member of the musical *avant garde* pushing the envelope, versus being yesterday's man, a complacent character about music. The later Wittgenstein realized there is more than one kind of logic and no hierarchy among logics.

Similarly, there are many worlds of music and one may inhabit one but not another, or one or more. Wittgenstein chose to inhabit the music of the Classical/Romantic tradition—music whose language or inner logic he understood—Bach, Mozart, Mendelssohn, Schumann, Schubert, through Brahms, Wagner, Mahler to Labor. This resolution,

---

46   Wittgenstein, *Culture*, 3.

however, raises questions of consistency: first about Wittgenstein's attitude to jazz, and second, to experiments in music and philosophy.

In early 1930, after having watched a very old film with his friend and relation Arvid Sjögren in the cinema, Wittgenstein's made remarks about jazz that should raise our eyebrows. He made the observation that a modern film is to an old one as a present-day motor car is to one built 25 years ago. The old ones, he thought, make a ridiculous and clumsy impression and:

> the way film-making has improved is comparable to the sort of technical improvement we see in cars. It must be much the same thing with modern dance music too. A jazz dance, like a film, must be something that can be improved. <u>What</u> distinguishes all these developments from the formation of a *style* is that spirit plays no part in them.[47]

This may be read as asserting that what is involved in the development of jazz seems to be merely a technical improvement and it is not to be compared to the development of an artistic style. Jazz, like car manufacture, progresses as it builds more complex and effective structures but spirit is not manifest in it or through it—its style is not expressive of value.

Such remarks may give the impression that Wittgenstein had no sense of, or curiosity about, the value of jazz as we understand it—a false impression on both counts. It is reported that Wittgenstein was interested in the language of jazz and approached Timothy Moore—a jazz pianist who also attended Wittgenstein's lectures and was the son of Wittgenstein's friend the philosopher G.E. Moore. We do not know of the substance of that discussion. What is important, however, is that Wittgenstein speaks of the development of modern dance music in general, mentioning jazz-dance music (*Jazztanz*) as an example, *not* of the development of jazz as we understand it today. He would have said the same thing about the waltz or the tango as he said about *jazztanz*. Modern dance music's aim, in his view, is to entertain and in this respect it is to be contrasted with music "expressive of the human spirit". What he actually says allows us to distinguish between jazz on the one hand and jazz-dance music on the other: spirit may be involved in the

---

47   *Ibid.*, 5.

development of jazz but jazz-dance music, like other modern dance music, is in his eyes more like *techne* than genuine artistic expression. Wittgenstein's own view then is *unlike* that of Theodor Adorno who held that jazz as such, like other mass music, was a mere commodity made for mass consumption.[48] For Wittgenstein, only jazz-dance music and "modern dance music" in general are candidates for such commodities, but *jazz* as such need not be. Adorno, on the other hand, sweepingly viewed both as mere distractions, as without revolutionary potential. Such an interpretation of Wittgenstein's remarks makes room for the role of spirit in the development of the art of jazz. To be sure, Thelonious Monk's *Straight, No Chaser*, Count Basie's *Lester Leaps In*, Miles Davis' *Kind of Blue*, John Coltrane's *Giant Steps* or *A Love Supreme* are modern classics that manifest genuine expression of spirit. To deny this says little about the music and more about oneself and one's ideological prejudices. That said, now I turn to the question of experiments in music.

3.   Musical Experiments: Wittgenstein, Cage and Family Resemblance

The question arises when we notice that the musical journey of modernism is in many ways parallel to Wittgenstein's own work in philosophy and architecture. *Wittgenstein-House*, the home he designed for his sister, was inspired by Adolf Loos, a pioneer of modernist architecture, an acknowledged influence on, and friend of, Wittgenstein. Wittgenstein, as we have seen, was keen to reject the philosophical tradition and modernize philosophy, yet seems to have refused to countenance similar moves in the music of his time. Why the different take on music? The inconsistency is not only surprising but conjures up a gloomy picture of the prospects for modern music. Moreover, it sits uneasily with Wittgenstein's later anti-essentialism and his idea of creative innovation within in a tradition.

The different take on philosophy and music is especially surprising since there are affinities between the early Wittgenstein and

---

48   Theodor Adorno, "Perennial Fashion—Jazz" in *Prisms,* trs Samuel and Sherry Weber, London: Neville Spearman, 1967.

Schoenberg. The *Tractatus* was highly syncopated, said C.D. Broad—a fellow Cambridge philosopher—of its aphoristic, stripped down style, and Wittgenstein, in retrospect, agreed: "Each sentence in the *Tractatus* should be seen as the heading of a chapter, needing further exposition".[49] Its logical rule governed structure with restrictions of what can be *said* appeals to the reader's sense of simplicity and clarity, yet also gives the reader a sense of claustrophobic confinement. Wittgenstein embraces modernity as he proposes a theory of propositional meaning privileging the propositions of science:

> The correct method in philosophy would really be the following: to say nothing except what can be said, i.e. propositions of natural science—something that has nothing to do with philosophy—and then, whenever someone else wanted to say something metaphysical, to demonstrate to him that he failed to give a meaning to certain signs in his propositions. (6.53)

To adopt such a procedure in philosophy renders absolute value—in ethics, aesthetics and religion—nonsense—but important nonsense: "There are, indeed, things that cannot be put into words. They *make themselves manifest*"(6.522). Such nonsense and the ensuing silence provides the space for the appreciation of transcendent values.

If meaning is confined this way, we are inclined to run up against the walls of our cage and as it were break on to the other side—yearning for transcendence:

> For all I wanted to do with them [with our ethical/religious expressions] was just *to go beyond* the world and that is to say beyond significant language. My whole tendency and I believe the tendency of all men who ever tried to write or talk Ethics or Religion was to run against the boundaries of language. This running against the walls of our cage is absolutely hopeless... which I personally cannot help respecting deeply and I would not for my life ridicule it.[50]

Of course, the idea of language as a cage, rather than an instrument

---

49   *Ludwig Wittgenstein Personal Recollections*, ed. Rhees, 173.
50   Ludwig Wittgenstein, "A Lecture on Ethics", in *Philosophical Occasions*, 44.

for communication and expression, strikes the later Wittgenstein as untenable if not absurd.

At this point surprising affinities between Wittgenstein and Schoenberg come into view and call for qualification of how we are to understand Ludwig's stand against modern music. Many of these affinities were pointed out and elaborated by James Wright in his book *Schoenberg, Wittgenstein and the Vienna Circle*, even though the focus of his comparisons is with the early Wittgenstein and the Vienna Circle. I expand and spell out the range of affinities to the later Wittgenstein as well. Schoenberg's atonal operatic composition *Moses and Aron* is similar to the *Tractatus* in its sparse desert like musical landscape is shaped by rules of atonality much like the cryptic propositions of the *Tractatus* are linked by rules of logic. Both early Wittgenstein and Schoenberg affirmed the fact/value distinction and the inexpressibility of absolute value: God and absolute value are beyond the reach of word and image. We can only speak meaningfully about the facts but not about value. The dichotomy between fact and value is embodied in *Moses and Aron*: at the end of the opera Moses is alone, prays to the God beyond expression and cries out "O word, thou word that I lack"—a direct parallel to the bid to silence at the end of Wittgenstein's *Tractatus*: "Whereof one cannot speak thereof one should remain silent". As we read the *Lecture on Ethics*, the thought may occur to us that Wittgenstein is a fusion of Moses and Aron in that, like Moses, he smashes the tablets, and, like Aron, he confesses that he (and we) cannot help but talk important nonsense.

"The true teacher of art", said Schoenberg, "guides his pupils toward a severe matter-of-factness".[51] Earlier, in his *Theory of Harmony*, Schoenberg is equally explicit:

> It is our duty to reflect over and over again upon the mysterious powers of art… [regarding] nothing as given but the phenomena…. Since we do definitely know the phenomena [as facts] we might be more justified in giving the name science [*Wissen-*

---

51   Arnold Schoenberg, "Problems in Teaching Art" in *Style and Idea: Selected Ideas of Arnold Schoenberg* (1st ed., 1975), ed. Leonard Stein, tr. Leo Black, Berkeley and Los Angeles: University of California Press, 1984, 368.

schaft] to our knowledge of the phenomena, rather than to those conjectures intended to explain them.[52]

We can see here a parallel with Wittgenstein's efforts to look at and do justice to the facts. The description of [relevant] facts, as the later Wittgenstein continued to stress, was important for philosophy,

Now turning to similarities to the later Wittgenstein. Schoenberg's idea is that "musical logic" must answer to facts about real material works of art. So, there is, as Wright argues, a particularism and realism about Schoenberg that sit uncomfortably with an often adopted extreme formalist reading.[53] What is assumed by those speculative "theoretical conjectures" is that tonality is natural and essential to music. In Schoenberg's view, however, this assumption is an effect of the normative dominance of the Austrian-German musical tradition that has blindsided us for so long that we forget we people can follow and appreciate such composers, for instance, as late Liszt, Fauré, Ravel and Debussy who made use of different scales from the diatonic. Traditional philosophy was also blindsided by an essentialist Platonist legacy. This of course already looks forward to similarities with the later Wittgenstein's view that we learn to use and understand many concepts without being able to define them formally. There is also a new element, *the imagining of fictitious concepts*. Both how things are or might be with us are important for our understanding. Likewise with Schoenberg in the case of music.

What is one of the most striking affinities between Schoenberg and Wittgenstein (early and later) is their "anti-theory stance". Wittgenstein stressed the importance of producing examples and of due attention to the particular case in teaching and understanding the use of a concept or word. Similarly with Schoenberg: "The pupil learns most through the example shown him by the masters in their masterworks... but the music theorist... seeks to create a substitute by replacing the living example with theory, with the system".[54] Again, and this time less patiently: "To hell with all these theories, if they always serve only to block the

---

52 Arnold Schoenberg, *Theory of Harmony*, tr. Roy E. Carter, Berkeley and Los Angeles: University of California Press, 1978, 8.

53 James Wright, *Schoenberg, Wittgenstein and the Vienna Circle,* Bern: Peter Lang, 2004.

54 Schoenberg, *Theory of Harmony*, 8.

evolution of the art and if their positive achievement consists in nothing more than helping those who will compose badly to learn it quickly".[55] Schoenberg's book *Harmonielehre* is a critique of musical theories and systems, in particular of the dominant major-minor harmonic system. Hence there is irony in the conventional English translation of its title as *Theory of Harmony*. Similarly, Wittgenstein's works constitute a critique of philosophical theories and systems as well as of the very idea of "theory" in philosophy. What matters for both is the renewed effort for a fresh look at things. "What matters is the search itself", remarked Schoenberg, and "I hope that [my students will know that… finding… can easily put an end to searching".[56] Indeed, theories and formulas tend to have a comforting effect on its holders.

Another family resemblance is the deep aversion both had to what they considered "philistine" and "bourgeois". A feature of the bourgeois is searching for:

> comfort and this intrudes even into the world of ideas and makes us far more content than we should ever be…. Here we can see most distinctly what the prerequisite for comfort is: superficiality. It is thus easy to have a… philosophy, if one contemplates only what is pleasant and gives no heed to the rest. The rest—which is just what matters most. In the light of the 'rest' these philosophies may very well seem made to order for those who hold them.[57]

This bears comparison with Wittgenstein's complaint that philosophical theories conveniently feed on a one-sided diet: examples that fit the mould are highlighted and those that do not are dismissed or explained away.

Another important affinity is the importance that a clearly arranged presentation plays in both Schoenberg and the later Wittgenstein. In Schoenberg the search for theory is replaced

> with a method of teaching… whose clarity is simply a *clarity of presentation* that avoids the mistake of confusing itself with the ultimate nature of the things presented. This helps the student to

---

55   *Ibid.*, 9.
56   *Ibid.*
57   *Ibid.*, 2.

attain such skills as needed to produce something of established effectiveness—something which in its materials and techniques resembles older compositions, but leaves room for creativity.[58]

Putting the factual material in a *clearly arranged presentation* is also of great importance for Wittgenstein:

> The concept of a perspicuous representation is of fundamental importance for us. It earmarks the form of account we give, the way we look at things.... A main source of our failure to understand is that we do not command a clear view of our words.—Our grammar is lacking in this sort of perspicuity. A perspicuous representation produces just that understanding which consists in seeing connections. Hence the importance of finding and inventing intermediate cases.[59]

Again, making comparisons is a crucial means of shedding light on things for both Schoenberg and, as we have seen, for Wittgenstein. Consider the following passage from Schoenberg:

> Efforts to discover laws of art can at best produce results something like those of a good comparison.... In making a comparison we bring closer to what is distant, thereby enlarging details, and remove to some distance what is too close, thereby gaining perspective.... However much I may theorize in this book—for the most part to refute false theories.... I do so with constant and full awareness that I am only presenting comparisons.[60]

Reading Schoenberg's preface to his *Harmonielehre* one is struck by the many affinities to later Wittgenstein—affinities of approach, themes and attitude. And reading the last sentence of Schoenberg's preface also puts in mind Wittgenstein's regard for skill and technique and his disregard for a vocabulary of criticism using 'beautiful' ["The word beautiful is bad... it is just so many words"[61]]: "I would be proud if... I could say: 'I have *taken* from composition pupils a *bad* aesthetics

---

58 *Ibid.*, 11.
59 Wittgenstein, *Investigations*, §122.
60 Schoenberg, *Theory of Harmony*, 11.
61 Wittgenstein, *Public and Private*, 403.

("These judgments 'beautiful', 'not beautiful', are entirely gratuitous excursions into aesthetics; some pretty talk".[62]] and have given them a good course in *handicraft*.'"[63] This bears comparison to Wittgenstein's remark: "The nimbus of philosophy has been lost. For now we have a method of doing philosophy, and can speak of *skilful* philosophers".[64]

In light of all this, we can, with justification, add Schoenberg's name to the list of thinkers Wittgenstein identifies with when he said: "Loos, Spengler, Freud & I all belong to the same class that is characteristic of this age".[65] Loos, we are not to forget, was a friend of, and an influence on, both Wittgenstein and Schoenberg. Significantly, Loos's name appears three times in Schoenberg's *Theory of Harmony* mainly as reminder to avoid ornament and decoration, but also as a reminder not to oversimplify or complicate needlessly.[66] The big theme that Wittgenstein may have in mind here is the theme of being true to one's time and historical moment: a new architecture, a new psychology, and new music. When standing side by side, the works of these thinkers show a striking affinity of face amounting to family resemblance. However, the fact remains: Wittgenstein could *not* bring himself to appreciate the new music.

In any event, with the Platonism of the *Tractatus* rejected, Wittgenstein's later philosophical perspective, as well as his remarks on thought-experiments in philosophy, can be extended to music with the consequence that the issue of musical experiments is left open. How then are we to bring Wittgenstein's later work to bear on musical experiments? In the *Philosophical Investigations* Wittgenstein offers a fresh perspective on meaning: "I am saying that these phenomena [of language] have no one thing in common which make us use the same word for all but that they are related to one another in many different ways... I can think of no better expression to characterize these similarities than 'family resemblances'".[67] A series of relationships connects each member of the family to all the others without there being any one thing which all the members of the family share. If upon

---

62   Schoenberg, *Theory of Harmony*, 9, 10.
63   *Ibid.*, 12.
64   Wittgenstein, *Public and Private*, 342.
65   *Ibid.*, 37.
66   Schoenberg, *Theory of Harmony*, 270, 340, 417.
67   Wittgenstein, *Investigations*, §65, §67.

exposure to a new musical work, we adopted a family resemblance perspective and searched for overlapping threads of similarities and differences, instead of a common element shared by all music, we are in a better position to understand and appreciate new music.

Consider then the prospects for experimentation through the lens of Wittgenstein's remarks on how to look at concepts. What he said to his student Norman Malcolm about his later philosophical perspective bears directly on our question:

> What I give is the morphology of the use of an expression. I show that it has kinds of uses of which you had not dreamed. In philosophy one feels *forced* to look at a concept in a certain way. What I do is suggest, or even invent, other ways of looking at it. I suggest possibilities of which you had not previously thought. You thought there was one possibility or only two at most. But I made you think of others. Furthermore, I made you see that it was absurd to expect the concept to conform to those narrow possibilities. Thus your mental cramp is relieved, and you are free to look around the field of use of an expression and to describe the different kinds of uses of it.[68]

In light of this we might say that the concept of music is an open concept and that formal definitions or narrow theories of music are hostile, if not incompatible, with creativity in music.[69] Different sorts of music, like different games, have no one thing in common that justifies our use of the same word for all music, but they are related to one another in many different ways. Wittgenstein can think of "no better expression to characterize these similarities than 'family resemblances'; for the various resemblances between members of a family: build, features, colour of eyes, gait, temperament, etc., etc. overlap and criss-cross in the same way.—And I shall say: 'games' form a family".[70] Playing a variation on this, consider different sorts of music: folk-songs, dirge, sacred music, chamber music, fugues, sonatas, symphonies, jazz, rock

---

68 Norman Malcolm, *Wittgenstein: A Memoir,* London: Oxford University Press, 1966, 50.

69 See Morris Weitz, "The Role of Theory in Aesthetics" in *The Philosophy of Art: Readings Ancient and Modern,* eds Alex Neill and Aaron Ridley, New York: McGraw-Hill, 1995, 188-189.

70 Wittgenstein, *Investigations,* §66 & 67.

and roll, rap and hip hop. We are *not* to say: "There must be something in common [to them], or they would not be called 'music'. Rather, listen if there is anything common to all. Don't think, but listen. We are likely to hear a complicated network of similarities overlapping and criss-crossing: sometimes overall similarities, sometimes similarities of detail. Wittgenstein's concept of family resemblance, we might say, encourages a positive attitude to the variety of possible musical expression and leaves room for musical experimentation.

To explore further Wittgenstein's later philosophical perspective as it relates to music, let's go, what might seem to some as "over the top", and ask if there is a family resemblance between John Cage and Ludwig Wittgenstein. In a thought provoking essay, the concert pianist Rita LaPlante Raffman applied Wittgenstein's later line of thinking to Cage's radically experimental piece for the piano titled *4'33"*. The so-called "Silent Sonata", she argued, is like a third cousin or an adopted orphan who at first does not look like his siblings but on closer scrutiny turns out to have many family resemblances to them. *4'33"* does not seem to resemble any paradigmatic work of music such as a Beethoven symphony or a Schubert string quartet nevertheless, she asserts, if we make careful comparisons then certain similarities can be discerned involving such basic elements of music as sound, rules, form and composer's intention. On the basis of such "family resemblances" she endorses *4'33"* as a work of music. It will be instructive to consider her striking claims and eventually relate them to Wittgenstein under an aspect she overlooks.

Cage's *4'33"* is a work in three movements and to perform it, the pianist, suitably dressed for a concert, goes on stage, sits at the piano, stays seated without playing for about 4 minutes and 33 seconds; then closes the keyboard and leaves the stage. During the performance he turns the pages of the "score" and, using a ticking stopwatch, opens and closes the lid of the keyboard at intervals specified by the length of a movement. Since the deliberate making of sounds is a basic minimal feature of music, and in *4'33"* the musician produces no instrumental sounds at all, one is inclined to think it cannot qualify as a work of music. LaPlante Raffman, however, reminds us not to forget that there are sounds in Cage's *Silent Sonata*: the ambient sounds the audience and the pianist make. "Sounds and silences", she asserts, "are components of Beethoven's *Fifth Symphony*, and they are components of the Cage.

The emphasis", she continues, "is obviously different, since the silences stop the flow of sounds in the Beethoven while the sounds stop the flow of silence in the Cage".[71]

Suppose that the venue for the performance is a concert hall. Then the ambient sounds may include the rustling of the pages of score being turned, sounds of throat-clearing, coughing, shuffling feet, whispers, the shrill sounds of cell phones going off. If the venue is the natural environment, the sounds may include the song of the nightingale, the sound of raindrops, of thunder, of waves of the sea, the sounds whales make. Now the objection is that even though such a collection of sounds is pressed into 4 minutes and 33 seconds as specified in the title, this involves too broad a construal of musical sound. The similarity cannot be a *family* resemblance, since the ancestral family background Wittgenstein assumes is the body of musical works in the Classical/ Romantic tradition of European music from Bach, Mozart, Haydn, Beethoven, Mendelssohn, to Brahms and Wagner. To propose that a random collection of sounds amounts to a *family resemblance* is to confuse the latter with a mere similarity and thus unacceptably stretch the boundaries of the concept of music.

Granted there are sounds, but could they count as *musical* sounds—what Wittgenstein would regard as musical communication? Such random sounds seem to lack expressive agency, and hence can have no musical *meaning* for us without further ado. Of course, this is not to deny that the sounds of the city can have meaning or significance for us. For instance, the ringing of the church bells may call the faithful to church or the sound of the gong at a factory may mean the work day's end; the shrill sound of the fire alarm or the police siren signify danger or caution. Such sounds have pragmatic meaning, but without further musical setting they have no *musical* meaning and hence are unlikely to provoke our aesthetic interest.

Now the question arises why should we have musical/aesthetic interest in sounds or noise we hear every day that ordinarily do not make the slightest impression on us? Wittgenstein took up this sort of question in his conversation with Engelmann regarding literature. "Only

---

71   Rita Laplante Raffmann, "Family Resemblance and Contemporary Music" in
      Ludwig Wittgenstein: Critical Assessments, ed. Stuart Shanker, London: Rout-
      ledge, 2004, 392-397.

the artist/musician, he claims, can give such things significance and elevate them so as to enable the audience appreciate them".[72] Through the imaginative application of their skill, artists enable us to see or hear things under a certain aspect, as this or that, and give them significance. While the sounds of the environment may be skillfully and effectively woven into a musical composition by an imaginative composer, traffic noise by itself does not count as a work of music. Instead of attentive listening, we try to escape it. Beethoven's sounds of thunder, the call of the cuckoo in Mahler's *First*, Gershwin's incorporation of the sounds of traffic into his *An American in Paris,* Messiaen's use of bird-call in *Birdsongs*, Karlheinz Stockhausen's use of the sound of helicopter blades in his *Helicopter String Quartet*, Bjork's whale-music—these are all elements woven into a larger work that renders such things intelligible as background. Material consisting exclusively of ambient noise or clatter is only material for musical exploration and composition; otherwise it fails to engage our musical interest even with the backdrop of a full orchestra poised to play. The hills are only "as it were" alive with the sound of music; in fact they are alive only with the sounds of nature, unless there is an outside concert going on. In this vein Eduard Hanslick crisply remarked that music owes more "to the gut of the sheep than to the song of the nightingale".[73]

There is another "family resemblance", suggests LaPlante Raffman, between *4'33"* and traditional works, namely "rule following". This may seem counter-intuitive, since Cage shuns the rules of the musical tradition—of harmony, counterpoint and so on, but this is not, she says, because Cage advocates chaos, rather "he is being creative! Just as much as any other composer, Cage is helping to define music". Does he not, she asks, introduce the rule that "any sound may occur in any combination and in any continuity?"[74] This only looks like a rule, one might say, because of its grammatical form. The "rule" really amounts to "Do whatever you want", since any and every move is compatible with it. Cage's purpose is the wholesale rejection of, and liberation from, the European musical tradition of the 18th and 19th centuries and hence a radical break from the ancestral connection

---

72 Wittgenstein, *Culture*, 6-7.
73 Hanslick, *On the Musically Beautiful,* 72.
74 LaPlante Raffman, "Family Resemblance", 395.

with the music and the family of composers who ground Wittgenstein's remarks about music.

Cage's instructions for his piece *Credo in Us*, featuring a record player or a radio as instruments, indicate that he regards the tradition as worn-out kitsch: "Use some classic, e.g., Dvořák, Beethoven, or Shostakovich". A record player squeaking odds and ends of Beethoven or Shostakovich is a musical parallel to Duchamp's painting a moustache on the Mona Lisa. To speak of *family resemblance* here between Cage and the tradition seems out of place. The distance between Cage and the tradition is even greater in Cage's *Music of Changes* where he leaves rules of composition behind and uses the Chinese *I Ching* to invent chance procedures aiming to eliminate authorial intention and causation from the process of composition. This amounts to an attempt to erase self, feeling and self-expression from his compositional process—an attempt not unlike some philosophical attempts to overcome problems of the self by translating sentences such as 'I am in pain' with 'There is pain'. Both attempts are as paradoxical as clapping with one hand, since they immediately bring to mind that something or someone is missing here.

In *Lectures and Conversations* Wittgenstein takes up the question of rules:

> The rules of harmony, you can say, expressed the way people wanted certain chords to follow—their wishes crystallized in these rules (the word 'wishes' is much too vague). But it is just a fact that people laid down such and such rules.... [In any event] all the greatest composers wrote in accordance with them.[75]

Then a student objects that all the great composers changed some rules and that was part of their creative greatness. Indeed, Bach, Haydn, Mozart, Beethoven, Brahms and Beethoven all changed the rules somewhat. "You can say", Wittgenstein replied, "that every composer changed the rules, but the variation was very slight; not all the rules were changed. The music was still good by a great many of the old rules".[76] If these are factual remarks about the family of composers in the history of European music, then, looked at sequentially, each

---

75   Wittgenstein, *Lectures*, 6.
76   *Ibid.*

composer, say, between Bach, Beethoven and Brahms changed the rules only slightly, with Mahler and Strauss much more so, and then with a lot of incremental change we can get the sea change that's Schoenberg. In order to recognize family resemblances and differences, we need to track the incremental alterations that eventually add up to warrant the ascription of a different style and a different musical face.

When we come to Mahler and Strauss, family resemblances are still readily discernible, although Wittgenstein picks up on the pronounced differences and anticipates what is to come. When we encounter Schoenberg, Bartók and Stravinsky, Messiaen, Stockhausen and Cage, in particular radical experiment *4'3"*, appreciation requires putting the salient differences right up front. The difference between Cage on the one hand and Bach, Beethoven, Brahms, Wagner and Mahler and Strauss on the other, is so radical that one is inclined to speak of Cage as rejecting the traditional rules wholesale or changing all the rules—both normative and constitutive—all at once. Now this is of great interest to the philosophy of music: Not only is Cage's music not good or bad by the old normative rules, but it seems absurd to speak of it as a work of music. To invoke Wittgenstein's notion of "family resemblance" here confuses rather than clarifies and misleads us in the appraisal of Cage's significance as a composer.

Do not take, Wittgenstein remarked, what is common as telling but at some point differences are crucial. Consider:

> A great architect in a bad period (Van der Null) has a quite different task from that of a great architect in a good period. You must again not let yourself be deceived by a generic term. Don't take comparability, but rather incomparability, as a matter of course. Nothing is more important though than the construction of fictional concepts which will teach us at last to understand our own.[77]

What is clear is that Cage's *4'33"* marks a drastic change: a wholesale rejection of the tradition altogether. It is *incomparability* what matters; otherwise its very status as opening space for a different kind of music is neglected. Whereas Laplante Raffman speaks of family resemblances and continuities, Wittgenstein would speak of *4'33"* as marking the

---

77   Wittgenstein, *Culture*, 84-85.

end of a certain world of music. In fact Cage is aware of this: "If this word 'music', he said, "is sacred and reserved for eighteenth and nineteenth century instruments [and composers], we can substitute a more meaningful term: organization of sound".[78]

Another "family resemblance" LaPlante Raffman discerns between Cage and the musical tradition is the importance given to the composer's intentions in the form of choices made. The tradition privileges the composer's intentions and choices in organizing sound, while Cage chooses to "include no planned sounds". When he "elects not to clothe his ideas in traditional garb, he is just replacing one method of organization with another. He is giving the lie to those who would deny him the name composer".[79] Unlike Beethoven, "who followed the procedures which were the accepted criteria of the day", Cage chose not to write in the traditional system, specified the duration of his work, selected the number of performers and instruments to be used, determined the genre of the work, and so on.

What this shows, I claim, is a radical difference rather than a family resemblance between Cage and the tradition. Leaving the ambient sounds to chance is a reason to say that Cage's intention is not to compose a work of music as traditionally understood, but to dismantle the musical tradition further by taking away the pride of place it gives to the composer to organize sound. Cage is interested in challenging us to re-think our assumptions about the nature and scope of music, about the role of the composer, and the conditions under which everyday sounds or noise are transformed into musical sounds and how they may become part or even the whole of, a work of music. His intention is not to contribute to or extend the traditional composer's authority or repertoire, but to undercut them. The gesture is one of defiant revolt, not a reformist attitude, even though his radicalism only made sense with the tradition as background—something of which Cage was well aware.

At this point it may be said that Wittgenstein's remarks about "slight or minor changes" in the rules of composition show a neglect of contingency, the changes in the historical/cultural/social context.

---

78 John Cage, "The Future of Music: Credo", in *Silence: Lectures and Writing,* London: Marion Boyars, 1978, 3.
79 LaPlante Raffmann, "Family Resemblance", 396.

With the arrival in music of Strauss' *Salome* and Schoenberg's atonal compositions the very foundations of traditional music were challenged. The avant-garde went so far as to claim that only music which showed a radical break from the tradition is worthy of being so called and anyone who composed according to traditional rules was composing a kind of kitsch or indulging in nostalgia. Such changes in twentieth century music were certainly not "slight variations" from the past—they were nothing short of fundamental. Many of the constitutive and normative rules have changed, so that not only was this music not good by the old rules, but its status as music was brought into question.

There are, however, two different questions here. There is the question of whether there is family resemblance and there is the question whether Wittgenstein would regard it as such. Schoenberg, Webern, Boulez, Stockhausen, and Cage, we might say, make sense only if they are understood with the tradition as background. In this sense they belong to the family, like revolutionaries do, even though they go on to compose in their own distinctive and original ways. Furthermore, we are unable to discern the family resemblance unless we fill in the family sequence—the intervening family members—who are the "slight variations" given what immediately went before. By shrugging off "modern music", Wittgenstein ignored the intervening family members and hence was unable to appreciate, or was indifferent to, how the moderns emerged out of the tradition. Roughly speaking, Charles Ives takes us some distance from Beethoven, and Schoenberg's twelve tone system; Hindemith's and Toch's phonograph concert of prerecorded sound, Boulez's hyper-activism in his *Second Sonata*, plus the new electrical instruments enlarging the range of sound, get us closer to Cage. Admittedly, Cage is a hard case and hence of critical interest. Even Boulez thought Cage had gone too far. But looking at Cage's development as a composer we might notice gradual changes. Think of his pieces for prepared piano which are, it seems to me, music but quite on the way to *4'33"*. Cage did not change the rules all at once; he seems to have done so only if we look at *4'33"* in isolation, as many writers tend to do.

4. Deterioration or Sea Change in the Culture of the West?

Wittgenstein, as Georg von Wright reminded us, "is much more deeply 'history-conscious' than is commonly recognized and his way of seeing philosophy was not an attempt to tell us what philosophy, once and for all, is but expressed what for him, in the setting of his times, it had to be".[80] Should this not go for music too? In his remarks about music, I suggest, he is not defining what music, once and for all is, but reflects on the musical world he inhabits, on what he takes to be the paradigm of great music. In doing so, he leaves room for other music—music for which he has little or no sympathy—for instance, music of the late 19th and early twentieth century. His awareness of contingency in the nature of performance comes through loud and clear in a striking conversation with Rush Rhees:

> Once when we were sitting in Trafalgar Square he spoke of the architecture of the buildings and especially of Canada House. We had been talking of music and of how hard it is to play Brahms at the present day. Myra Hess [a distinguished British pianist of the first half of the twentieth century] played Brahms exactly in the way which had been right during Brahms' life time. But to play him that way *now*—with just the same emotional emphasis to fit the emotional reactions of people then—this made the music meaningless for us. There was only one man he heard in recent years who really did know what the music meant and played it—'and that was the *great* Brahms.' A nose for what was music and what was rhetoric. The way Myra Hess played it would have been music in Brahms' day, but now it was just rhetoric; and whatever it gives us, it just isn't Brahms. Wittgenstein pointed to Canada House, which the builders were just finishing. This architecture has followed a tradition by taking over certain rhetorical forms, but it says nothing in them. Large scale, meant to fit within a great culture. But—waving his hand towards it—'that's *bombast*: that's Hitler and Mussolini.' [Wittgenstein] would not have said that another architect might have built one that *wasn't*. Not today, and not here. Canada House helped to

80 Henrik von Wright, "Wittgenstein in Relation to his Times", in *Wittgenstein and His Times,* ed Brian McGuinness, 216.

show why Hitler and Mussolini had to work with bombast, as it
showed how truly they were one in spirit with us.[81]

An authentic rendition of Brahms today requires playing him differently
than he was played in his own times and an authentic architect must refrain
from borrowing rhetorical forms of previous times. "Architecture is a
gesture.... [it] immortalizes and glorifies something. Hence there can
be no architecture where there is nothing to glorify".[82] If so, then there
is such a thing as a false gesture—one that expresses a self-deceptive,
kitschy or otherwise inauthentic feeling. Greek Revival architecture—
of which Canada House is a fine example—but is not a style to be used
for building additions in the late 1930s. The gesture it expresses is a
feeling of pretended reverence, since the required object of reverence
is no longer there to glorify. The whole exercise is one of bombast and
nostalgia. "Today the difference between a good architect and a bad
architect consists in the fact that the bad architect succumbs to every
temptation while the good one resists it".[83] It is in this sense that the
spirit of the age was that of Mussolini and Hitler who used bombast and
inflated rhetoric when on the podium appealing to the masses. There
can be little doubt that, in contrast, Wittgenstein was thinking of the
architecture of Adolf Loos and the house in Vienna he [Wittgenstein]
designed for his own sister Gretl. These works make no false gestures
and are notable for their clarity, simplicity of design and absence of
ornament: "Everything ritualistic (everything that, as it were, smacks of
the high priest) is strictly to be avoided because it at once putrefies".[84]

Similarly, today's composers can not just like that adopt and
employ the old forms and style without bombast or false sentimentality.
They can however, restore an old style in a newer language; perform it
afresh so to speak in a manner that suits our times. If they do that, really
they only reproduce. This is what Wittgenstein did in his building work,
with the help of Loos's architecture. What Wittgenstein says here is not
to be mistaken for giving an old style a new trim. He aims at something
deeper: "You don't take the old forms & fix them up to suit today's taste.
No, you are really speaking the old language, maybe unconsciously, but

---

81   *Ludwig Wittgenstein Personal Recollections*, ed. Rhees, 225-226.
82   Wittgenstein, *Culture*, 49; 74.
83   *Ibid.*, 5.
84   *Ibid.*, 10.

speaking it in a manner that belongs to the newer world, though not on that account being necessarily one that is to its taste".[85]

If so, then the case for new music, for musical experimentation, looks not only promising but essential for cultural self-expression today. The stress on contingency comes through loud and clear in a telling passage about appreciation:

> What does appreciation consist in?… It is not only difficult to describe what appreciation consists in, but impossible. To describe what it consists in we would have to describe the whole environment…. There is an extraordinary number of different cases of appreciation. And of course what I know is nothing compared to what one could know…. You can get a picture of what you might call a very high culture, e.g., German music in the last century and the century before, and what happens when it deteriorates. A picture of what happens when in architecture when you get imitations—or when thousands of people are interested in the minutest details. A picture of what happens when a dining room table is chosen more or less at random, when no one knows where it came from.[86]

For instance, to appreciate Mahler *this way*, you have to know a great deal about the history of European classical music and the culture of Vienna. To hear Mahler's music as deterioration, as Wittgenstein at first does, requires placing Mahler in a line in that history, comparing him with the others and attend to differences. A lively, healthy musical culture exists in a period when extraordinary care is lavished on certain details, when people know where a theme or musical line comes from. When Wittgenstein does this with Mahler, Mahler comes up short. Of course, it takes a lot of training of the ear to get this, as it takes a lot of training of the eye to appreciate painting or architecture. To situate and relate a piece of music historically is one sort of musical appreciation; to play it with the right expression or savour it while listening is another. These are different cases of musical appreciation.

The role of contingency in artistic appreciation is further brought out in Wittgenstein's remarks about putting figures in the arts side by side and making comparisons between them:

---

85   *Ibid.*, 69.
86   Wittgenstein, *Lectures*, 7.

> You can sometimes find the similarity between the style of a musician and the style of a poet, or a painter who lived at the same time.... Take Brahms and [the Swiss poet] Keller. I often found that certain themes of Brahms were extremely Kellerian. This was extraordinarily striking. First I said this to people. You might say: 'What would be the interest of such an utterance?' If I say this theme of Brahms is extremely Kellerian, the interest this has is first that these two lived at the same time. Also that you can say the same sort of thing of both of them—the culture of the time in which they lived. If I say this, this comes to an objective interest. The interest might be that my words suggest a hidden connection.[87]

If Brahms is to be put beside Keller for appreciation, who is the figure in the visual arts to put beside John Cage in music? Marcel Duchamp is a natural choice. So, we might say that Cage's concerns and style are very Duchampian. This says something of interest because roughly speaking they lived at the same time and shared the same culture. To tease out the connection, something has to be said about Dada and other developments in 20th century art. Cage and Duchamp also wear the same face or perform similar expressive gestures even though Cage was rightly perceived as serious and Duchamp as playful in the sense that he played practical jokes on classic works of art. The case of cultural similarity is rather different from that of faces.

> With faces you generally soon find something which makes you say: 'Yes, that's what made them so similar.' Whereas I couldn't say now what it is that made Brahms similar to Keller. Nevertheless, I find that utterance of mine interesting. It derives its interest from the fact that these two lived at the same time. 'That was [or wasn't] written before Wagner.' The interest of this statement would lie in the fact that on the whole such statements are true when I make them. One can actually judge when a piece of poetry was written by hearing it, by the style. You could imagine that this was impossible, if people in 1850 wrote the same way as they did in 1750, but you could still imagine people saying: 'I am sure that was written in 1850.'[88]

---

87   *Ibid.*, 32.
88   *Ibid.*

Although Wittgenstein and Cage were, roughly speaking, a generation apart, nevertheless drawing comparisons between them may be illuminating despite Wittgenstein's willingness to listen only to music from Bach to Brahms, Wagner, Mahler and Labor. Reading some work of philosophy, we may say: "This was written before (or after) Wittgenstein." Similarly, hearing a piece of music, we may say: "This was written before (or after) Cage." And that could be an important remark for appreciating the piece. The old rules of music exclude the Cage, since his work shows a decisive break from the tradition. When we look at Cage's face, we may see a few interesting expressive features that remind us of Wittgenstein's face (especially when we insert Schoenberg's between them), but then again differences become more prominent and important. In the visual arts, on the other hand, the analogous case to Cage's *4'33''* is Marcel Duchamp's *Fountain*—they show the same expression, the same face as Cage—the differences are negligible.

Suppose a work of art to be an artifact, chosen to be suitably played or displayed, is of aesthetic interest and accepted by the artistic community. But how could, we might ask, a urinal—an artifact not even made by Duchamp but mass produced by the J.L. Mott Iron Works and plumbing supply company—bearing the signature R. Mutt, baptized as *Fountain*, be considered a work of art? Well, it is. That's how art has changed and the changes have been radical, not slight. Duchamp's reactions to objections from the old standpoint are revelatory of a new conception of art: "Whether Mr. Mutt with his own hands made the fountain or not has no importance. He CHOSE it. He took an ordinary article of life, placed it so that its useful significance disappeared under the new title and point of view—created a new thought for that object".[89] The only issue here is whether the *objet trouvé* is of any aesthetic interest. Duchamp's ready-made object becomes a work of art because "looking at it in a certain way makes it into a work of art". The artist chose to "lift it out of the limbo of disregarded objects into the living world of works of art".

The same logic seems to apply to Cage's *4'33''* and this connection is no accident, since his *Music for Marcel Duchamp* preceded *4'33''*.

---

89   Marcel Duchamp, Beatrice Wood and H.P. Roche, *The Blind Man No. 2* (May 1917), 5.

Cage's, like Duchamp's, contribution is minimal: it is an auditory ready-made consisting of found sounds. Cage lifts the sounds occurring during 4 minutes and 33 seconds of the performance out of the everyday and presents this ensemble of sounds for our musical/conceptual appreciation. Listening to it under this aspect makes it into a brilliant invention of a musical/conceptual experiment and Wittgenstein, had he known of it, would have appreciated Schoenberg's allusion to Cage as an "inventor". The composer, we might say, chose to lift the ambient sounds out of the limbo of the unheard and into the living world of music. He created a new thought for what is usually unheard, ignored or forgotten. If Duchamp's *Fountain* is one of the most influential works in the plastic arts, Cage's *4'33"* is its match in the world of music, broadly conceived. Ironically, the most influential work of art does not exist: the urinal that was *Fountain* no longer exists, except as a replica of Stieglitz's photograph; nor does the original Cage *4'33"* exist any longer. Perhaps this does not matter, since what counts is a fresh appreciation of what our everyday environment provides whether by way of sounds or sights.

Is this not a clear case of deterioration or is it a sea change in the musical culture of the West? The question seems to demand a *theory* of what counts as decline or deterioration. Wittgenstein, recall, does not have a theory of deterioration. "Do you think I have a theory [of deterioration]? Do you think I am saying what deterioration is? What I do is describe different things called deterioration. I might approve of deterioration".[90] And here his awareness of the social/political motivations of the musical avant-garde's program comes through loud and clear: "All very well your fine musical culture; I am very glad children don't learn harmony now". So, deterioration does not always imply disapproval; rather it might even be an expression of approval. It is as if Cage was saying "All very well your fine musical culture, but look how it narrows our range of hearing/listening, how it underwrites past practices without questioning them, while the sounds surrounding us, of our environment, of nature and the value of silence turn on deaf ears. Those rules of harmony facilitate automatic obedience and conformity to the status quo, prevent us from individual self-expression, from paying due attention to the music of our everyday life."

---

90   Wittgenstein, *Lectures*, 10-11.

4'33" plainly raises issues of deterioration and fraudulence in modern music. If Cage and modern experiments in music are seen as paradigms of deterioration and decline, there is a short step from this to saying "That's not music". But that does not go deep enough as an objection: The charge against Cage is that he is pulling a fast one, that he is mocking the musical conventions of the tradition as well as the expectations of the audience. Wittgenstein had a strong sense of cultural deterioration and decline:

> My own thinking about art & values is far more disillusioned than would have been possible 100 years ago. However, that does not mean it is more correct on that account. It only means that there are examples of decline in the forefront of my mind, which were not in the *forefront* for those people then.[91]

This sense of decline was likely prompted by Wittgenstein's own experience as well as by reading Oswald Spengler and Leo Tolstoy. Tolstoy's *What is Art?*—a book that Wittgenstein referred to and commended as much to learn from despite its false theorizing"—raises issues of deterioration and fraudulence in modern art. [92] "Art", Tolstoy avers, "that does not move us… is either bad art or not art at all".[93] The argument that "in order to feel art, one must understand it (which, in fact, merely means get accustomed to it), is the surest sign that what is offered to our understanding in this way is bad, exclusive art, or not art at all".[94] If understanding is a necessary condition for "feeling music", then appreciating music's meaning is a matter of intellect, perhaps a matter of instruction in learning music theory and history. Both Tolstoy and Wittgenstein reject the claim that understanding the importance (meaning) of art/music is a matter of cleverness or intellectual training. However, the insight Wittgenstein teases out of Tolstoy is that what is hard is the struggle to resist our inclination to perceive what most of us *want* to perceive. "Art in its latest manifestations, Tolstoy continues, "has even lost all the properties of art and has been replaced by simulacra of art…. This art has in the course of time even ceased to be

---

91 Wittgenstein, *Culture*, 91.
92 *Ibid.*, 67.
93 Tolstoy, *What is Art?*, 81.
94 *Ibid.*, 82.

art and has come to be replaced by counterfeits of art". Responding to those spoiled classes who looked for mere amusement and enjoyment from art, "artists were compelled to develop methods by which they could develop objects simulating art. These methods comprised of "borrowing, imitation, effectfulness and diversion".[95] Wittgenstein's initial critique of Mahler as a thief who imitates and borrows from the tradition is reminiscent of the vocabulary and substance of Tolstoy's observations about modern art, until it dawns on him [Wittgenstein] that it is a mistake for a contemporary composer to compare himself to the greats of former times—to evaluate himself in line with past standards.

One big difference, as mentioned before, between Wittgenstein and Tolstoy is that Tolstoy had a *theory* of deterioration and fraudulence while Wittgenstein explicitly disavows theorizing cultural deterioration or fraudulence. Another is their distinct appraisals of particular composers and works of music. Tolstoy judged Beethoven's late quartets to be exercises in self-indulgence characterized by chaotic sounds lacking expressive power; Wittgenstein on the other hand heard them as *tremendous*, original achievements of a master composer. Again, Tolstoy dismissed Wagner's music as obscure inaccessible rubbish, while Wittgenstein thought highly of Wagner, without ignoring regions of Wagner's music where, as we have seen, genius was lacking and mere skill shows through. While both Wittgenstein and Tolstoy regard music as expressive communication, Tolstoy wanted particular feelings and emotions communicated, while Wittgenstein saw this demand as an instructive error—the byproduct of bad theorizing. To ask for the specification of emotional content, as opposed to music's expressive gesture or face—to demand from the audience the uptake of what the composer may have felt at the time of composition, is a fundamental error in Tolstoy as well as in other expression theories of art.

---

95   *Ibid.*, 84.

Chapter VII
Philosophy, Music and Therapy

Cage is like Wittgenstein at least in this respect: the latter breaks away from the prison house of the philosophical tradition, while the former breaks away from the prison house of the musical tradition. Cage may also say to fellow composers: "For heaven's sake, don't compose music the old way; it's frankly disgusting. It just keeps on repeating the same old message in the same old ways, with a few variations on the same old themes. It's not for us today". Wittgenstein had an aversion to modern musical culture because it was resonant with and incapable of (musically) resolving the strife and conflict of the twentieth century. One might think therefore that modern music and his philosophical perspective have little or nothing in common—that the differences outweigh all the similarities.

This, as I argued, is partly right. On the other hand, it is partly wrong, since there are noteworthy and instructive affinities between Wittgenstein's version of modern philosophy and modern music. Like the musical moderns, the *Tractatus* repudiates the tradition with its metaphysics and theorizing. When modern composers said "That's not music", they denied musical status to then current compositions done in the traditional mode; when the Tractarian Wittgenstein said "That's not philosophy", he relegated to the rubbish heap then current philosophy done in the traditional mode.

Such negative gestures, however, are insufficient unless they accompanied by a positive, affirmative direction for new music and new philosophy. Cage encourages us to remove the wax of the tradition from our ears and listen to the music of the everyday. His concern to retrieve everyday sounds is reminiscent of the later Wittgenstein's concern with the language of the everyday and the ordinary. They bring music and philosophy down to earth as it were, urging us to attend to what is generally overlooked and under-heard, what is taken for granted because it is ordinary and everyday.

Cage's "I have nothing to say and I am saying it"[1] resonates with early Wittgenstein's saying in *Tractatus* 7 "Whereof one cannot speak, thereof one must be silent". Nor did, as we have seen, the later Wittgenstein abandon the say/show distinction but reconceived it. In the later philosophy the inexpressible is no longer the transcendent; rather, "[t]he inexpressible (what I find enigmatic & cannot express) provides the background, against which whatever I was able to express acquires meaning".[2] As late as 1947 Wittgenstein writes: "We might say: Art *shows* (*zeige*) the miracles of nature to us. It is based on the *concept* of the miracles of nature. (The blossom just opening out. What is so *marvelous* about it?) We say: 'Look, how it's opening out!'"[3] In philosophy too we are to *look* and see what language game is played. In Cage, silence enables us to attend to the sounds in our environment, to retrieve and appreciate unnoticed ambient sounds, including noise.

Cage's love of noise, however, contrasts sharply with Wittgenstein's deep aversion to it. Even in Brahms, a composer Wittgenstein's admired, he was beginning to hear the noise of machinery. Cage, on the other hand, was noise obsessed: "I believe, he remarked:

> that the use of noise to make music will continue and increase until we reach a music produced through the aid of electrical instruments which will make available for musical purposes any and all sounds that can be heard. Photoelectric, film, and mechanical mediums for the synthetic production of music will be explored. Whereas, in the past, the point of disagreement has been between dissonance and consonance, it will be, in the immediate future, between noise and so-called musical sounds. The present methods of writing music, principally those which employ harmony and its reference to particular steps in the field of sound, will be inadequate.[4]

The complaint is that the tradition excludes a wide range of sounds, while Cage's idea of "experimental music" is to be inclusive, to radically expand the range of sounds acceptable for composition and

---

1   John Cage, "Lecture on Nothing" in *Silence: Lectures and Writing,* London: Marion Boyars, 1978, 109.
2   Wittgenstein, *Culture*, 23.
3   *Ibid.*, 64.
4   Cage, "The Future of Music" in *Silence*, 3-5.

listening. In his hands, the essence of music implodes. An interesting affinity to be noticed here is that the later Wittgenstein expands the regions of language relevant to philosophical investigation; he becomes more inclusive as he moves beyond the traditional preoccupation with reference, description and information, attending to multifarious language games including promising, requesting, expressing, and so on. In his hands, the essence of language fragments.

Attempts to eliminate melody and harmony—as it were the surface of music—and compose music by electronic means or through the application of mathematical formulas are like the efforts of the early Wittgenstein and the Logical Positivists to re-conceive philosophy as nothing but logical analysis of the deep structure of "the proposition". The charge "That's not philosophy" was leveled at anyone who did otherwise. "That's not music" was used in a similar way by avant-garde composers and anyone who worked in a different spirit was not contributing to musical progress, was not composing real music. If Cage was the Dada of music, the early Wittgenstein was the Dada of philosophy—a thought that crossed his mind judging by a 1931 remark: "It occurred to me today as I was thinking about my own work in philosophy & said to myself: 'I destroy, I destroy, I destroy.'"[5] But this is true just in the sense of pulling down the edifice to expose the foundations: "I am not interested in erecting a building but having the foundations of possible buildings transparently before me".[6]

Twentieth century music, like twentieth century philosophy, interrogates its own identity. Modern philosophy then is hardly unique in this respect, although it may be uniquely relentless in such self-questioning. The young Wittgenstein imagined himself to have killed traditional philosophy by having solved, in one fell swoop, its problems. Later on, when he realized that his own solution was problematic, he drew our attention to the "un-theorized" use of concepts to resolve philosophical problems. Cage imagined himself to have killed traditional music and to have restored our sensitivity to ambient sound. The material of music, he said, was sound and silence and integrating these was his conception of composition.

Philosophical theorizing for Wittgenstein is like conventional

---

5 Wittgenstein, *Culture*, 19.
6 *Ibid.*, 9.

composing for Cage: baggage we need to throw overboard, since they are the source of problems and tensions. Beethoven, the icon of the tradition, Cage asserted, "was in error, and his influence which has been as extensive as it is lamentable, has been deadening to the art of music".[7] He went on to explain that Beethoven was guilty of two major misdeeds: passing on to subsequent composers a conception of music as narrative motivated by the composer's self-centred purposes and perpetrating "the vogue of profundity". What did Cage mean here by the "vogue of profundity"? If he meant to rid us of the illusory idea that music *in itself,* regardless of everything else, embodied depth, then perhaps well and good. It is quite another thing, however, to deny that a piece of music can have the character of depth.

Wittgenstein deflates the illusion of depth without denying that a piece of music may rightly be said to be deep. In his view a philosophical problem is deep in the way a poem or a face in or a piece of music is deep. You can't call a poem or a piece of music deep unless much connected with the poem or piece of music was already known. The depth cannot be separated from all the other things connected with it. Wittgenstein traces the depth of philosophy to misunderstanding the forms of our language:

> The problems arising through a misinterpretation of our forms of language have the character of *depth.* They are deep disquietudes; they are as deep as the forms of our language and their significance as great as the significance of our language.— Let us ask ourselves: why do we feel a grammatical joke to be deep? (And that is what the depth of philosophy is.)[8]

"That's not philosophy"; "that's not music".[9] These issues arise in a historical/cultural context where cultural and personal identities are under threat. Such recriminations when leveled at oneself as a philosopher or composer may serve as a spur toward a turn in one's own creative endeavours. When leveled, however, against

---

7   Richard Kostelanetz, *Conversing with Cage,* New York and London: Routledge, 1983, 81.

8   Wittgenstein, *Investigations,* §111.

9   Here I am indebted to the stimulus of 'That's not philosophy!'—a presentation by my colleague Rob Piercey, reflecting on twentieth-century philosophy.

other philosophers or composers, they often show an invidious competitiveness. Ideologically combative composers of the era issued manifestos arguing for the emancipation of dissonance and a deliberate turning away from an audience whose expectations of "comfort and joy", of an affirmation of the status quo, seem to block the composer's creative freedom. For such combative modernists the traditional composer was a kitsch-monger to an audience who stands in the way of "musical progress". Sadly, once a composer turns his back on the audience and becomes exclusively absorbed in a "private language of pure self-expression", music as expressive communication is at risk of being dismissed as musical nonsense, much like the plain nonsense of philosophical theorizing. With the loss of audience comes the end of meaningful composition—music becomes a sort of self-indulgence rather than meaningful communication.

Like Wittgenstein in philosophy, Cage in music issued reminders. What is *4'33"* if not a reminder that silence makes possible the appreciation of everyday sounds and musical sound itself? A reminder that the sounds of music emerge out of the sounds of non-music? If Wittgenstein brings back the sounds of everyday language/speech to the workings of philosophy, Cage brings back to music the sounds and the noise of the neglected backdrop of our everyday life:

> I said that since the sounds were just sounds, this gave people hearing them the chance to be people, centered within themselves where they actually are, not off artificially in the distance as they are accustomed to be, trying to figure out what is being said by some artist by means of sounds. Finally I said that the purpose of this purposeless music would be achieved if people learned to listen; that when they listened they might discover that they preferred the sounds of everyday life to the ones they would presently hear in the musical program; that that was alright as far as I was concerned.[10]

Such purposeless play is an "affirmation of life—not an attempt to bring order out of chaos nor to suggest improvements in creation, but

---

10   Paul Griffiths, *Modern Music: The avant garde since 1945,* New York: George Braziller, 1981, 124.

simply a way of waking up to the very life we are living…".[11] This is a project with a therapeutic aspect that has a striking resemblance to Wittgenstein's later philosophical goal.

Cage, like Wittgenstein, aimed to cure us from bad habits. One such habit is that of listening to music to escape from *this* world to *another* world. This legacy from Schopenhauer's Platonist metaphysics severs music from our everyday world and locates its value as a way of escape from our ordinary world of appearances. Like Wittgenstein, Cage had no sympathy for such an otherworldly view of, or way of listening to, music: "For many years I've noticed that music—as an activity separated from the rest of life—doesn't enter my mind".[12] For him, strictly musical questions, such as the distinction between musical sounds and noises, "are no longer serious questions…. We no longer discriminate against noises". Cage dismantles dichotomies: of musical sound versus noise, of music and the world, of composer versus listener. Wittgenstein too helps us to let go of transcendence, but without reduction. For him, everything is what it is and not another thing. As we have seen, he wants to compare some music to language games; other music to architecture; yet other music to nature.

Cage thinks of the traditional building blocks of music as elements of a confining and oppressive architecture and he attempts, through the creation of new music and advocacy of new listening, to restore the wholeness of our being in the world:

> New music: new listening. Not an attempt to understand something that is being said… just an attention to the activity of sounds. One needs to give up the desire to control sound, clear one's mind of music, and… let sounds be themselves rather than vehicles for man-made theories…. [13]

If this means the end of music as traditionally understood, so be it, since the absence of such music does not necessarily diminish society. "The end of music" chord struck by Cage is similar to the one Wittgenstein

---

11   John Cage, "Experimental Music" in *Silence: Lectures and Writing,* London: Marion Boyars, 1978, 12.

12   John Cage, "The Future of Music" in *Empty Words,* Middletown, Connecticut: Wesleyan University Press, 1979, 177.

13   Cage, *Silence,* 10.

struck when he imagined the disappearance of music and the arts: "The disappearance of the arts [music] does not justify a disparaging judgement on a whole segment of humanity.... [for] the disappearance of culture does not signify the disappearance of human value but simply of a certain means of expressing this value". In such times "genuine & strong characters simply turn away from the field of the arts & somehow the value of the individual finds expression".[14]

There is strong textual support for seeing Wittgenstein's philosophy, early and later, as having a therapeutic dimension. There is, however, no reduction: no proposed *theory* to the effect that philosophy is a branch of psychotherapy, nor does Wittgenstein *equate* a philosophical problem with illness. Rather, readers are to take his remarks as pointing to a useful analogy that sheds light on the practice of philosophy. "Like" is the guiding word here. The philosopher is looking for the "saving word" to cut a clear path through the problems that trouble us and provide relief from our deep disquietudes. "The task of philosophy is to soothe the mind about meaningless questions. Whoever doesn't tend to such questions doesn't need philosophy".[15] In the *Investigations* the therapeutic analogy is made explicit: "The philosopher's treatment of a question is *like* the treatment of an illness".[16] Again, "There is not *a* philosophical method, though there are indeed methods, like different therapies".[17]

The most vivid characterization of the philosopher's troubled condition is that of the fly trapped in a fly bottle: "What is your aim in philosophy?—To show the fly the way out of the fly bottle".[18] What is involved in "showing the way out" is no mere intellectual exercise —the fly is no fly on the wall—but an existential crisis: the fly's very survival is at stake. Joachim Schulte gives a striking description of the philosophical fly's predicament:

> The fly in the trap does not behave like the traveler in a strange city: Having landed on the sticky surface, it is in grave danger. Lack of orientation is not the only problem: the fly suffers

---

14 Wittgenstein, *Culture*, 8-9.
15 Wittgenstein, *Public and Private*, 73.
16 Wittgenstein, *Investigations*, §255.
17 *Ibid.*, §133.
18 *Ibid.*, §309.

confusion in every part of his being, and is unable to escape from
what has seized it. Being rescued from this sort of predicament
would be to be rescued from the greatest distress. [19]

Like the fly, the modern composer is attracted into the narrow bottle
by scraps of food, a promise of nourishment the tradition offers. Like
the fly, she is frustrated, buzzing and bumping against the sides of the
bottle, missing the narrow opening that would restore her freedom of
movement in nature. Cage, it seems to me, would embrace this analogy.
His intention, we might say, is to help the trapped musical fly out
of the narrow bottle of the tradition that constrains and shuts things
down, while he opens things up. He looks around, listens and hears
musical nourishment in the many kinds of possible sound surrounding
us: the "music" of nature, of the city, of our machines, radios, tapes,
of electric instruments, of modified [such as his prepared piano] or
newly invented instruments, and of the buzz of recent technology. The
appeal to "chance procedures" is intended to extricate ourselves from
an anthropocentric music, a privileging of human feeling and concerns,
of musical constructions that narrow our listening and hearing, ignoring
the variety and richness of other sounds. It's as if Cage opens the door
and breaks on to the other side.

Criticism, including self-criticism, is big for Wittgenstein too.
Wittgenstein's philosopher, like a patient in psychotherapy, suffers from
errors that must be described and acknowledged as the right expression
for what he feels or is inclined to do. These problems may arise in
different ways: a one-sided way of looking at things skews our vision
of a concept. A narrow diet of examples or a misguided conception or
application of a prototype tend to result in over-simple generalizations
that distort our appreciation. Fixations or obsessions with the standard
case produce grammatical illusions that constrain our thinking and
listening. All too often these "devices" have been used to build "an
official theory" or devise "a sanctioned method" that are like what Cage
alludes to as ossifying musical architecture. For Cage there is no one
way to compose music or integrating sound and silence, just like for
Wittgenstein there is no single philosophical method. There is no such
thing as *one* big philosophical problem, nor is there *one* big musical

---

19   Joachim Schulte, *Wittgenstein An Introduction,* Albany: State University of New
     York Press, 1992, 102.

problem. Different philosophical problems call for different therapies; different musical tasks in different periods call for different ways of composing. If we are open to the variety of language and sound, then the characteristic paralysis when we confront a question or task abates and our agency is restored. If philosophers and composers go about their practice this way, they will be no longer haunted by unmanageable, monumental problems.

Can the therapeutic analogy concerning music and philosophy be further extended? We seem to reach the limits when we consider Wittgenstein's remark that:

> the real discovery is the one that makes me capable of stopping doing philosophy whenever I want to.—The one that gives philosophy peace, so that it is no longer tormented by questions which bring *itself* into question.[20]

Imagine a composer of music saying: the real discovery is that I can stop composing music whenever I want to. This sounds strange, if not absurd, and the analogy seems to break down. But no so fast. What might the composer mean? She might say this because the preoccupations of traditional music still haunt her. She might be haunted by the question 'Is what I am writing really music?'

Such foundational concerns may have a paralyzing effect on her creative endeavours and lead her to think that she has to have a theory to answer the big question about what music really is. Unless you answered the question what is music nothing you do in music is reliable, for whatever you do is vulnerable to corrosive doubt. Unless you have a theory, you do not really know what you are doing. There is, Wittgenstein and Cage suggest, no peace for such composers and philosophers unless they avoid a certain prejudice, namely, that there are two sorts of problem in the intellectual sense: "essential, great, universal, & inessential, as it were accidental problems. Our conception on the contrary is that there is no great essential problem in the intellectual sense".[21] On the old view, composers and philosophers who aim to do original work must do foundational work and start with a fresh slate. This is a natural but misguided tendency that creates further tensions

---

20 Wittgenstein, *Investigations*, §309.
21 Wittgenstein, *Culture*, 20.

and friction instead of resolving them. If we adopt Wittgenstein's perspective, then there are no eternal problems in music or philosophy, and we do not need to start at the beginning, with the original data of philosophy (written or spoken sentences) or music (scores of past compositions or folk songs). "'Everything is in flux'. And perhaps that is the very point at which to begin".[22]

Another point at which the analogy seems to break down is when Wittgenstein tells us that philosophical work is really a working on oneself, on one's own conception, on how one sees things and what one expects of them.[23] If so, then each of us need to do philosophy for ourselves. Suppose that this goes for philosophy. Now imagine a composer saying: composing music involves a working on oneself, on how one looks at things etc. If so, then music is something each person needs to do for him or herself—you need to listen to music that you compose for yourself. Is this not a bizarre idea tantamount to abandoning one's responsibilities as a composer? Not on Cage's view, since his "new music/new listening" involves "democratizing" the role of the composer. Consider his response to the objection that if experimental music is simply happening sounds, "I could write it as well as you": "Have I said anything that would lead you to think that I thought you were stupid?"[24] The upshot: that's the point, be your own composer.

I have been arguing that there is a striking resemblance between the therapeutic aspect of Cage's musical and Wittgenstein's philosophical activity. A prominent feature of their activity is a return to the everyday but with a fresh "enlightened" attitude and ways of attentiveness that bring peace to philosophical and compositional practice. Big differences, however, remain. Melody for Wittgenstein, *unlike* for Cage, is a *must* for music, for the sort of music he can appreciate. It is expressive of the human spirit and the value of the human individual. With the disappearance of melody a certain means expressive of the human spirit is lost. Like the loss of a language, "it is always a tragic thing when a language dies…. But it doesn't follow that one can do anything about to stop it doing so.[25]

---

22   *Ibid.*, 11.
23   *Ibid.*, 24.
24   Cage, "Experimental Music" in *Silence*, 17.
25   *Ludwig Wittgenstein Personal Recollections*, ed. Rhees, 152.

The drift of the "language of music" changed direction. That's the way it is, Wittgenstein would say. Different cultural eras express themselves differently. The music of the second half of the twentieth century are so different from what has gone before that new names, such as 'electro-acoustic music', 'sonic art', 'sound-scapes', had to be invented to mark them off from what has gone before. New musical or aural experiences have become possible through new means of expression. When we look at these movements of music, we are inclined to look on them as continuations of one another, but Wittgenstein thinks this may be an illusion: "The possibility of a number of closed systems which, once one has them, look as if one is the continuation of another. And all this has to do with the thought that we do not consider how much can be taken away from—or given to a human being".[26]

But melody and harmony have not disappeared, even though their dominance has ended. Struggling to emerge out of dissonance, out of primordial or techno-noise, when melody finally surfaces and soars, even if briefly, only the wax in our ears due to theoretical bias prevents appreciation.

Cage recollects:

> When Schoenberg asked me whether I would devote my life to music, I said, 'Of course'. After I had been studying with him for 2 years, Schoenberg said, 'In order to write music, you must have a feeling for harmony.' I explained to him that I have no feeling for harmony. He then said I would always encounter an obstacle, that it would be as though I came to a wall through which I could not pass. I said, 'In that case I will devote my life to beating my head against that wall.[27]

Cage kept banging his head against the wall—somewhat reminiscent of Wittgenstein's philosopher running up against the walls of the cage of our language. But this is where Wittgenstein and Cage part company— this is where Wittgenstein drew the line. Despite their different views on the nature of melody, for Wittgenstein, like for Schopenhauer, the deep significance of music has to do with "how the connected

---

26 Wittgenstein, *Public and Private*, 25.
27 John Cage, "Indeterminacy" in *Silence: Lectures and Writing,* London: Marion Boyars, 1978, 261.

melody, progressing in high, light, and quick notes, is to be regarded as expressing the life and efforts of man, connected by reflection".[28] While the accompanying harmonies are important, they lack the continuity and progress possessed by melody. Perhaps this is why Wittgenstein remarked that:

> I often think that the highest I wish to achieve would be to compose a melody.... That is why I am thinking of it as such a high ideal because I could then in a way sum up my life; and set it down crystallized. And even if it were but a small, shabby crystal, yet a crystal. [29]

Yet in 1931 Wittgenstein did compose a small musical crystal: a passionate fragment consisting of four bars, lasting about thirty seconds. It is as if he started to say something, realized that it could not be said, and then he turned to music.

---

28   Schopenhauer, *World As Will*, vol. 1, 154.
29   Wittgenstein, *Public and Private*, 18-19.

Bibliography

Adorno, Theodor. 1967. *Prisms*. (trs Samuel and Sherry Weber). London: Neville Spearman.

——. 1995. 'On the Fetish Character in Music and the Regression of Listening' in Neill and Ridley (1995): 526-538.

Barrett, Cyril. 1998. 'Changing the Rules in Art' in Johannessen (1998): 1-17.

Bell, Clive. 1931. *Art*. London: Chatto and Windus.

Blaukopf, Kurt and Herta. 1976. *Mahler: His Life and Work*. (trs Paul Baker and others). London: Thames and Hudson.

Botstein, Leon. 2002. 'Whose Gustav Mahler? Reception, Interpretation, and History' in Painter (2002): 1-54.

Bouwsma, O.K. 1950. 'The Expression Theory of Art' in Black, Max (ed.) *Philosophical Analysis: A Collection of Essays*. Ithaca: Cornell University Press: 71-96.

——. 1986. *Wittgenstein Conversations 1949-1951*. Indianapolis: Hackett.

Braithwaite, R.B. (ed.) 1931. *The Foundations of Mathematics*. London: Routledge and Kegan Paul.

Bullough, Edward. 1995. '"Psychical Distance" as a Factor in Art and as an Aesthetic Principle' in Neill and Ridley (1995): 297-311.

Burns, Steven. 2002. 'Flock of Nightingales: Wagner's Music and German Philosophy' in *AE Canadian Aesthetics Journal* 7 (on line).

Cage, John. 1978. 'Experimental Music' in *Silence: Lectures and Writings*. London: Marion Boyars: 7-12.

——. 1978. 'Experimental Music: Doctrine' in *Silence: Lectures and Writings*. London: Marion Boyars: 13-17.

——. 1978. 'Indeterminacy' in *Silence: Lectures and Writings*. London: Marion Boyars: 260-273.

——. 1978. 'Lecture on Nothing' in *Silence: Lectures and Writings*. London: Marion Boyars: 109-127.

——. 1978. 'The Future of Music: Credo' in *Silence: Lectures and Writings*. London: Marion Boyars: 3-6.

——. 1979. 'The Future of Music' in *Empty Words: Writings '73-'78*. Middletown, Connecticut: Wesleyan University Press: 177-187.

Campbell, Peter and Béla Szabados. 2012. 'Wittgenstein on Self-Deception in Science, Psychology and Philosophy' in *Wittgenstein-Studien* 4(1): 147-170.

Carroll, Noël. 1994. 'Cage and Philosophy' in *The Journal of Aesthetics and Art Criticism* 52(1): 93-98.

Cross, Charles R. 2005. *Room Full of Mirrors: A Biography of Jimi Hendrix*. New York: Hyperion.

Danto, Arthur. 1964. 'The Artworld' in Neill and Ridley (1995): 202-212.

Daverio, John. 1997. *Robert Schumann, Herald of a New Poetic Age*. New York: Oxford University Press.

Dickie, George. 1964. 'The Myth of the Aesthetic Attitude' in *American Philosophical Quarterly* 1(1): 56-66.

——. 1969. 'Defining Art' in *American Philosophical Quarterly* 6: 253-266.

Drury, Maurice. 1981. 'Conversations with Wittgenstein' in Rhees (1981): 112-189.

Duchamp, Marcel, Beatrice Wood and H.P. Roche. 1917. *The Blind Man 2*. New York.

Engelmann, Paul. 1967. *Letters from Ludwig Wittgenstein with a Memoir*. Oxford: Blackwell.

Fann, K.T. 1967. *Ludwig Wittgenstein: The Man and His Philosophy*. New York: Dell Publishing.

Gillock, Jon. 2009. *Performing Messiaen's Organ Music*. Bloomington: Indiana University Press.

Goehr, Lydia. 1998. *The Quest for Voice: Music, Politics, and the Limits of Philosophy*. Berkeley: University of California Press.

Gorlée, Dinda. 2008. 'Wittgenstein as Mastersinger' in *Semiotica* 172: 97-150.

Grice, H.P. 1968. 'Utterer's Meaning, Sentence Meaning, and Word Meaning' in *Foundations of Language* 4: 225-242.

Griffiths, Paul. 1981. *Modern Music: The avant garde since 1945*. New York: George Braziller.

Hagberg, Garry. 2006. Review of *Schoenberg, Wittgenstein and the Vienna Circle* by James Wright (New York: Peter Lang, 2005) in *Philosophy in Review* 26(6): 449-452.

Hanslick, Eduard. 1986. *On the Musically Beautiful* (tr. Geoffrey Payzant). Indianapolis: Hackett.

Janik, Allan. 2001. *Wittgenstein's Vienna Revisited.* New Brunswick, New Jersey: Transaction.

Janik, Allan and Stephen Toulmin. 1973. *Wittgenstein's Vienna.* New York: Simon and Schuster.

Johannessen, Kjell (ed.) 1998. *Wittgenstein and Aesthetics.* Bergen: University of Bergen, Institute of Philosophy.

King, John. 1981. 'Recollections of Wittgenstein' in Rhees (1981): 83-90.

Kivy, Peter. 2002. *Introduction to a Philosophy of Music.* Oxford: Clarendon Press.

Kostelanetz, Richard. 1983. *Conversing with Cage.* New York and London: Routledge.

LaPlante Raffman, Rita. 2004. 'Ludwig Wittgenstein's Concept of Family Resemblance and Contemporary Music' in Shanker, Stuart (ed.) *Ludwig Wittgenstein: Critical Assessments.* London: Routledge: 392-397.

Lewis, Peter B. 1977. 'Wittgenstein on Words and Music' in *British Journal of Aesthetics* 17: 111-121.

——. (ed.) 2004. *Wittgenstein, Aesthetics and Philosophy.* Aldershot, England: Ashgate.

Loos, Adolf. 1908. 'Ornament is Crime' in Miller, Bernie and Ward, Melony (eds) *Crime and Ornament.* 2002. Toronto: YYZ Books.

Lugg, Andrew. 2000. *Wittgenstein's Philosophical Investigations 1-133: A Guide and an Interpretation.* London and New York: Routledge.

——. 2003. "Wittgenstein's Tractatus: True Thoughts and Nonsensical Propositions" in *Philosophical Investigations* 26(4): 332-247.

Lurie, Yuval. 1992. 'Culture as a Human Form of Life: A Romantic Reading of Wittgenstein' in *International Philosophical Quarterly* 32: 193-204.

——. 2012. *Wittgenstein on the Human Spirit.* Amsterdam: Rodopi.

Mahler, Alma. 1971. *Gustav Mahler, Memories and Letters* Donald Mitchell (ed.). Seattle and London: University of Washington Press.

Malcolm, Norman. 1966. *Wittgenstein: A Memoir.* London: Oxford University Press.

Mann, Thomas. 1985. *Pro and Contra Wagner.* (tr. Allan Blunden) (Introduction by Erich Heller). Chicago: The University of Chicago Press.

McGuinness, Brian (ed.) 1982. *Wittgenstein and His Times.* Oxford: Blackwell.

——. 1988. *Wittgenstein: A Life, Young Ludwig.* Berkeley: University of California Press.

——. (ed.) 1995. *Wittgenstein in Cambridge: Letters and Documents, 1911-1951.* Oxford: Blackwell.

——. 2002. *Approaches to Wittgenstein.* London and New York: Routledge.

Moore, G.E. 1959. 'Wittgenstein's Lectures in 1930-1933' in Klagge, James and Nordmann, Alfred (eds) *Wittgenstein: Philosophical Occasions* .Indianapolis: Hackett: 46-114.

Neill, Alex and Aaron Ridley (eds). 1995. *The Philosophy of Art Readings Ancient and Modern.* New York: McGraw-Hill.

Painter, Karen (ed.). 2002. *Mahler and His World.* Princeton and Oxford: Princeton University Press.

Piercey, Robert. 2013. 'That's not Philosophy'. Paper presented at the *Philosophy Cafe* (Artisan, Regina, Saskatchewan).

Pinsent, David. 1990. *A Portrait of Wittgenstein as a Young Man.* Oxford: Basil Blackwell.

Ramsey, F.P. 1931. 'Philosophy' in Braithwaite (1931): 263-269.

——. 1931. 'General Propositions and Causality' in Braithwaite (1931): 237-255.

Redpath, Theodore. 1990. *Ludwig Wittgenstein: A Student's Memoir.* London: Duckworth.

Rhees, Rush (ed.). 1981. *Ludwig Wittgenstein Personal Recollections.* Oxford: Oxford University Press.

Ross, Alex. 2007. *The Rest Is Noise: Listening to the Twentieth Century.* New York: Picador.

Schoenberg, Arnold. 1975. *Style and Idea.* (tr. Leo Black). Berkeley and Los Angeles: University of California Press.

——.1978. *Theory of Harmony* (tr. Roy E. Carter) Berkeley and Los Angeles: University of California Press.

Scholes, Percy A. 1970. *The Oxford Companion to Music.* 10th Edition. (ed. John Owen Ward). London: Oxford University Press.

Schopenhauer, Arthur. 1958. *The World As Will and Representation.* 2 vols. (tr. E.F.J. Payne). Indiana Hills, Colorado: The Falcon Press.

Schulte, Joachim. 1992. *Wittgenstein An Introduction.* Albany: State University of New York Press.

——. 1995. *Experience and Expression: Wittgenstein's Philosophy of Psychology.* Oxford: Clarendon Press.

Scruton, Roger. 2004. 'Wittgenstein and the Understanding of Music' in *British Journal of Aesthetics* 44(1): 1-9.

Sharpe, R.A. 2004. 'Wittgenstein's Music' in Lewis (2004): 137-150.

Shiner, Roger. 1978. 'On Giving Works of Art a Face' in *Philosophy* 53(205): 304-324.

Sparshott, Francis. 1987. "Aesthetics of Music: Limits and Grounds" in Alperson, Philip (ed.) *What is Music?* University Park, PA: The Pennsylvania State University Press.

Spengler, Oswald. 1945. *The Decline of the West.* (tr. Charles Francis Atkinson). New York: Knopf.

Stern, David. 1995. *Wittgenstein on Mind and Language.* New York and Oxford: Oxford University Press.

——. 2001. 'Was Wittgenstein a Jew?' in Klagge, James (ed.) *Wittgenstein: Biography and Philosophy.* Cambridge: Cambridge University Press: 237-272.

——. 2004. *Wittgenstein's Philosophical Investigations, An Introduction.* New York and Oxford: Oxford University Press.

Stravinsky, Igor. 1975. *Autobiography.* London: Calder and Boyars.

Szabados, Béla.1999. 'Was Wittgenstein an Anti-Semite? The Significance of Anti-Semitism for Wittgenstein's Philosophy' in *Canadian Journal of Philosophy* 29: 1-28.

——. 2006. 'Wittgenstein and Musical Formalism' in *Philosophy* 81(318): 649-658.

——. 2012. 'Wittgenstein on Musical Irony' in *Wittgenstein-Studien* 3(1): 187-204.

——. 2013. 'Wittgenstein's Reception of Wagner' in Bru, Sascha, Huemer, Wolfgang, and Steuer, Daniel (eds) *Wittgenstein Reading.* Berlin: De Gruyter: 171-195.

Tanner, Michael. 1995. *Wagner.* Princeton and Oxford: Princeton University Press.

——. 1999. *Schopenhauer.* London: Phoenix.

Tietz, John. 1999. *Redemption or Annihilation? Love and Power in Wagner's Ring.* New York: Peter Lang Publishers.

Tovey, Donald Francis. 1935. *Essays in Musical Analysis.* Volume II, London.

Tolstoy, Leo. 1995. *What Is Art?* London: Penguin Classics.

Wagner, Richard. 1910. *Judaism in Music.* (tr. Edwin Evans). London: W. Reeves.

——. 1964. *Wagner on Music and Drama* (tr. H. Ashton Ellis, selected and arranged with an introduction by Albert Goldman and Evert Sprinchorn). New York: E.P. Dutton.

Waugh, Alexander. 2008. *The House of Wittgenstein A Family at War*. New York: Doubleday.

Waismann, Friedrich. 1979. *Ludwig Wittgenstein and the Vienna Circle*. (ed. Brian McGuinness, trs Joachim Schulte and Brian McGuinness). Oxford: Blackwell.

Weitz, Morris. 1995. 'The Role of Theory in Aesthetics' in Neill and Ridley (1995): 188-189.

Wimsatt, W.K. and Monroe C. Beardsley. 1946. 'The Intentional Fallacy' in *Sewanee Review* 54: 468-88.

Wittgenstein, Ludwig. 1953. *Philosophical Investigations*. (ed. and tr. G.E.M. Anscombe). Oxford: Basil Blackwell. Revised second edition, 2001.

——. 1961. *Notebooks 1914-1916*. Oxford: Basil Blackwell.

——. 1963. *Tractatus Logico-Philosophicus*. London: Routledge and Kegan Paul.

——. 1964. *The Blue and Brown Books*. Oxford: Basil Blackwell.

——. 1967. *Lectures and Conversations on Aesthetics, Psychology and Religious Belief*. (ed. Cyril Barrett). Berkeley, Los Angeles: University of California Press.

——. 1979. *Wittgenstein and the Vienna Circle*. Conversations Recorded by Friedrich Waismann. (ed. Brian McGuinness, trs Joachim Schulte and Brian McGuinness). Blackwell, Oxford, England.

——. 1980/1998. *Culture and Value*, (ed. G.H. von Wright, tr. Peter Winch). (rev. 2nd ed by Alois Pichler). Oxford: Basil Blackwell.

——. 1988. *Remarks on the Philosophy of Psychology*. Volume II. Oxford: Basil Blackwell.

——. 1993. *Philosophical Occasions 1912-1951*. (eds James C. Klagge and Alfred Nordmann). Indianapolis & Cambridge: Hackett.

——. 1993. "A Lecture on Ethics" in *Philosophical Occasions*: 36-44.

——. 1993. "Philosophy" in *Philosophical Occasions*, 158-199.

——. 2003. *Public and Private Occasions* (eds and trs James Klagge and Alfred Nordmann). Lanham, Maryland: Rowman & Littlefield.

Wollheim, Richard. 1995. "Criticism as Retrieval" in Neill and Ridley (1995): 185-204.

Worth, Sarah. 1997. 'Wittgenstein's Musical Understanding' in *British Journal of Aesthetics* 37: 158-167.

Wright, G.H., von. 1982. *Wittgenstein*. Oxford: Basil Blackwell.

——. 1982. "Wittgenstein in Relation to His Times" in McGuinness (1982): 108-120.

Wright, James. 2004. *Schoenberg, Wittgenstein and the Vienna Circle*. Bern: Peter Lang.

Zwicky, Jan. 1998. *Songs for Relinquishing the Earth*. London, Ontario: Brick Books.

Index